D0955342

Praise for
Trade Show and Event Marketing

The exhibition and event's industry witnessed dynamic change the past few years. Ruth Stevens Trade Show and Event Marketing Handbook delivers a fresh perspective on trade shows and corporate events. It rightly focuses on the strategic rather than tactical elements of this strong marketing channel. This is an excellent reference to help you get the most out of your marketing investment.

> **MIKE BANDY**
> **President**
> **Trade Show Exhibitors Association**

My first job out of college in 1979 was as a junior marketing communications specialist at Westinghouse, where I was responsible for, among other things, trade shows for one of our divisions—and I wish I had this book back then. It shows the complete novice how to create and manage trade show exhibits and events successfully . . . yet also contains many tips, ideas, and resources that even the old pro like me will find helpful.

> **ROBERT BLY**
> **Author of *The Copywriter's Handbook* and**
> **(forthcoming) *The White Paper Marketing Handbook***

Finally, a definitive and comprehensive guide to the strategic use and measurement of trade shows and events written specifically for the sales and marketing exec. Long overdue for the events marketing industry.

> **SKIP COX**
> **President**
> **Exhibit Surveys, Inc.**

A comprehensive "A to Z" on this very important marketing topic. It shows the reader how to organize, plan, strategize, execute, and even measure results. And even better: It's not only easy to follow, it's a joy to read. Anyone who wants to improve marketing productivity and effectiveness needs to keep this great reference handy for repeated use.

MARY DONATO
Associate Director
Institute for the Study of Business Markets (ISBM)
SMEAL College of Business, Pennsylvania State University

Do your homework! Trade shows are expensive and time-consuming. Instead of just winging it, consider this practical, nuts and bolts approach to maximizing your return on investment.

SETH GODIN
Speaker, Author, *Purple Cow* & *Free Prize Inside*

Extremely useful advice (backed up by data) on the strategy of trade show marketing—including strengths and weaknesses of marketing via corporate events and seminars versus trade shows. Few books give you this thorough a strategic overview so you can make informed decisions about your events budget.

ANNE HOLLAND
Publisher
Marketing Sherpa

Ruth Stevens has written another book filled with great ideas and practical advice that will maximize your effectiveness at trade shows, where the selling, prospecting and relationship-building possibilities are endless.

RICK KEAN
Executive Director
Business Marketing Association

Ruth really "gets it." This is the first work I've seen that clearly identifies the opportunities for strategic marketers to maximize their business event investments and the importance of measuring their effectiveness. I highly recommend the book for event organizers and their clientele.

DAVID KORSE
President IDG World Expo

It's no surprise that business to business guru Ruth Stevens would write the **must-read book** on trade show and event marketing. She zeroes in on today's issues that corporations, agencies, and exhibitors all face. Stevens lays out a compelling case that shows how trade show and event marketing, if done right, can fulfill an untapped role in bridging the marketing and sales process—strategically, operationally, and financially.

PAM LARRICK
Chair McCann
Relationship Marketing

"Finally . . . a resource that provides an easy-to-follow effective guide for delivering a great customer experience—at a trade show or event. I'm impressed with the research and the recipe, and found the chapters on objective setting, customer acquisition, and appropriate metrics most rewarding.

A must-read for ensuring a flawless event!"

DIANE MCGARRY
Chief Marketing Officer
Xerox Corporation

"A great practical guide to getting better results, with step-by-step guidelines for anyone handling trade shows and events. Goes way beyond the 'theory of the case,' right down to specific techniques on how to get better ROI—with illustrations and cases showing you how.

"A 'bible' for beginners, a look at the "state-of-the-art" for the more experienced—a 'must read' for anyone handling trade shows and events as part of their marketing mix."

RALPH A. OLIVA
Executive Director, Institute for the Study of Business Markets
Professor of Marketing, Smeal College of Business, Penn State

"A long-needed, strategic view of Trade Shows and Event Marketing. Clearly illustrates how these critically important activities fit into the overall marketing mix plus the bonus of all the nitty-gritty details of how to develop and manage the entire spectrum of activities. Don't plan a show or exhibit without this handbook."

DON E. SCHULTZ
Professor—Integrated Marketing Communications
Northwestern University

Trade Show
and Event Marketing

Plan, Promote & Profit

RUTH P. STEVENS

RÃCOM
COMMUNICATIONS

Australia • Canada • Mexico • Singapore • Spain • United Kingdom • United States

THOMSON

✦ ™

Trade Show and Event Marketing: Plan, Promote & Profit
Ruth P. Stevens

CONTENTS

iii

PREFACE

A Business Marketing Parable

How often have you experienced this situation? A business-to-business company decides to exhibit at a trade show. A coordinator in the marketing department is charged with the logistics. So, she organizes a booth, creates the signage, packs up some collateral material, orders some giveaways, makes the travel arrangements, and manages the set-up and tear-down. A handful of sales reps are told to show up and help work the booth.

The show attracts 1,000 people, of whom about 100 are solid prospective buyers for this company's product. Some of these solid prospects happen by the booth, and the sales reps are able to engage with them. But no appointments have been made in advance, so it's hit or miss.

A fishbowl is placed out in front of the booth, and it captures hundreds of additional contacts. These are sorted through after the show and handed over to the sales team for follow-up. Some of the newer sales people give it the college try, but are quickly discouraged by the poor results.

Word spreads through the company that the show was unproductive. How did this happen? There were 100 solid prospects in attendance at the show. Each of the five sales reps could have easily managed 20 productive conversations during a three-day show. Why did this company miss the boat on that opportunity?

The answer lies in strategy. This company treated the show like a mere sales and marketing exercise, and failed to apply any strategic thinking to it. Had they considered the show within the context of their entire go-to-market strategy, they would have recognized the value of such improvements as:

- Researching the nature and needs of the show attendees.
- Setting measurable objectives for everyone involved in the show.
- Creating pre-show promotions to drive the solid prospects to the booth.

- Making appointments with the prospects and current customers known in advance.
- Training the sales reps on how to work a booth effectively.
- Eliminating the fishbowl, which simply gathers random contacts and does nothing to identify solid prospects and begin a relationship. (As Hank Riefle, former co-owner of Hardach Travel, says, "Business cards can't swim. Fish bowls are for fish.")
- And the list goes on and on.

Consider another tale from the annals of trade show marketing: the one about the exhibit manager who opens a cabinet when assembling the booth on the show floor—and out spills an avalanche of lead forms from last year's show. Is this possible? I have heard the same story from so many sources, about so many companies, that it has taken on the status of an urban myth.

It's stories like these that compelled the development of this book. As a matter of fact, the book's original roots are buried in a monthly column I used to write for *DMNews*, a weekly trade publication in the direct marketing industry. As it happened, over the three-year period of my column's existence, I wrote two pieces describing my experiences as an attendee at The National Center for Database Marketing (NCDM), a show targeted to direct marketers who use database technology to target customers and prospects. The first column, which coincided with the dotcom boom, related my frustration at stopping by booths of new technology companies eager to sell new database systems and services—many of them of course Web-based—and finding that they could not explain their value proposition. I would ask, "So, what do you guys do, anyway?" and they didn't have a coherent answer. As a marketer, I found in this situation ample opportunity for a juicy column on how to develop a compelling elevator speech.

The second column, about a year later, related my frustration with the signage at NCDM—the same show. I noticed that exhibitors were falling short of providing signs that gave me a clue about whether I should stop at their booths as I walked by. Worse, when I did approach the booth, the signage did not help me understand what their companies did and why I should care. On the whole, I was not being "sold to" effectively at this show.

My columns in *DMNews* elicited a steady stream of feedback over the three years, but I was always struck in particular by the response to the two random discussions on trade shows. While hardly inundated, I got more than average feedback, and all of it supportive.

Clearly, I had struck a chord. Everyone in business marketing is a trade show veteran—whether as an exhibitor or an attendee. Everyone recognizes the frustrations. So why do we keep on with ineffective trade show marketing? I decided to look into this further.

What I found on cursory examination is that business-to-business marketers are spending big bucks on trade shows—this explains why everyone has been to one at some point. But no one seems to have a clue about their value. So I decided to dig a bit deeper.

I thought I could give the subject some special attention, given my training and experience as a direct and database marketer in business-to-business. After all, the major reason marketers exhibit at shows is lead generation. So what's the problem? Let's apply the lead-generation discipline developed over decades in the world of business-to-business direct marketing.

But as I looked into it, I realized that the subject is more complicated—and interesting. Trade shows represent a bigger marketing opportunity than simply as a lead generating machine. They have capabilities in customer management, in public relations, in new product launches—across the entire marketing mix.

At the same time, trade shows are widely misunderstood and misapplied. They are used for mere awareness, or for junkets, or because someone in the corporation thought "we ought to be there." The more research I did, the more I realized that there is:

1. Real business opportunity in trade shows.
2. Wide misunderstanding of how to take advantage of the opportunity.

I also learned something interesting: as trade shows become more fragmented and noisy, business-to-business companies are diverting show dollars to proprietary corporate events where they can control not only the attendance, but the message and the entire customer experience. I quickly added a section on this topic, because the thinking, the strategy, and the budgets are one of a piece. They seek to answer the question: how do we identify and engage with our audience more efficiently, in an atmosphere where they want to learn about products, where they are seeking answers to business problems?

Thus, this book. As I looked into the matter, and talked to a bazillion experts in the field (with thanks to them all), I recognized that there is a need for a book that concentrates on business events as a marketing strategy.

When Myron Gould, a seasoned direct marketing professional, heard I was working on this book, he said, "Trade show marketing? Hmmm. Isn't that an oxymoron?" He has a point. Business events are typically dismissed as merely tactical. But my hope is that this will change.

This book is targeted to the people who are responsible for marketing and marketing communications in business-to-business companies of all sizes and in all industries. These people—whether marketing manager, director, vice president or even CEO—need to understand the strategic value of trade shows and corporate events as an important part of the marketing mix. Too many of them have relegated complete responsibility for business events to the junior staffer who manages event logistics. With this book, I hope that business-to-business marketers will give business events more serious—and more informed—consideration, and will learn how to get more measurable value from investing in event marketing.

This book is organized sequentially, beginning with an overview of the business event marketing business today, and a set of strategic options that business-to-business marketers can use to frame their thinking about the best uses of event marketing for their businesses. It then moves into the more tactical applications of business event planning, management, and post-event follow-up activity. The two-fold objective of this book is to help business marketers:

1. Make trade shows and corporate events a valuable and effective part of their entire go-to-market strategies.
2. Manage their business event investments in a way that provides a demonstrable ROI.

I hope readers will find that this book helps them move their event strategies to new heights, and take maximum advantage of this powerful marketing tool.

ACKNOWLEDGMENTS

A large number of trade show and corporate event marketing experts generously shared their time and experience with me.
Among them, I would like to thank:

Betti Abbas, Harris Interactive

Candy Adams, "The Booth Mom," of Trade Show Consulting

Mark Amtower, Amtower & Company

Marlys K. Arnold, ImageSpecialist and author of *Build a Better Trade Show Image*

Rob Aston, HP

Barbara Axelson, Axelson Communications

Judy Baker-Neufeld, TradeShows PLUS!

Michael Bandy, Trade Show Exhibitors Association (TSEA)

Don Barshinger, Slack Barshinger & Partners, Inc.

Dan Belmont and Nancie Freitas, Carat

Beth Blake, Reed Expositions

Ann Boyrazian, T&G Ingredient Tops Plus

Cathi Brozina, Johnson & Johnson

Bob Burk, King Industries, Inc.

Grace Chan, RBC, Canada

Alan Cordial, Calan Communications

Skip Cox, Ian Sequeira, and Debbie Baldwin, Exhibit Surveys, Inc.

Chet Dalzell, Harte-Hanks

Jefferson Davis, Competitive Edge

Carling Dinkler, Custom Conventions

Doug Ducate and Tracey Nickless, Center for Exhibition Industry Research

Wayne Dunham, Dunham Communications

Angela L. Eastin, Primedia Business Exhibitions

Tracy Emerick, Taurus Marketing

Richard Erschik, Leads to Sales, Inc.

Glenn Feder, National Trade Productions Inc.

Carol Fojtik, Hall-Erickson, Inc.

Sean Forbes, RightNow Technologies

Mark Foster, Condit Exhibits

Dennis Frahmann, Best Software

Carrie Freeman-Parsons, David Gauthreaux, Allen Reichard, and Rick Halvorson, The Freeman Companies

Marshall Gage, Performark, Inc.

Jane Gentry, Epoch, Inc.

Barry Gold, sales & marketing consultant to Quaero

Mim Goldberg and Marc Goldberg, Marketech, Inc.

Deborah Goldstein, IDG List Services

Srinath Gopalakrishna, University of Missouri-Columbia

Jim Grace and Marilyn Monohon, CAS

Cyndi Greenglass, DMS Group, Inc.

John Guthrie, Guthrie & Company

Stephen Hacker, IAEM

Andy Hallock and Carlin Stamm, The Hubert Company

Mike Hamilton, Synchronicity

Marilyn Harrington, Infinity Expo Group

Jim Hasl, Ziff-Davis

Matt Hill, The Hill Group

Rachel Honig Peters, G.S. Schwartz & Co., Inc.

Susanne Hyatt and Stacey Burbach, Siebel Systems

Pat Jaglowitz, Open Text Corporation

Dan Janal, PR Leads

John Kahan, Microsoft

Melinda Kendall, MediaLive International, Inc.

Lee Knight, *Exhibitor* magazine

Dr. Allen Konopacki, Incomm Center for Research & Sales Training

Gloria Kurant, Kurant Direct, Inc.

Joyce P. Lake and Mary McFadden, The Lake Group

Connie LaMotta, LaMotta Strategic Communications

Sandy Lane, Allied Van Lines

Jim Lenskold, The Lenskold Group, and author of *Marketing ROI*

Niel Lichtman, Marketing4Profit, Inc.

Jeff Little, George Little Management LLC

E. Jane Lorimer, Lorimer Consulting Group

Patrick McGuiness and Joscelyn Spencer, Saab Aircraft

Laura McGuire, Qgenisys, Inc.

Mac McIntosh, Sales Lead Experts

Douglas MacLean, MacLean Marketing

Laura L. McLeod, Trade Show Solutions Center LLC

Mike Maguire, Structural Graphics

Darby Mason, Xilinx

Laurie Meacham, The Broadmoor Hotel

Wayne Messick, iBizResources.com

Elise Morin, Beverly Tomb, and Cheval Force Opp, IBM

Ken Mortara, ShowValue, Inc.

Carol Myers, Unica Corporation

David C. Nelson, Hole-in-One USA

Ed Niehaus, Niehaus Ryan Wong

Gary Nolan, MC^2

Linda Nosko, Mayflower Transit

Jim Obermeyer, Reveal

Paul O'Brien, Persist Technologies

Fred O'Keefe, Geo Creative

Victoria Pace, Goldstein Communications Ltd.
Pamela Parker, *ClickZ*
Lynne Parry, Apple Rubber Products, Inc.
Nancy Perkins, Xerox Corporation
Jim Prendergast , JWP Group

Jane Quinn, Replogle Globes, Inc.

Janet Rapp, MTS Systems Corporation
Jim Rapp, Market Central, Inc.

Anne Schaeffer, Dave Smith, and Susanne Sicilian, The DMA
Michael Seymour, Heritage Exhibits
Ted Seward, BCC Software
Peter Shankman, The Geek Factory
Ellen Shannon, Publication and Conference Development Partners
Rich Simms, DialAmerica Marketing
Barry Siskind, International Training and Management Company, and author of *The Power of Exhibit Marketing*
Gary Slack, Slack Barshinger & Partners, Inc.

Marci R. Snyder and Kathryn Munn, Woolpert LLC
Ken St. John, NoteSystem.com
George Stadnik, LuckyGolfer, Inc.
Judy Studenski, Bob Irving, and Marilee Summers, American Slide Chart
John Suhler, Veronis Suhler Stevenson

Mike Thimmesch, Skyline Exhibits
Diane Tiberio, Reed Exhibitions

Brian Vanden Broucke, Articulate Creative
George L. Vanik, Northrop Grumman
Anne Vargo, CDW Computer Centers
Karen Vidoni, Perrygraf

Steve Wallis, AIRxpert Systems, Inc.
Margit B. Weisgal, Sextant Communications
Jacques Werth, High Probability Selling
Michael Westcott, The George P. Johnson Company
Charles S. Whiting, Jr., Astoria Graphics

I would also like to thank my long-suffering husband, Jim Spencer, my indefatigable editor, Rich Hagle, and his brilliant copyeditor, Margaret Maloney, for their support.

1

Introduction to Trade Shows and Corporate Events

Trade shows and corporate events provide an efficient opportunity for face-to-face contact with customers and prospects—an essential component in the business-to-business sales and marketing process.

When chief marketing officers are asked what's on their minds, they talk about demand generation, revenue productivity, and the link between sales and marketing. While there may be a chasm between sales and marketing in many companies, at the top of the marketing food chain, the chasm is generally bridged. All parties at the top of the pyramid are firmly focused on business results.

Trade shows and corporate events are perfectly suited to serve as a buttress in support of that bridge. Business events uniquely combine elements of marketing, marketing communications, and sales. They can identify high-potential prospects, accelerate the sales process, introduce new products, assist in entering new markets, boost public relations, nurture relationships with existing customers—the functions are many and varied.

However, the power of business events is little understood by marketers today. Business event marketing is viewed as a tactical, logistical function, and frequently delegated to a junior staffer who happens to have an operational bent. Worse, business event marketers frequently manage to evade the requirement that their investments demonstrate a return. But for their power to be exploited fully, business events must be viewed strategically, as part of an integrated go-to-market process.

Business events represent a significant line item in the business marketing budget. American businesses spend $21 billion on trade show marketing annually, according to the Center for Exhibition Industry Research (CEIR). In a 2003 poll of its members, the Business Marketing Association found that trade shows represent 18.6% of marketing budgets. According to *Meetings & Conventions* magazine, in 2003 companies spent $15 billion on corporate meetings, of which 67% were devoted to sales and marketing objectives.

It's clear that business events are a big part of the marketing mix. But when senior managers are asked what they get from their investment in business events, most are unable to give a satisfactory answer. "Well, we are there every year," they may say. Or, "We do a lot of business at trade shows." Or, "Our customers tell us they enjoy our events."

At the same time, business event spending continues to escalate. Trade show productions have grown ever more elaborate over the years: triple-decker booths, plasma television walls, live theater with Broadway actors—one-ups-manship abounds. Corporate events represent one of the highest cost-per-contact elements of the marketing mix.

Is this any way to spend $21 billion, or $15 billion? This book proposes to shed some light on trade show and corporate event marketing, from the point of view of business marketing strategy as a whole. Its intended audience is a marketing manager, director, and vice president, or a senior finance or management executive who thinks about sales and marketing strategy.

The twin themes of this book are:

1. Trade shows and corporate events can be an effective component of an integrated sales and marketing strategy, but they must be applied to their best use. Business events support some marketing objectives extremely well. But business marketers tend to pay little attention to business events—$21 bil-

lion and $15 billion in budget notwithstanding. Or, if they are paying attention, they seem to expect the event to deliver against an objective for which it is ill-suited. Simply put, business events need to be managed strategically.

2. Investments in trade shows and corporate events can be—and must be—measured. Business events need to be compared on a return on investment (ROI) basis to the other tactical levers available in the marketing toolkit. In short, business events must pay their way and justify their existence. Many people claim that business events are hard to measure. Hogwash.

The Focus of This Book

Book topics must be bounded, or they rapidly turn into lifetime projects. This book has been fenced off to consider trade show and corporate event marketing within three categories.

First, the book focuses on business trade shows and corporate events, versus consumer shows or events. The target reader is a business-to-business marketer for whom business event marketing is a potentially important part of the go-to-market strategy. This marketer must consider business events in comparison and in concert with other sales and marketing options, like advertising, direct mail, telemarketing, Internet marketing, and direct sales calls. This marketer expects all marketing activities to demonstrate results.

Second, this book defines business events to mean trade shows and proprietary corporate events, where companies invite customers, prospects, and business partners to meet with them for mutual business benefit. Originally, this book was conceived to be about trade shows alone, and how business marketers can get the most value from their trade show investments. However, it quickly became clear that corporate events are gaining in importance and share of budgets as an alternative approach to obtaining similar results, so business marketers are shifting some of those monies into corporate events. This book covers both trade shows and corporate events, which together offer many similarities and synergies.

But broaching the topic of "business events" opens a sizable can of worms. Business event marketing is subject to very broad interpretation these days. This book limits itself to trade shows and corporate events, and does not consider the wider world of business marketing, such as sports event sponsorship, cause marketing, entertainment marketing, such as music concerts and comedy, mobile marketing, publicity stunts, guerilla or field marketing, and the myriad other business event-related marketing activities that are intended to create an interactive experience with a brand.

Third, this book has a domestic focus. Business event marketing on an international scale deserves a book of its own.

Business event marketing suffers from widespread confusion about the meaning of "business event" and what categories should be included in the discussion. Any attempt at bringing some order to the subject risks legitimate complaints about overlap and subjectivity. With apologies in advance, this book organizes events as shown in Exhibit 1.1.

Exhibit 1.1: The Taxonomy of Business Events

Business Events		
Trade Shows	**Corporate Events**	**Other Events ***
• Vertical, horizontal, and niche • National, regional, and local • Association or not-for-profit • Conferences, conventions, and meetings	• Road shows • User groups • Client conferences • Partner conferences • Single-customer events • Educational seminars • Executive seminars • Webinars • Entertainment events	• Sports sponsorships • Mobile marketing • Guerilla marketing • Cause marketing • Publicity stunts • Consumer events

*not covered in this book

Defining Our Terms

This book uses fairly narrow definitions for several key terms in business-to-business event marketing:

- *Business event* is an umbrella term encompassing trade shows and proprietary corporate events designed to serve customers, prospects, and resellers. As previously noted, this book does not deal with the broader world of events, such as sports sponsorships and mobile marketing.
- *Trade show* means a conference, convention, or meeting organized and managed by a company or association that brings multiple sellers together with multiple buyers. A defining characteristic of a trade show is that sellers can display their wares in some type of exhibit hall.
- *Corporate event* is defined in this book as a proprietary event for the organization's customers, prospects, or business partners. A corporate event may or may not include an exhibit area of some sort. A defining characteristic is that it is owned by the marketer, versus a third party.
- *Show organizer* or *show manager* is the company that attracts the registered attendees and recruits the exhibitors, and may or may not select the program content for a trade show. The *show sponsor* is the organization—often an industry association—that provides vertical knowledge, expertise, and connections to attract program content and drive attendance.
- *Lead*, or *sales lead*, is used to mean a contact that has been assessed and deemed worthy of adding to the marketing database for later follow up and conversion. A *qualified lead* is one that has been developed to the point where it is ready to be passed to a sales person. These definitions are intended to counter the overuse of "lead" to refer to contacts of all sorts, even those that will never be a candidate to make a purchase.

The Trade Show and Corporate Event Industry Today

Business events are big business. As a category, trade shows are the more mature, and enjoy considerable support from trade and professional associations that track and report on industry statistics. Information about corporate events is somewhat harder to find, but clearly proprietary events are a growing category, and trade groups are beginning to form around them.

The leading research organization supporting the exhibition industry, meaning trade shows, is the Center for Exhibition Industry Research (CEIR), based in Chicago. According to CEIR's *Exhibition Industry Census*, in the U.S. and Canada combined, there were 13,185 trade shows in 2000, of which 85% were business-to-business trade shows. Two-thirds of these business trade shows are owned by nonprofit groups, like industry and trade associations. The rest are owned by for-profit companies. In the U.S. alone, CEIR identified 11,094 shows. Between 1986 and 2000, exhibitions with over 10,000 net square feet of space grew at a compound annual growth rate of 7.36%. The average net square feet of exhibit space per show in 2000 was 38,066, and, together, these trade shows attracted 44 million qualified buyers and 1.5 million exhibiting companies.

According to *Tradeshow Week*, the average company in 2003 participated in 46 trade shows. The average business-to-business trade show in 2003 had 337 exhibitors and 127,301 net square feet of exhibit space, attracting 7,099 attendees. This is big business, as an industry, and big opportunity for marketers.

Business buyers use trade shows as a decision-making environment. When asked what actions they had taken at the last show they attended, 26% said they had signed a purchase order, and 51% said they had requested a sales person call on them. Even more broadly, 76% said they had requested a price quote, and 77% said they had found a new supplier. This is an environment where buyers are looking and sellers are getting connected with them.

Business events are gaining in prominence within the business marketing mix. Between 1996 and 2000, the percentage of company marketing budgets spent on trade shows grew substantially, from 14% to 24%, according to CEIR. According to the George P. Johnson Company, in North America more than 1 million "event-scale" meetings were held, including proprietary corporate events as well as trade shows.

The buyers are there, and the sellers are there. The marketer's job is to make the sales magic happen.

Trends in Trade Show and Corporate Event Marketing

The business event industry has experienced some difficulties over time. Companies and associations continue to consolidate, reducing the number of potential exhibitors and sponsors. Travel budgets tend to be slashed during economic downturns, and of course domestic travel safety has become an issue in recent years. Initially, the arrival of the Internet raised some questions about whether people would be getting together online instead of at conferences—a concern that has not, in fact, materialized.

But perhaps most problematic for the industry is exhibitors' difficulty in proving the value of the business event to the company bottom line. If 18.6% of your marketing budget is devoted to a category that cannot demonstrate results, questions will inevitably arise, and budgets will be shifted to other, more apparently productive activity. This book is intended to address this very issue.

The Center for Exhibition Industry Research—albeit a source with an agenda—remains bullish on the future of trade show and corporate event marketing. CEIR points out a number of positive trends that will continue to drive exhibition industry growth:

- The importance of face-to-face marketing continues unabated. But as the cost of direct sales calls continues to climb, trade shows and corporate events provide a comparatively efficient venue for customer meetings.
- Associations, which own two-thirds of business-to-business trade shows, continue to grow as a category, and trade shows are an important part of their service to members as well as their revenue.
- Large trade shows continue to spawn smaller niche and vertical trade shows, to meet the needs of marketers for more targeted venues.

- There continues to be demand for exhibit space. CEIR's 2000 *Exhibition Industry Census* estimated that 18% of business events enjoy sold-out exhibit halls, with potential exhibitors on waiting lists.
- Business events attract a higher quality audience than ever. In a 2001 study, 53% of CEOs said they would attend between three and five trade shows in the year. And 84% of overall trade show attendees stated that they have buying authority for their companies.

From a business marketer's perspective, additional trends in the world of trade shows and corporate events are apparent:

- The efficiency of trade shows as a medium for reaching qualified buyers is trending down. According to Skip Cox of Exhibit Surveys, traffic density in the average exhibit hall has slipped from 4.1 in 1980 to 2.3 attendees per 100 square feet in 2002. Worse, the percent of attendees who say they are attending with plans to buy is down from 62% in 1990 to 53% in 2002. Cox concludes that marketers must work harder to make the trade show productive.
- Exhibitors are gaining in market savvy. They are pressuring trade show organizers to control costs, and to provide reliable metrics on attendee quantity and quality. They are buying more adaptable booth apparatus for lower costs, better portability, and re-configurable use at multiple business events. They are renting booths instead of buying, to gain flexibility and speed. They are voting with their feet, shifting from large horizontal trade shows to smaller, more targeted vertical trade shows.
- Exhibitors are adding proprietary corporate events to their mix. According to CEIR's new study *The Role and Value of Face-to-Face Interaction*, 47% of exhibitors now hold proprietary corporate events, and 71% of trade show attendees say they also go to proprietary corporate events. The study reported that respondents attend an average of 3.5 trade shows and 3.3 proprietary corporate events per year. Similiarly, Mike Westcott, Vice President of Marketing at the George P. Johnson Company, reports

that his 2003 *Event Trends* study found that 47% of senior executives intend to give a high priority to corporate events, compared to 40% when the study was conducted in 2002. The appeal of corporate events to business marketers—the control, and the dedicated market access they offer—is apparent.

- Corporate event spending differs across industries. In the George P. Johnson 2003 *Event Trends* study, there was considerable variation within the 47% of executives who consider corporate events increasingly important. Pharmaceutical and healthcare executives said their corporate event spending would decrease between 2002 and 2003. The industry breakout underlying the 47% was as follows:

    —Financial 56%
    —Automotive 47%
    —Healthcare 38%
    —High tech 28%
    —Consumer/other 52%

- Marketers are consolidating their corporate event business with preferred vendors, seeking cost efficiencies, standard practices, and well-managed event portfolios. For example, Microsoft selected Freeman as its corporate event management company, and IBM placed its worldwide corporate event portfolio with George P. Johnson.

- As key accounts become a larger part of the revenue base at many companies, trade show programs are being combined with invitation-only pre-show events. Power buyers insist on an early—even exclusive—look at new products before the rest of the pack. For example, at New York's spring Toy Show, vendors are adding a special pre-show viewing in December for key customers.

- Corporate events are on an upswing. *Meetings & Conventions* magazine's *2004 Meetings Market Report* indicated a sizable increase in business meetings between 2001 and 2003, from 844,100 to 890,994. Expense in the same period jumped from

$10.2 billion to $15 billion, suggesting substantial growth in the category.

- Independent observers note that, while trade shows have suffered in recent years, the outlook is generally positive for the category. Veronis Suhler Stevenson, investment banker to the communications industry, forecasts 4.8% compound annual growth for business-to-business spending on trade shows and exhibitions from 2002 to 2007, according to the company's 2003 *Communications Industry Forecast & Report.*
- Some questions still remain about the future of business events, as younger buyers' habits shift from traditional channels to

Exhibit 1.2: Perceived Value of Business Events

Business Event	Value Based on ROI or ROO	Value Perceived by Senior Management
Vertical trade shows (covering an industry segment)	68%	56%
Horizontal trade shows (covering an entire industry)	56%	40%
National/international trade shows in the U.S. and Canada	54%	45%
Regional trade shows	51%	28%
Conferences/meetings focused on educational sessions	27%	24%
International trade shows held outside the U.S. and Canada	19%	18%
Private trade shows (corporate events)	21%	23%
Other	1%	21%

Source: *Tradeshow Week's* Executive Outlook Survey, March 2003.

Tradeshow Week's March 2003 Executive Outlook survey reported on the business event types perceived as the most valuable based on ROI or ROO and senior management.

other media, such as the Internet. In business-to-business today, the Internet has not shown any signs of replacing the need for face-to-face contact, but as new generations emerge, the balance may tip.

The Marketer Versus the Event Manager

This book is aimed at the marketing executive in business-to-business companies of all sizes. Most books and trade publications on business events speak primarily to the needs of the exhibit manager or event manager, the person in the company with day-to-day responsibility for exhibiting at a trade show or pulling together a corporate event. This unsung hero deserves a lot of respect, for the management of the myriad details involved in the trade show and corporate event activity. Consider what is on the event manager's plate:

- Contracts, sourcing, and paperwork.
- Travel, lodging, and entertainment.
- Packing, shipping, drayage, set-up and tear-down, where Murphy's Law rules.
- Labor issues, regulations, and flaring tempers.

The exhibit manager who takes the company to a trade show is blamed by all, and appreciated by few. And the same holds true for event managers, who plan and organize proprietary corporate events. In fact, these people have many of the responsibilities of a show organizer, scouting locations, arranging for registration of attendees, recruiting speakers and session content, and all the logistics of travel, food and beverage, hotel nights, lighting, music—an enormous task. Sales and marketing management simply has no idea how much work it is to pull off a business event.

In recent years, as pressure grows on business event marketing to become more disciplined about results metrics and to justify budgets, the exhibit manager and event manager have been forced to take on some strategic marketing roles. Making decisions about selection.

Setting objectives. Deciding on key messaging. Arranging pre- and post-event marketing programs. This is asking too much. The marketing strategy for business events must come from a trained marketer, and it must be part of a fully considered program for meeting sales and marketing objectives.

Viewed from the other direction, business-to-business marketers themselves must become very familiar with business events as a strategic marketing tool. They must be able to incorporate events into their integrated go-to-market strategies. This means taking responsibility for this huge investment and ensuring that it drives the business profitably. It is the purpose of this book to open the door to a profitable, measurable, fully integrated business event marketing strategy for your company.

Exhibit 1.3: Marketing Budget Spent to Support Direct Sales

Marketing Budget Spent to Support Direct Sales	Percent
Trade shows	18.6%
Specialized business publication advertising	13.8%
Internet/electronic media	13.5%
Promotion/market support	10.9%
Publicity/public relations	10.8%
Direct mail	10.0%
Dealer/distributor materials	5.6%
Market research	4.1%
General magazine advertising	3.2%
Telemarketing/telecommunications	2.5%
Directories	1.6%
Other	5.5%

Source: Business Marketing Association 2003 Marketing Reality eSurvey.

Business marketers spend more on trade shows than any other category, according to a 2003 survey conducted among 250 of its members by the Business Marketing Association.

Trade Shows and Corporate Events as a Business Marketing Tool

Business-to-business selling, for the most part, involves face-to-face contact between buyer and seller. Business events, including trade shows and corporate events, provide an efficient venue for companies to meet their current and prospective buyers for personal interaction. Thus, business events can be a powerful component in a business-to-business go-to-market strategy.

This book concentrates on two key areas of business event marketing: trade shows and corporate events. Together, they form a productive part of the marketing mix. In many respects, they can be viewed together for planning purposes, but there are several differences as well. Exhibits 2.1 and 2.2 show how these two categories are similiar and how they are different.

Exhibit 2.1: The Convergence of Trade Shows and Corporate Events

- Face-to-face, quality time with customers and prospects
- High per contact cost compared to other marketing communications channels, but low cost per contact compared to direct sales
- Focus on identifying sales opportunity, whether leads into new accounts or penetration in existing accounts
- Typically considered part of the same function internally, for budgeting, organization, and management
- Best applied as part of an integrated end-to-end program, with pre-event communications and post-event follow-up

Exhibit 2.2: The Divergence of Trade Shows and Corporate Events

Trade Shows	Corporate Events
• Focus on prospects • Competitive clutter diffuses messaging and attention • Event schedule, content, and attendee population arranged by show organizer • Abundant PR opportunity	• Focus on current customers • Dedicated corporate focus allows more message control • Event entirely arranged by corporate marketer • Costs can be defrayed by including business partners or by charging attendees to come

Trade Shows and Corporate Events in the Marketing Mix

Trade shows and corporate events can be a powerful tool, but they are widely misunderstood, and consequently, misapplied. Let's review the strengths and weaknesses of these potent elements of the marketing toolkit, beginning with trade shows.

THE STRENGTHS OF TRADE SHOWS

Trade shows have been an important part of business marketing, probably since the days of their predecessors, bazaars and fairs, and for good reason. Here's why:

- Trade shows offer the opportunity to interact with customers and prospects in a face-to-face environment, but with more efficiency than in a series of single sales encounters. At a trade show, a sales rep will find more buyers in the room in one day than he or she can visit in a month. Many of your major customers and prospects will be there looking for ideas, information, and solutions.
- Trade shows attract active buyers. According to Center for Exhibition Industry Research (CEIR), 57% of trade show attendees are planning a purchase in the next 12 months. Furthermore, 93% have some buying influence, 66% recommend purchases or vendors, 40% specify a vendor, and 36% are the final purchase decision-makers.

- Business people value trade shows for information that supports their purchase decisions. A Yankelovich/Harris Interactive study in 2001 found that 49% of business people in 12 industry categories rate trade shows as valuable, second only to the 51% who valued trade publications, and higher than the 44% who valued websites.
- Interaction at a trade show accelerates the sales cycle. According to CEIR, sales leads generated from a trade show cost 56% less to close than those from direct field sales contact. While a field-only sale takes 3.7 calls to close, a lead from a trade show closes in only 1.6 calls. The Yankelovich/Harris Interactive study showed trade shows compelled 64% of respondents to buy or recommend a product, compared to trade publications (58%) and websites (50%).
- Trade shows help you identify new prospects. According to CEIR, only 12% of attendees will have been called on by an exhibitor's sales person in the past year. The trade show provides an opportunity to find these fresh prospects and begin a relationship.
- Trade shows are more than just another marketing communication medium. They uniquely combine sales with marketing—taking advantage of the power of each. You get the benefit of a face-to-face conversation combined with the ability to position your product and company, generate qualified leads, talk with industry press, research customer needs, keep an eye on competitors—a bonanza of sales and marketing opportunity.
- Trade shows are an expensive way to merely gather names, but an efficient way to gather qualified leads. Qualified buyers are coming to you at the show, and they are eager for information and solutions. While there certainly are some junkets and parties involved, the trade show business is about business.
- Trade show attendees include often hard-to-reach decision-makers and influencers—the people who won't take a meeting with a sales person, but will certainly go to a conference to keep up with their industry. In the 2001 Yankelovich/Harris Interactive study, 76% of business people said they had attended at least one trade show in the previous year. These people attended

three shows on average, and spent eight days at trade shows per year. And according to a 1996 CEIR study, 91% of CEOs surveyed said they planned to attend more than three trade shows in the year.

- People wear many hats at trade shows. Other exhibitors may also be your customers and prospects. Your competitors may also be your business partners. The atmosphere of a trade show is about business, and just about everyone there is worth influencing.

Exhibit 2.3: Reasons for Attending Trade Shows

Reason for Attending Trade Show	Percent of Respondents
See new technology or products	81%
Personal development	79%
Better job performance	76%
Recharge motivation	67%
Networking	66%
Hands-on experience	64%
Meet other users	61%
Learn about regulatory issues	61%
Seminars	60%
See what large institutions are doing	60%

Source: Center for Exhibition Industry Research.

THE WEAKNESSES OF TRADE SHOWS

Trade shows have been problematic for business marketers over the years. Representing a large chunk of the marketing budget, they are ripe for questions and for cuts. Shows can be vexing, on several fronts:

- Compared to other marketing communications channels, trade shows are expensive. You need a good reason to invest in a cost-per-contact number such as $250 with a trade show, when you can make a direct mail touch for $1 or conduct a webinar for $2 per contact.

- Without clear metrics and clear reporting on results, a trade show budget can seem like a big black hole.
- Many companies over-spend on the obvious elements—the booth, parties, premiums—and under-spend where it really counts, on the planning, promotion, data capture, post-show follow-up, and metrics.
- Marketers over-delegate to the exhibit manager, whose skills and training are closer to logistics than to marketing. It's unreasonable to expect this person to manage marketing strategy as well as the practical details of carpet rentals and drayage.
- Industry trade shows are a relatively high-risk form of marketing. Most come around once a year and soak up major budgets. If you've blown the trade show, you've blown it big.

It's no wonder that suspicion and confusion reign among business marketers and senior executives on the subject of trade show effectiveness.

Exhibit 2.4: Strengths, Weaknesses, and Best Applications of Trade Shows

Strengths	Weaknesses	Best Applications
• Concentrates many face-to-face contacts into a short time • Combines sales results with marketing impact • Gives access to hard-to-reach decision-makers • Cuts through the marketing communications clutter	• Expensive relative to other marketing communications media • Dependent on sales lead management systems to demonstrate ROI • High-risk investment—little ability to test the variables	• Prospecting among highly qualified audiences • Moving prospects along the sales cycle • Retaining and cross-selling current customers • Industry/competitive positioning and research • Introducing new products or entering new markets

THE STRENGTHS OF CORPORATE EVENTS

Proprietary corporate events offer the following key advantages to marketers:

- When creating a proprietary corporate event, the marketer has nearly complete control of the customer's experience with the company. You can shape the event to suit the needs of your audience—and meet your corporate sales and marketing objectives.
- Corporate events are an excellent venue for relationship building with key customers, from end-users, to technical personnel, to purchasing officials, to senior executives. The relationship can be deepened on both sides: you get more focused selling time, and the customers provide you with more insights into their needs and business problems.
- Corporate events are designed to allow higher level conversations than can be expected in the hustle and bustle of a trade show.
- Customers and prospects can focus on your message, without distractions from competitors.

THE WEAKNESSES OF CORPORATE EVENTS

Corporate events have their downsides, as well. Among them:

- Corporate events are expensive—most are either fully paid for or deeply subsidized by the marketer. On a cost per contact basis, corporate events can outstrip even the cost of a sales call.
- Proprietary, customized corporate events require considerable skill to organize. A bad event can do serious harm to your relationship with customers.
- Persuading the right customers to attend can be difficult.
- Some customers resist attending proprietary corporate events, preferring the chance to interact with multiple vendors simultaneously.
- When they gather together in one place, customers are prone to comparing notes about pricing, service issues, and other topics that can harm your relationship with them. Managing these unintended interactions presents a challenge.

**Exhibit 2.5: Strengths, Weaknesses, and
Best Applications of Corporate Events**

Strengths	Weaknesses	Best Applications
• Controls the customer's brand experience • Eliminates competitive distractions • Can sometimes be designed to break even	• Expensive cost per contact • No ability for customers to compare competing products • Can be difficult to persuade important clients to attend	• Enhancing relationship with current customers • Cross-selling and upselling • Moving qualified prospects along the sales cycle • Learning about customer problems and needs

The 10 Essential Principles of Business Event Marketing

With a little effort, business marketers can, in fact, have it all. Your objective is to get the most out of the enormous opportunity found in personal contact with a targeted audience of qualified buyers. First and foremost, you must consider the fundamental principles that drive successful business event marketing, whether at trade shows or corporate events. These boil down to an essential 10.

1. Business events are a hybrid sales and marketing activity. They combine elements of selling, of lead generation, of public relations, of research, of brand awareness building, of account penetration, to name a few. In fact, among marketing activities, business events are about as close to sales as you can get. You might say they are akin to a sales call combined with an ad and a PR campaign. If you think of them as simply "sales" or simply "marketing," you'll lose some of the leverage available to you. When you consider the business event opportunity, wear a very strategic marketing hat, so you don't miss anything.

2. Business events must be an integral part of the marketing mix. Consider them within the larger context of the entire go-to-market strategy. When seen as mere tactics, something "we do

every year because we always have," they will quickly devolve from an investment into an expense. Marketers must consider the entire marketing mix—the annual program—and fit in the business event opportunity where it will drive the most business. Marketing departments are responsible for pulling a variety of levers, and business events are just one of them. In many cases, a business event is not the right lever to meet the business objective.

3. Targeting is everything. A great business event is only as great as the visitors it attracts, and their value to you as customers and prospects. At a trade show, a fabulous booth is useless in front of the wrong people. So, trade show selection deserves your attention and your discipline. When you plan your participation at a business event, design your activities to attract the real potential buyers and minimize the number of non-prospects. Be very clear about whom you want to meet, and what conversations you want to have. Don't forget that current customers are, in fact, your best prospects for new business. So, target them as part of your trade show strategy as well as with your corporate events.

4. Set clear, specific objectives. Plan—and fund—the metrics by which you will measure your results. This should go without saying, but business events have been managed with less than due diligence in this area. As a result, business events as a whole have developed an undeserved reputation for being "difficult to measure." They are no more difficult than any other marketing activity. Events can be, and must be, measured,

5. Don't ask a business event to deliver on its weaknesses. Trade shows, for example, tend to be inefficient venues for generating awareness. They are an expensive way to build a mailing list. If those are your objectives, you will find other more compelling options in the business marketing toolkit. Neither are business events effective opportunities to keep up with the Joneses. If your competitors at a trade show have fancier booths, a bigger footprint, or splashier sponsorships, you can congratulate yourself. You are probably driving better business results than

they, with your focused, targeted, and measurable business event marketing activities.

6. The business event itself is only a few days in the midst of a larger, multi-month program. It's the tip of the iceberg: it's what you see, but it's only a minor part of business event marketing. Some companies think that if they pull together a booth and show up at the trade show, they are all set. Keep in mind that you are conducting an end-to-end marketing campaign, with the business event itself as a part of it. Also, remember that business event expenses tend to be incurred in various departments throughout a company. In order to understand the true investment your company is making in the business event, and its cost to the company, all these costs must be gathered from all departments, and analyzed as a whole.

7. Promote your business event. At a trade show, you cannot simply rely on show management to get you all the possible business opportunities at the show. Pre-show promotions are perhaps the greatest under-leveraged opportunity in trade show marketing today. This is where the right targets are identified, and attracted to meet with you face to face. For corporate events, promotions are required to drive attendance in the first place.

8. Capture and follow up on your business event contacts. Post-event is where the real revenue-driving business is done. At a trade show, go for the quality, versus the quantity, of contacts. Lead capture and management is a process; it simply requires attention and diligence. If you don't have a lead management process in place at your company, stop now. Go build one before you invest another dollar in business event marketing.

9. It's all about people. If business events are an efficient face-to-face medium, then the leverage to be gained is in the people involved on both sides of the interaction. Success is about targeting the right audience and persuading them—and only them—to interact with you at the business event. It's equally about selecting, training, and motivating a strong staff to communicate with them.

10. The business event serves business goals. Don't neglect the forest for the trees. Managing events is an extremely complicated activity, what with the glamorous exhibit and the fun hospitality on the one hand, and the rigors of the logistics and the myriad details on the other. But these activities are simply the trees—they are a means to an end. The forest lies in the business result and the planning that drives it. If you are paying attention to the trees alone, you miss the true power of event marketing.

Challenges and Considerations in Business Event Marketing Strategy

Business events work best when they fit into an integrated go-to-market plan. Unfortunately, in many companies business events are relegated to a very tactical role, and under-leveraged at the strategic level. Marketers would do well to take charge, recognizing that business event marketing has enormous potential, and elevating it to its rightful role at the strategic marketing table.

But before marketers can migrate business event marketing into the mix, they must consider a number of basic issues in business marketing today.

Ask any random person who has passing familiarity with business-to-business marketing the following question: When you think of "marketing" in business-to-business, what do you mean? The overwhelming majority of respondents will say "advertising." No surprise. The concept of marketing in business-to-business has been demoted, essentially, to marketing communications, with advertising being perhaps the most visible of the communications media. This is a distortion of the concept, and it excuses the need to plan and budget strategically and responsibly.

Part of the confusion is semantic. Marketing communications is simply the most common meaning for marketing. There are others. In some companies, sales reps are referred to as marketing reps, so marketing is really a euphemism for sales. In other companies, engineers are called product marketers, in an effort to make product development more responsive to market needs. The upshot? A jumble of legacy terms muddies the waters. Everyone is confused about the meaning of marketing in business-to-business. And it gets worse.

SALES VERSUS MARKETING: WHO'S IN CHARGE HERE?

Marketing's relationship to sales is another problem area. Considerable confusion reigns regarding the relative roles of sales and marketing in a business-to-business company. If marketing is not just marketing communications—or even if it is—what should marketing be doing, and what should be the province of sales? The roles can vary from industry to industry, across company sizes, and from company to company. There is little agreement to be found.

Relegating the function of marketing to mere marketing communications is a waste of talent, resources, and productivity. That's bad enough. Even worse, when roles and responsibilities are unclear, the result is inefficiency, staff conflict, and annoyed customers. So it benefits the business marketer to gain some clarity—and agreement—throughout the company on the optimal role for marketing.

The truth is, in business-to-business, marketing is typically in a service role to sales. Marketing's job is dedicated to optimizing the sales function. But it is not just marketing communications. It should serve a far broader strategic and tactical role.

As marketing supports sales, it conducts research to uncover the market opportunity and to gain insight into customer needs for product development and positioning; it builds awareness of the offerings in the marketplace using tools like advertising and public relations; it provides customer-facing opportunities like parties, trade shows, and meetings; it develops the communications materials—collateral, signage, letters, gifts—that keep the relationship moving. It generates qualified leads to make the sales force more productive. It regularly evaluates and reports on its results, and seeks continual improvement.

The roles are that of a partnership, with separate but complementary duties. Business-to-business companies are most effective when the sales people are selling and the marketers are identifying sales opportunity and keeping the pipeline full.

This stands in sharp contrast to the role of marketing on the consumer side. In consumer package goods, for example, marketing essentially runs the business. Marketing holds P&L responsibility, sets strategy, decides on optimal products, pricing, promotion, and distribution. Sales is just one of the many levers marketing pulls to go to market effectively. And some observers of the business-to-business world hold out hope, vainly, that this is the way things might work in their world as well.

But in business-to-business, sales typically runs the P&L, and marketing is seen as a cost center—something to be cut when times are tough or when sales fails to meet its revenue targets.

HOW MARKETING CONNECTS
WITH BUSINESS EVENTS

When it comes to business events, confusion about the role of sales and marketing translates into uncertainty about who should do what to whom. In some companies, business events are viewed as so critical to the sales effort that the trade show and event function reports, organizationally, to sales management. Marketing in such companies is typically responsible only for marketing communications, meaning awareness advertising, setting brand image standards, public relations, corporate communications, collateral materials, and market research. For the business events, they might be called upon to supply graphics and maybe arrange a hospitality suite.

But the ideal role for marketing in business-to-business is a more strategic one. As the business-to-business marketing thought leader Tracy Emerick has so colorfully opined, marketers should be like eagles—flying around above the plains, seeing the large picture, exploring the opportunity, and identifying the best prospects. Sales people, on the other hand, are like the buffaloes—heads down, focusing on the grass, persistently working the opportunity, and closing the business. Marketing's role is to observe, identify the opportunity over the longer term, and then make sure sales has the near-term resources it needs to go get the revenue.

In the world of trade shows and corporate events, the implications are clear: business events are the province of marketing and part of its mission to make sales more effective. Whether this is defined as a service or a partnership is best left to the culture of the organization. The point here is that marketing is most effective when it has all the marketing options available, to manage them as an organic whole, and get the most value from each piece.

If we are clear that trade show and corporate event management belongs in marketing, then what is the role of sales in events? The sales team is responsible for:

- Working the business event, as requested by marketing.
- Contacting current customers for appointments or invitations.
- Working the business event leads that have been generated, qualified, and distributed.
- Providing information to marketing on lead disposition status.

There needs to be some clarification of the respective roles of marketing and sales in lead generation and management. One of marketing's key roles in business-to-business is generating qualified leads for sales. This means that, when it comes to the lead process, marketing is responsible for the following functions:

- Lead generation.
- Fulfillment.
- Qualification.
- Nurturing.
- Lead distribution.
- Tracking and analysis.

Here too, the implication is clear. Lead management belongs in marketing, not in sales. Marketing's job is to deliver the right number of qualified leads, at the right time, to support the sales team's quota requirements. If marketing hands over unqualified leads, it has failed in its mission. If sales takes on the qualification process, it is wasting its precious resources.

A cautionary tale about how unclear roles can lead to business event marketing disasters comes from George Stadnik, Vice President of LuckyGolfer, Inc., an interactive entertainment media company in Stamford, Connecticut. Stadnik was on the trade show and corporate event staff at Data General, years ago, when the company was ready to roll out a new suite of office automation products via a 10-city national road show tour.

"My job at the time was trade show logistics. Marketing, sales, and PR were all responsible for the outcome of the tour, but the event design was developed unilaterally by marketing and ended up being somewhat confused. The event was only about marketing's vision of the Data General brand, about "here we are, aren't we great and by the way, here's our stuff," says Stadnik ruefully. "An architectural design company was hired to design and produce the set pieces for the tour, and what they ended up building, we couldn't set up or break down quickly with the available union help. Worse, the local sales teams were left out of strategy development, and they pulled their support for the program. As a result, the only customer invitations that went out came from corporate marketing contact lists. At the first event in Chicago, the press showed up, but there were zero customers there. We were already committed to run the next event in New York, but we cancelled the rest of the dates. It was embarrassing, especially in light of the very successful sales driven events our competitors were doing on a cruise ship in Boston Harbor." Stadnik's conclusion: Sales is the client of marketing when it comes to events. If marketing is only thinking about communications, image, and brand, versus driving revenue for sales, much opportunity will be lost.

POSITIONING THE BUSINESS EVENT MARKETING FUNCTION INTERNALLY

Business event marketers—especially the exhibit managers and event managers—have had it tough. They are expected to handle every tiny logistical detail required to pull off a successful event, but are often blamed for every snafu, even those beyond their control. In the corporate hierarchy, business events people are relegated to the same outpost as other "below the line" functions such as direct marketing and sales promotion, and even may inhabit separate floors, buildings, or cities, from the rest of the marketing function.

Many companies don't know how to think about managing the business event function organizationally. Business event marketers might report to public relations, to corporate communications, to marketing communications, to sales, or even to the president's office.

But business event marketing—18.6% of the average marketing budget—needs to be taken seriously, and managed actively. Like the other marketing levers, business events should report to marketing management. Business marketers need to view business events holistically, recognizing that they contain various elements of sales and marketing functions. They must not be seen as mere logistics.

Neither should business events be seen as merely another form of marketing communications. Business events combine elements of so many marketing, sales, and marketing communications functions, they cannot be pigeon-holed solely as a communications channel, such as direct mail or advertising. In order to take advantage of the true power of business events, marketers must be educated as to their best uses, and close enough to their management to integrate them effectively into the go-to-market process.

LEADS VERSUS BRANDING: WHICH ARE WE DOING HERE?

A fierce debate rages on about the appropriate objectives to be pursued by marketing—actually marketing communications—in business-to-business. One camp, populated heavily by marketers with an advertising bent, argues that the objective of marketing communications is to build awareness and deliver a consistent brand experience to customers and prospects. Awareness is typically measured by such indicators as recall and attitude. Consistency is ensured by the use of stylebooks and "brand stewardship" review boards who keep an eye on the art, copy, and logo usage that appears in various media channels, including trade show graphics and business event signage.

The other camp is populated with a combination of sales people and marketers who have sales promotion or direct marketing inclinations—those who live "below the line," in agency-speak. They argue that the role of marketing is to drive revenue, specifically by making the sales force more productive. They respect the power of a consistent brand image to help the sales effort get a foot in the door and encourage customer retention. But their primary focus is on revenue. And at a trade show, it's on generating qualified leads and offering sales people plenty of opportunity to meet with their customers. At a corporate event, it's arranging for plenty of face-to-face time for sales people with customers and prospects, and with a focus on upselling and cross-selling opportunity.

If you have not already gathered, the bias of this book is firmly toward the latter camp. Here is the argument, as it relates to business events: business events provide an ideal environment for face-to-face interaction between company representatives and current and prospective buyers. Buyers come to shows and meetings to do business, to learn about new products, and to solve business problems. This is exactly the right opportunity to begin, nurture, and even close sales conversations. If the primary objective for the business event is building awareness or image, a major revenue-generating opportunity is wasted. Furthermore, when you consider the expense per impression of business events versus other communications channels, a trade show or corporate event is simply the least efficient brand awareness medium available.

This is not to say that communications should not be carefully structured at a business event. Business events are, after all, an important component in the brand experience. As Don Barshinger of the Chicago communications agency, Slack Barshinger, points out, "Everything communicates. The trade show booth does deliver a message. That message must be deliberate." No element of the business event program should do anything to harm the reputation and the image of the brand.

But that is a given for any form of marketing communications. All messages must be consistent with what customers and prospects expect to see and hear from your company.

The important point here is that marketing—and marketing communications—share responsibility with sales for driving revenue. Somehow, in the last several decades, some marketers have retreated from this responsibility. In the "old days," businesses expected their marketing communications to drive sales. Why else spend the money? If the new ad campaign didn't lift sales results, the ad agency was fired.

But somewhere along the line, marketing communicators converted their goals from sales to something called branding. Essentially, this meant brand awareness and image, as measured by surveys about whether customers remember the ad, and felt good about the company. Marketers also measured purchase intent, as stated by survey respondents—but there was no direct link to purchase behavior. A sizable gap can exist between what prospects say they will do and what they actually do. In this environment, if the customers didn't buy, marketing could point their fingers at sales and say "That's your job, not ours."

In some business-to-business companies, especially large enterprises, this "branding" view of the proper role of marketing has gained some traction. But in most companies, marketers are still on the hook to drive revenue, as they should be. Business owners want tangible results they can take to the bank. This is where business event marketing has a superb role to play.

EVENTS VERSUS OTHER ELEMENTS OF THE MARKETING TOOLKIT

If business events are to be integrated into the marketing mix, they must be applied to their best use. Analyzing each element of the business-to-business marketing toolkit is an essential step in this process. The marketer who sets objectives and selects the best elements for a program to meet those objectives must consider the entire universe of options available.

The marketing mix, however, is complicated. It includes a variety of channels, which can be hard to classify. The most appropriate taxonomy of marketing activities will be a function of your products, industry, company size, corporate culture, and a host of other factors. But for the sake of discussion, here is a sample classification system.

1. Sales channels
   —Field sales
   —Inside sales
   —Ecommerce/call center
   —Third-party distributors

2. Marketing functional channels
   —Events
   —PR
   —Sales promotion
   —Packaging
   —Customer service

3. Marketing communications channels
   —Direct mail
   —Email
   —Outbound telemarketing
   —Inbound telemarketing
   —Website
   —Search engine marketing
   —Print
   —Television
   —Radio
   —Banners

As discussed earlier, trade shows and corporate events contain within them elements of numerous sales and marketing elements. So, any attempt to segment events out and compare them to the other functions is fraught with problems. However, to shed some light on the relative merits of the elements of in the marketing toolkit, Exhibit 2.6 provides a brief comparative analysis.

Exhibit 2.6: Comparative Analysis of Marketing Tools by Channels

Marketing Tool	Considerations	Best Applications
Sales Channels		
Field sales	High cost per contact Narrow market coverage ability	Close sales Work qualified leads Key account management
Inside sales	Broader coverage Lower cost per contact	Team with outside sales Coverage of lower-value accounts
Ecommerce/call center	7 x 24 customer access Supports deep product SKUs Lowest cost per contact	High-volume, low-value product lines Replacement parts Occasional buyers
Third-party distributors	Broad market coverage Loyalty issues Control issues	Value-added sales Market coverage
Marketing Functional Channels		
Events	Low cost for face-to face Targeted, motivated audience	New product introduction Lead generation Customer relationship management
PR	Low cost High credibility Control issues	Awareness New product introduction
Sales promotion	Erodes brand value perception	Short-term sales driver
Packaging	Customer's first physical experience with the product	Positioning
Customer service	Costly but essential to customer satisfaction	Customer relationship management

(continued)

Exhibit 2.6: *continued*

Marketing Tool	Considerations	Best Applications
Marketing Communications Channels		
Direct mail	Targeted Personal Expensive in low quantities Long planning cycle	Lead generation Customer relationship management
Email	Includes solo email and newsletters Customer concerns with spam Very low cost per touch Fast turnaround and results	Retention Lead qualification Lead nurturing
Outbound telemarketing	Highly flexible Intrusive Penetrates small universes	Lead generation Lead qualification Lead nurturing
Inbound telemarketing	Can be outsourced or in-sourced	Customer service Response management
Website	Multi-functional Easy to update Passive medium	Awareness Lead generation Response management Retention
Search engine marketing	Highly targeted Difficult to manage	Lead generation
Print	Trade media and busi- ness media available Broad reach Efficient cost per thousand	Awareness Lead generation
Television	High fixed cost of production	Awareness for broadly focused product or brand Lead generation
Radio	Highly flexible Regional selectivity	Awareness for broadly focused product or brand
Banners	Best with highly targeted media Fast turnaround and results	Lead generation

A number of useful studies have contributed insight to our understanding of the relative value of business events as part of the marketing toolkit. *Tradeshow Week*'s June 2003 Executive Outlook survey asked corporate marketers to rate the value of various marketing mediums. Exhibit 2.7 provides the percent selecting "very" or "somewhat" valuable. Notice how critically important event marketing is viewed by these respondents.

Exhibit 2.7: The Importance of the Marketing Mix Elements

Marketing Medium	Percent of Corporate Marketers Rating Marketing Mediums "Very" or "Somewhat" Valuable
Sales force	97%
Website	97%
Event marketing (in all forms)	96%
Trade magazine advertising	87%
Direct mail	85%
Marketing partnerships	81%
Email, outbound	78%
Fax marketing	46%
Call center telemarketing	42%
Retail in-store positioning and incentives	40%
Newspaper advertising	31%
Television advertising	22%
Radio advertising	19%

Source: *Tradeshow Week's* Executive Outlook Survey, June 2003.

CEIR's 2002 study, *The Role and Value of Face-to-Face Interaction*, asked trade show attendees and exhibitors to value various elements of the sales and marketing toolkit. The following numbers represent the percent of respondents who rated the element "very valuable" or "extremely valuable." Notice how the level of agreement between attendees and exhibitors is closest on the subject of the value of business events. Marketers would do well to pay more attention to the views of their customers when it comes to selecting elements of the event marketing mix.

Exhibit 2.8: The Value of Marketing Levers

Elements of the Sales and Marketing Toolkit	Respondents	
	Attendees	Exhibitors
Exhibitions	70	77
Sales calls	71	95
User groups	57	75
Technical conferences	60	64
Mobile truck exhibits	45	78
Permanent briefing/demo centers	52	86

Source: Center for Exhibition Industry Research, *The Role and Value of Face-to-Face Interaction,* 2002 study.

CEIR also reported how corporate marketers apportion their budgets, by percent, among the various sales and marketing options available to them. Exhibitions comprise 14% of the entire sales and

Exhibit 2.9: How Marketing Dollars are Allocated

Sales and Marketing Options	Industries				
	High Tech	Food/ Beverage	Manufacturing	Healthcare	Overall
Direct/ Field sales	41%	42%	47%	40.5%	47%
Exhibitions	18%	17%	18.6%	21.3%	14%
Advertising	13.6%	16%	14%	11.6%	1.5%
Direct mail	11%	5.6%	7.1%	8.6%	9%
Public Relations	4.4%	7.4%	8.2%	8.3%	6.5%
Telemarketing	6.4%	4.4%	3.7%	4.5%	5%

Source: Center for Exhibition Industry Research, *The Role and Value of Face-to-Face Interaction,* 2002 study.

marketing budget—very close to the 18.6% number reported by the Business Marketing Association.

American Business Media commissioned a 2001 study by Yankelovich/Harris Interactive to explore the value of various business communications media among 505 executives in companies with revenues larger than $5 million. From the point of view of consumers of business information, versus advertisers or communicators, the respondents named the following relative strengths of the three media under consideration.

Exhibit 2.10: Comparing Strengths of Trade Shows, Trade Magazines, and Websites

Media	Strengths
Business magazines	Highly credible sources Provides information you can trust
Business websites	Primary source for research Access to the latest information
Trade shows	Interaction with industry peers Personal interaction with company representatives Direct experience with products and services

Source: Yankelovich/Harris Interactive, 2001 study.

Strategic Approaches to Event Marketing

Business events are at their most powerful when they are part of an integrated go-to-market strategy. Integration can be viewed from at least two perspectives:

1. The business event is one of many marketing and sales levers, all working to their individual best advantages, where together they create a whole that is greater than the sum of its parts. In this approach, business events are added to the mix along with direct mail, telemarketing, field sales, public relations, websites, and a grand plan emerges containing the best elements for the job.
2. The business event is internally integrated. The business event itself is seen as part of a larger campaign or program, where all

elements of the marketing mix are put to work, before, during and after the event. Databases, direct mail, telemarketing, public relations, sales promotion, advertising, entertainment, and sponsorship marketing all work together to maximize results. The business event itself is only the shortest—albeit perhaps the most expensive—element in a four-to-six month campaign, end to end.

Integration sounds logical, but how do you actually pull it off? First, you have to have control—or at least influence—over all the elements of the marketing mix. That's a given. Then, you must decide on which of several approaches to strategic marketing planning make the most sense for your company. Business marketers tend to select from among strategies based on the following:

- Customer life cycle.
- Customer value segmentation.
- Product life cycle.
- The customer's buying process.
- Quarterly (or periodic) sales objectives.

BUSINESS EVENT PLANNING BASED ON THE CUSTOMER LIFE CYCLE

A company's relationship with a customer or set of customers goes through a natural series of stages known as the customer life cycle. At each stage, the needs of the customer are different, so the strategies the marketer applies to meet those needs must be different, too. Ultimately, in life cycle marketing, the marketer's objective is to move every customer along the continuum toward the "core," where the customer is a loyal, frequent, satisfied buyer. Once there, the company's strategy converts to defection prevention and customer value optimization.

Business event marketing can be applied neatly to support company objectives at each stage of the customer life cycle. Consider the following chart, which outlines in a typical series of life cycle stages the marketing strategies that might be associated with each stage, and the business event levers that can best serve those marketing objectives. Keep in mind that this is an oversimplified view, intended to illustrate the thought process that goes into applying events to the customer life cycle.

**Exhibit 2.11: Marketing Strategies
for a Typical Customer Life Cycle Stage**

Life Cycle Stage	Marketer's Objective	Best Business Event Applications
Prospect	Evaluate potential and stimulate trial or purchase	Trade show
Trial user or first time buyer	Ensure satisfaction and stimulate repeat purchase	Road show
Repeat buyer	Ensure satisfaction and stimulate multi-product purchase	User group
Core customer	Keep them happy and buying; solicit referrals	Client conference
Defector	Solve problems and win back	Entertainment event

Do not take this chart as a turnkey formula for making life cycle marketing decisions. Business event types can be applied to a variety of objectives—that is one of their key advantages. Trade shows, for example, are equally effective tools for communicating with current customers and for finding new prospects. And client conferences can help you persuade qualified prospects to join the customer fold.

BUSINESS EVENT PLANNING AROUND CUSTOMER VALUE

Companies that segment customers by value, or potential value, are looking to optimize the return on the customer asset. They seek to enhance the value of each account, either by improving sales and margins, or reducing the cost to serve, or a combination. To this end, each account's potential is assessed, and differentiated strategies are put in place. On a tactical level, this means that different customers will receive different treatment. For example, a high-value account might be covered by a face-to-face sales team, while a low-value account is directed to purchase through the Internet. Or, a set of new products might be developed to offer into particular accounts to capture a larger share of their spending in the category.

Business events can be applied similarly to the objective of customer value maximization and differentiated treatment. The strategy might be applied on an account-by-account basis, or within an account, for example, treating key decision-makers differently from purchasing officials or junior staff, or client conferences may be limited to senior executives in large accounts. User group meetings may be organized along with a special concurrent VIP conference. At trade shows, marketers will set up invitation-only dinners for key clients and prospects. The possibilities are endless. However you decide to apply your business event options, customer value considerations can provide a helpful strategic base for your thinking.

BUSINESS EVENT PLANNING DRIVEN BY PRODUCT LIFE CYCLE

Marketers have long viewed business events as a natural fit with the product life cycle as it moves from introduction, to growth, maturity, and decline. For example, a new product may be scheduled for launch at a major industry trade show, where plenty of press representatives are in attendance. Road shows lend themselves well to a more thorough introduction to the features and benefits of a new product. User groups are ideal for managing customer usage and satisfaction with more mature products that are already in wide use in the marketplace.

Since business events are an efficient form of face-to-face marketing, they can be applied effectively at various stages of the product life cycle, with the possible exception of the stage of decline. While most marketers consider trade shows to be best applied at the product introduction stage, the CEIR conducted a study reporting that exhibiting has value through the stage of maturity. In the study, executives were asked to rate the effectiveness of various marketing options at the four stages of product life cycle. They ranked trade shows equally effective as print advertising, and second only to direct selling, in the first three stages of the product life cycle—introduction, growth, and maturity. In the stage of decline, however, they rated both advertising and trade shows as far less important than direct selling.

BUSINESS EVENT PLANNING BASED ON THE CUSTOMER'S BUYING PROCESS

Fortunately for marketers, most business buyers follow a fairly well defined process as they evaluate options and make purchase decisions. In some companies, the process is so well defined that it is codified, and prospects will share with you the exact steps they must go through to buy. The more marketers understand the buying process of their prospects, the more efficient they can become with their selling processes. The secret is to map the selling activity to the prospect's buying process stage.

See Exhibit 2.12 for a list of the typical steps a business buyer goes through. Of course, these steps will vary by industry and by company

Exhibit 2.12: Marketing Objectives at Each Stage of the Buying Process

Customer's Buying Process Stage	Marketer's Objectives
Identify need	Arouse interest
Research solutions	Be known to the research team
Develop short list	Be selected for short list
Request proposals/quotes	Submit winning proposal
Review proposals/quotes	Create preference
Negotiate	Preserve margins
Select vendor	Win!
Install and use	Satisfy and support usage
Upgrade	Upsell, cross-sell

size. On the right of the table is a list of the seller's objectives at each
stage. Notice how the seller's objectives vary as the prospect's needs
and activities evolve.

The successful marketer will analyze the buying stages for each account, or customer segment, and understand who is involved at each
stage. The marketer will then craft strategies to help the prospect
move to the next stage—preferably toward a purchase from the
seller, versus the competition. The ideal approach is to develop a
contact strategy for each prospect or customer appropriate to the
buying stage. Exhibit 2.13 suggests some of the tools the marketer
may appropriately use to influence the buyer's behavior.

**Exhibit 2.13: Marketing Tools to Influence Buyers
at Each Stage of the Buying Process**

Marketing Objectives	Options in Marketing Toolkit
Arouse interest	Advertising, PR
Be known to the research team	Advertising, PR, search engine, trade show
Be selected for short list	Direct mail, email, telephone, website, trade show
Submit winning proposal	Face-to-face sales, inside sales
Create preference	Face-to-face sales, inside sales, direct mail, webinar, road show
Preserve margins	Face-to-face sales, telesales
Win!	Face-to-face sales
Satisfy and support usage	Support, website, e-newsletter, user group
Upsell, cross-sell	Telesales, direct mail, trade show, client conference, webinar

There are two lessons for business event marketers embedded in the
notion of the business buying process.

1. Trade shows and corporate events are not the optimal marketing tool for every stage, but can be superb when applied at the
   right point in the buying process.
2. Every visitor to your booth at a trade show or to your corpo-

rate event will be at some stage of the buying process himself or herself. The qualification process is designed to help determine that stage. Once you grasp that information, you can craft the best next step to offer the prospect.

When it comes to trade shows, for example, as Matt Hill of the Hill Group points out, visitors come to your booth because they want to talk to you, they want to hear an overview of what your company does, they have customer service issues to resolve, or they want to be allowed to grab a brochure and be on their way. Your job is to manage their expectations, and deliver on their needs.

BUSINESS EVENT PLANNING TIED TO SALES OBJECTIVES

Perhaps the simplest strategy for business event planning is based on periodic sales requirements. The sales pipeline must be filled with enough prospective business to meet revenue goals. It is marketing's job to keep the pipeline stocked with the right amount of quality leads that will allow sales quotas to be met, at the company, region, or territory level.

Business events can play an important role in generating the sales leads needed to fill the pipeline. If you understand how many qualified leads are needed in any given territory and during any given period, you can back your way into the appropriate marketing programs to support those objectives. Of course, you need to take into account the following challenges:

- Trade shows are scheduled on their own calendars, not yours. So, a certain amount of inflexibility must be considered. The best approach is to plan on exhibiting at your most productive trade shows to start, and building the rest of the plan to fill in the lead generation gaps.
- Business events may not provide the geographic specificity you need for the pipeline supporting each sales territory. Other than regional shows, your trade show lead output is going to be fairly unpredictable in these terms. You will need to supplement the trade show leads with road shows, direct mail, outbound

telemarketing, and other lead generation activities that allow more geographic control.

- Business events can produce a glut of leads at one time, depending on their productivity. You will smooth the flow a bit with your post-event qualification and nurturing process. But there is the risk that an unusually high volume of leads will reduce the sales force's enthusiasm for working them all, resulting in a lower lead-to-sales conversion rate than usual.

Despite these potential pitfalls, planning your business events to support lead flow requirements is a fairly straightforward procedure. First, you examine the quota of each territory concerned, and subtract out the amount that will be self-generated through the natural course of territory management. The remaining amount is what needs to be supported by lead generation programs. You divide this amount by the average order size in your company or category to arrive at the number of closed leads required. Then divide again by the lead-to-sales conversion rate, to arrive at the number of qualified leads required per rep. An example appears in Exhibit 2.14.

Exhibit 2.14: Sample Lead Requirements Worksheet

Revenue quota per rep	$3,000,000
Percent of quota self-generated	40%
Quota requiring lead support ($3 million*1-.40)	$1,800,000
Revenue per order	$90,000
Converting leads required ($1.8 million / $100,000)	20
Conversion rate	25%
Qualified leads required per rep (20 / .25)	80

In this situation, each rep needs 80 qualified leads in the territory per year. Review your event calendar, and estimate how many of these leads will be generated from the programs you have planned. Fill in the gaps with other marketing programs. And make sure you are buying the highest ROI leads first. You will need to adjust the integrated marketing program to optimize the results.

BUSINESS EVENT PLANNING BY TARGET AUDIENCE

Another strategy for integrating business events into your marketing plan is based on target audience analysis. Select the key audiences you seek to acquire or retain, and apply the most effective marketing tools to those objectives. Events and trade shows can play an active, and effective, role.

The chart in Exhibit 2.15 analyzes the best event applications against marketing objectives targeted to various audience segments. Here, the segments are organized by buyer type. But you can also set this up by any relevant business segment, like industry, company size or geography.

BUSINESS EVENT PORTFOLIO PLANNING

If every business event has its most productive applications, then the ideal business event program would balance the business event plan against the sales and marketing objectives. The goal is that each business event drive optimal business and each business event pull its own weight relative to the other business events and to the other elements of the marketing mix.

Forward-thinking companies go through a process known as business event portfolio planning, whereby all the business events operational around the company are analyzed for their effectiveness, their contribution to objectives and any possible duplication that might have cropped up. This process only works if, organizationally, the marketing team has control—or influence—over all the business events that may be scattered around. It can pose a bit of a political problem, as well, when interested parties around the company hear that marketing is evaluating their favorite activities with an eye to gaining efficiency.

The George P. Johnson Company, a business event agency headquartered in Auburn Hills, Michigan, and with offices around the world, shares a telling example of a corporate client's results from a portfolio planning exercise. With a judicious shift in the business event mix over a three-year period, the client was able to reduce its business event budget overall by 33%, while increasing its business

Exhibit 2.15: Best Event Applications by Target Audience

Target Audience	Marketer's Objectives	Audience's Objectives	Optimal Business Event Options
End-users, current customers	Product information delivery Repurchase/cross-purchase Identify problems and needs Product demo	Learn about new solutions Solve problems/troubleshoot Network with peers	User group meeting Partner conference Single-customer event (if a large account) Webinar Educational seminar (product topics)
End-users, prospects	Awareness Consideration Preference Product demo	Learn about new solutions	Road show Trade show Webinar
Influencers, specifiers	Consideration Preference Product information delivery Product demo	Learn about ways to do job better Compare vendor solutions	Trade show Webinar Road show Single customer event (if a large account)
Decision-makers, department heads	Preference Purchase Repurchase/cross-purchase	Solve business/financial problems Network with peers	Executive briefing Entertainment event Educational seminar (business topics)
C-level, senior management	Preference Purchase Repurchase/cross-purchase	Solve business/financial problems Network with peers	Executive briefing Entertainment event

event productivity by 400%. The company migrated from a portfolio concentrating on trade shows to a more equal mix of key account workshops and executive seminars, which allowed them to educate customers and prospects and close more business.

Exhibit 2.16: Portfolio Planning

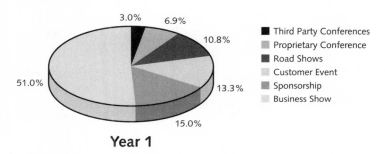

Year 1

Third Party Conferences
Proprietary Conference
Road Shows
Customer Event
Sponsorship
Business Show

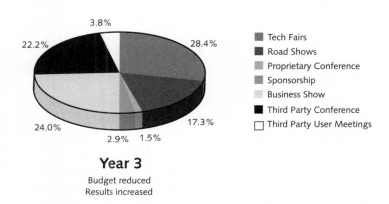

Year 3

Budget reduced
Results increased

Tech Fairs
Road Shows
Proprietary Conference
Sponsorship
Business Show
Third Party Conference
Third Party User Meetings

Source: The George P. Johnson Company. Reproduced with permission.

The first step in business event portfolio planning is to analyze all the business events in operation and rank them based on their performance against the objectives set for them. Mike Westcott, Vice President of Marketing at George P. Johnson, recommends that you ask the following kinds of questions about the business events under observation:

- Which business events represent the largest budgets? It makes sense to start with the largest areas of potential opportunity for savings or re-direction of the marketing investment dollars.
- Which business events provide access to the most valuable target audiences, decision-makers, influencers and the like?
- Are there any business events demonstrating growth or particular vitality? The buzz factor may be important.
- Are there any particular sponsorship opportunities at the business events that match your strengths?
- What was the return on the business event investment? Or, if the business event was not managed properly in the past, what is the potential ROI on the business event?

Once these questions have been answered, the business events should be ranked by their potential to deliver results by each criterion. Next, the business events need to be analyzed for duplication on two dimensions:

1. Are there business events that are reaching the same target audiences? If so, consider consolidation or elimination of the weaker performers.
2. Are there business events taking place during the same time periods or locations, allowing opportunities for consolidation or de-duplication?

Finally, analyze the portfolio for gaps. Are there target audiences that are underserved? Are there marketing objectives that are not being met? There may be business events—or other marketing vehicles—that can be found to enhance the program.

Westcott offers an analytic framework for thinking about the business event portfolio. With an X-axis describing "leadership," or brand strength, and a Y-axis representing "share of voice," or the competitive environment, Westcott arranges the event categories as follows.

Exhibit 2.17: Balancing Your Business Event Portfolio

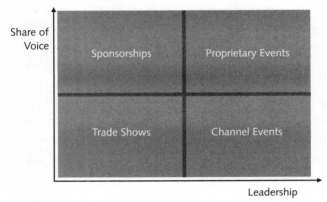

Source: The George P. Johnson Company. Reproduced with permission.

This analysis provides some revealing insights into the nature of the event portfolio. Trade shows are a highly competitive environment, best suited to very strong brands that can rise above the noise. Channel events, put on by a company's own customers or channel partners, involve competitive pressure but also deliver, by virtue of being selected to participate, a leadership message. These are best used by companies who depend heavily on channel partners for distribution, for example, software developers. Sponsorship of sports or cultural events provides a captive audience but is more about good will than brand leadership. These are best suited to companies with a few large accounts, like the automotive industry. Proprietary corporate events hold the most desirable position in the matrix, showing strength in both areas.

WHERE AGENCIES PLAY

If this were a discussion of business-to-business advertising or direct marketing, we would have a clear notion of how agencies support their clients' marketing objectives. General agencies do advertising, and direct response agencies do direct marketing. Some, of course, claim to do both. Particularly in the business-to-business world, agencies dedicated to business marketers will handle all kinds of marketing communications functions, from lead generation campaigns to collateral fulfillment and response capture.

However, as odd as it may seem, when it comes to trade shows and corporate events, all bets are off. Most business marketers find themselves using a combination of resources—ad agencies to create their booth graphics, direct marketing agencies to conduct pre-show campaigns, exhibit houses to design and build their booths, and lead management companies to follow up on their show contacts. There does not seem to be a tradition of one-stop shopping for business event marketing services. This scenario raises a number of important challenges:

- Recruiting and coordinating multiple vendors to create a single program.
- Encouraging them to work together in a cooperative spirit, rather than competitively for client favor and budgets.
- How to ensure consistent output in terms of quality and timing, as well as consistent brand messaging and image.
- The lack economic efficiencies that results from piece-part billing.

Despite these problems, marketing agencies are loath to offer a complete solution. Don Barshinger, Chief Creative Officer of Slack Barshinger, a Chicago agency that specializes in business marketing, puts it this way: "We are a communications agency. We help our clients with their trade show programs all the time. We are very competent in marketing planning, driving attendees to the exhibit, creating the messages, training the staff, even organizing the databases and managing lead follow-up. But we can't get into the booth building business. We are never going to be carpenters."

Another explanation is offered by Doug Ducate, President of CEIR in Chicago. "Ad agencies in the past showed little interest in helping with exhibits because the medium was not commissionable. As agencies move to fee-based arrangements with their clients, they are getting more involved."

At the other end of the spectrum lies the exhibit company that has recognized the client need for strategic marketing support, and has added such services as marketing planning, direct marketing communications to drive attendance, lead fulfillment and management, and business event portfolio strategy and planning. Service integration is a clear trend in the business event marketing world.

For companies who plan to use business events as part of their go-to-market strategy, the options are still fairly muddy. You will almost certainly end up managing a mix of suppliers, perhaps a communications agency and a business event marketing company, or a combination of an ad agency and an exhibit house. When searching for the best solution, the right approach is to hire the suppliers who understand your marketing objectives and communicate your key messages to your target audiences.

And the challenge remains to motivate them to work together effectively. As the client, you need to clearly communicate up front that the mission is to meet the marketing objectives, and that you expect your supplier partners to suppress their natural competitive instincts and to cooperate with one another in achieving your marketing objectives.

3

Prior Planning:
Do It Right
the First Time

Setting Objectives

Why set objectives? Well, if you don't know where you are going, any road will take you there. And once you're there, you'll still be lost. Regrettably, 71% of exhibitors go to a trade show without any specific objectives, according to the Center for Exhibition Industry Research (CEIR). How can this be?

For some of us, defining objectives is the most difficult part of a marketing campaign. We dawdle. We prefer action to thought. We may even hope that, without particular goals, we won't have to disappoint ourselves, or others.

But that's the entire point. Marketers are under increasing pressure to be accountable, to demonstrate the value of their expenditures. So it's imperative that you set down, in writing, exactly what you expect to deliver as a result of the trade show marketing program, whether it's a single show, or an entire year of integrated trade show marketing plans.

If you don't clarify your objectives, you will be well advised to cancel the show and stay home.

CHOOSING YOUR OBJECTIVES

Select one or two primary objectives and no more than two secondary objectives. This will keep your efforts focused, and avoid the dilution that can imperil marketing programs that try to be all things to all people.

Selecting one or two primary objectives has the further benefit of allowing you to line up every strategy, every tactic, under the objectives themselves. When considering various activities, you can ask yourself the question: "Does this support our mission?" If not, don't do it. You'll find that this approach helps win arguments when wacky ideas come out of the woodwork and you have to explain to various parties around your company why they don't make sense.

Make your primary and secondary objectives as specific as possible. No fluff. No jargon. Example: 65 demos given, 350 qualified leads generated, 10 new business partners recruited, or a 20% increase in new product awareness from before to after the event.

Make the objectives realistic, but challenging. You don't want them to be unattainable, but neither do you want to short change your results and leave opportunity on the table.

Make your objectives measurable. If you can't measure it, you can't manage it, goes the old adage. We marketers suffer from an occasionally deserved reputation for spending without delivering measurable results. But in trade show marketing, there is no excuse for that.

Map your trade show objective to your go-to-market strategy. If, for example, you are in a business with a long, complex sales cycle, your trade show objective is likely to be about sales lead generation. If your sales cycle is short, and the trade show puts you in front of decision-makers (and permits on-floor sales), the logical objective for the trade show is revenues closed on site.

As an example, consider the case of Northrup Grumman.

Northrop Grumman, whose sales cycle can extend as far as seven years, exhibits at as many as 300 shows around the world every year. George L. Vanik, Marketing Communications Manager for the electronic systems division, handles 30 of them, including tabletop exhibits. His division's trade show objectives are all around meeting specific people. "In the defense industry, there's no way we are going to get any orders at a show. Our customers aren't even the decision-makers—Congress is. So we don't even track show leads," says Vanik.

Northrop Grumman's trade show objectives are two-fold:

1. Conduct meetings with customers.
2. Establish teaming arrangements with business partners, like Raytheon, Lockheed, and Boeing. For some business opportunities, these customers are competitors, but they are just as likely to be partners.

OBJECTIVES CHECKLIST

Businesses set marketing objectives that serve their business strategies. So marketers set trade show objectives that support the greater marketing objectives.

At a high level, there are myriad possible objectives that a trade show marketer may use as a focus. This checklist will serve to stimulate your thinking:

- ☐ Introduce a new product.
- ☐ Generate qualified sales leads.
- ☐ Gather new prospects for the database and for later cultivation.
- ☐ Enter a new market.
- ☐ Sell, sign contracts, or generate RFPs.
- ☐ Build awareness.
- ☐ Recruit channel partner.
- ☐ Recruit new employees.
- ☐ Recruit strategic employees.
- ☐ Conduct market research, such as competitive intelligence, industry trends, or learning about a new industry.
- ☐ Achieve an ROI.
- ☐ Retain current customers, penetrate current accounts.
- ☐ Influence the press or financial community.
- ☐ Support your industry.

An agricultural machinery company planning to exhibit at a trade show attended by farmers might set its primary objective as generating new sales leads and its secondary objective as retaining current customers. A telemarketing services company announcing a new inbound service offering at a conference of business marketing professionals might set its primary objective as a new-product introduction and its secondary objective recruiting new employees. A company entering an entirely new market segment where it is unknown is likely to have brand awareness as its primary goal at a trade show that attracts attendees from the new market.

You know your business and your marketing objectives. At this stage in the business event marketing process, you are seeking clarity, specificity, and agreement.

CONNECTING OBJECTIVES TO METRICS

Next, you must link your primary objective to metrics that will allow you to measure your results. Exhibit 3.1 provides examples of metrics that might be associated with various primary objectives.

Marketers' Trade Show Objectives

CEIR surveyed marketers in the manufacturing sector in 2000, to identify their objectives in trade show marketing. Listed in order of importance, the objectives were ranked by percent of selection by respondent:

1. Generating sales leads from existing customers.
2. Generating sales leads from new customers.
3. Educating customers about products and services.
4. Showing dealers how to promote effectively.
5. Promoting awareness of company and capabilities.
6. Introducing new products and services.
7. Accumulating competitive information.
8. Gaining publicity and press.
9. Identifying new customers.
10. Conducting business with other exhibitors.
11. Reaching high-quality prospects.
12. Meeting key customers.
13. Entering new markets.

Exhibit 3.1: Setting Specific Metrics Around Your Objectives

Primary Objective	Associated Metrics
Introduce new product	Number of demos given Number of visitors to booth Number of samples ordered Number of press mentions Number of qualified leads generated by product Number of RFPs requested
Generate sales leads	Number of qualified leads Cost per qualified lead
Gather new prospects	Number of prospects gathered Cost per new prospect contact Number of new accounts added to the database
Enter new market	Number of prospects gathered by industry Number of qualified leads generated by industry Number of RFPs requested
Sales	Revenue Number of transactions closed Number of purchase orders signed Expense to revenue ratio (E:R) Return on investment ratio (ROI) Number of new accounts/customers
Awareness	Number of visitors to booth Number of demos given Number of flyers distributed Number of attendees to pass by booth Number of visibility opportunities (sessions, events, press conferences, etc.) or number of resulting impressions Pre-post show awareness levels Number of press mentions
Recruit channel partners	Number of partners recruited Cost per recruited partner Geographic penetration of recruited partners
Recruit new employees	Number of employees recruited Cost per new employee Employees recruited by skill category
Competitive research	Number of competitors at the show Competitive analyses completed
Market research	Customer surveys completed Focus groups conducted

Exhibit 3.1: *continued*

Primary Objective	Associated Metrics
ROI	Return on investment ratio Expense to revenue ratio
Retain current customers	Number of customer appointments scheduled and held Number of new product demos to current customers Revenue closed from current customers
Support your industry	Number of association functions attended Dollars invested in association function sponsorship

CALCULATING REALISTIC GOALS

If your goals are tied to metrics, and you commit to deliver on them, the metrics must reflect reality. How do you set goals that are achievable? You calculate back from the data available about the trade show attendance, the exhibit hall hours, and the staffing, and you develop a feel for the art of the possible.

The first step is to research the trade show attendance by reading the exhibitor guide and talking to show management and prior exhibitors. Let's say your objective is to introduce a line of pneumatic seals to a new industry segment, namely, plastics.

Through your research, you discover that, last year, of the 5,000 attendees, 15% were from the plastics industry. Of those 750 targets, show management estimates that 45% to 50% could be expected to pass by your booth during the exhibit hall hours. So, your metric might be to give a demo to as many of those 375 prospects as possible.

But the next step is to ensure that this is a realistic goal, given your resources. If a one-to-one demo takes 15 minutes and you plan three sales people and demo stations in the booth, then you are talking 31 hours of full-throttle demonstrating during exhibit hall hours. Here's how that calculation worked:

375 prospects / 4 demos per hour / 3 sales people = 31.25
hours of demos needed

But what if the trade show's prime exhibit hall hours total only 25? You must either add another sales person and demo station, or reduce the number of demos you can realistically expect to give during the trade show.

Use a similarly specific analysis of the viability of each of your metrics. Make sure each metric is both attainable and as aggressive as possible, given the realities of the trade show, the audience, and your resources.

The table in Exhibit 3.2 shows an example of how you might calculate reasonable goals for prospecting results at your booth. By multiplying the numbers in the first column, you will come up with a set of goals relating to leads and sales. Once you've done the math, then apply your judgment.

Exhibit 3.2: Calculating Prospecting Goals

Resources Available	Calculations
Number of sales reps in the booth	Assume 10 contacts per hour during busy hall hours
Number of busy hours	Find out the typical busy hours from show management
Lead conversion rate	Say 20% of contacts become qualified leads
Sales conversion rate	Say 40% of qualified leads convert to sales during or after the show

RETURN ON OBJECTIVES

As marketers find themselves under the gun to demonstrate the results of their efforts, the management rallying cry has become ROI, or return on investment. For every dollar invested in a marketing campaign, management demands a return, meaning revenue or margin directly attributable to that effort. ROI is a financial measure.

In most business-to-business situations, however, connecting a particular dollar of sales revenue to a particular marketing investment is a difficult proposition, for several reasons:

1. Buying cycles are long and complex, involving multiple sales and marketing "touches." How can you reasonably claim the show was the driver of that piece of revenue? A lead generated at a trade show will go through many interactions before it converts to sales.

2. Most business-to-business companies market through many channels. Logically, revenue is recognized at the point where the deal was completed. If the revenue is also attributed to other sales and marketing channels, i.e., double counting, life can get very complicated, for marketing, for sales, and for finance.

3. Furthermore, it can be difficult to secure reporting on sales results attached to a specific event. When third-party channels are involved, sales reporting may be impossible. Even with in-house sales teams, a long sales cycle gets in the way of clearly connecting a sale to a particular lead.

When it comes to assigning revenue results to a single tactic, such as a trade show or an event, marketers can get into serious squabbles about double counting, about commissions, about budgets—in essence, about power and influence.

Some marketers struggling with these issues have decided to change the conversation altogether. Instead of fighting over revenue attribution, they have declared themselves in the business of delivering a return against their stated marketing objectives, a concept known as ROO, or return on objectives. They set objectives for the business event, as well as associated metrics, and report only on their ability to meet those objectives. In effect, they set activity-based objectives that involve areas firmly under marketing's control.

For measuring marketing tactics in a multichannel, complex business-to-business world, this approach makes some short-term sense. However, corporate management is looking for all elements of its marketing mix to drive revenue and profits. So, the sooner you set up systems and processes to tie your programs to sales results, the more likely your trade show programs will receive the attention and the budgets they deserve. Hiding behind ROO is just a distraction.

SETTING OBJECTIVES FOR TRADE SHOW STAFF PARTICIPATION

When your staff is visiting a trade show merely as an attendee, prior planning is still critical to getting the best value from the investment.

The veteran marketing and association management executive, Jim Prendergast, shares his advice to trade show attendees:

1. Protect what you've got. Recognize that the trade show is organized to give your current customers exposure to your competitors. Prendergast tells his people to get busy—way in advance—organizing client-retention activities, like meetings and social events. "I always send an event planner to the town in advance to scout out a great restaurant. We host a client-only dinner for 40 or 50 people at nearly every show."
2. Develop new business. Even if you are not exhibiting, Prendergast advises that you use the event as an opportunity to cultivate new prospects, in a nice way. "I instruct my people to come away with plenty of business cards and plans for follow-up calls."
3. Learn something. The sessions, the exhibit hall, all programs are there for your education. Make sure you absorb some new information about your industry.
4. Have a ball. Prendergast recognizes the opportunity for fun and relaxation at an event, and he encourages his people to take advantage.

Selecting the Right Show

With as many as 11,094 events run in the U.S. in 2000, 85% of which are business-to-business trade shows, according to CEIR, it's a challenge to decide on the most productive trade shows for your company. Fortunately, narrowing down the field is a fairly straightforward process. Here are the steps that will ensure success.

First, develop a list of candidate trade shows. Sources of ideas include:

- Customers and prospects—ask them which trade shows they plan to attend next year.
- Sales people's suggestions—this will be one of your best sources of input.
- Business partners, distributors, and resellers.
- Vendors—ask for their trade show attendance and exhibiting plans.

- Trade shows where you exhibited in the past.
- Competitors—their websites may very well list their annual event calendars.
- Directories.
- Industry associations.
- Trade publications.

Then, organize the possible candidates by their fit against your criteria, such as buyer type, level of authority, industry, and so forth. The most appropriate trade shows will emerge from this process.

Generally, you'll find the best access to prospects if you attend the trade shows catering to your customers' industries, versus your own. So, if you are a manufacturer of pneumatic seals targeting the plastics industry, skip the manufacturers' show and instead head to the plastics industry event, where you'll have less competition and a denser concentration of prospective buyers.

Once you have a short list, it's time to investigate the show's credentials. Here are some tips for establishing a sense of the show's quality:

- Visit the trade show as an attendee before exhibiting. Get a feel for the activity in the exhibit hall, the buzz, the standards set for the conference sessions, and the profile of the visitors. If you are a prospective exhibitor, show management will offer you a complimentary pass to inspect the trade show in advance. "We encourage potential exhibitors to walk the show," says Marilyn Harrington, formerly General Manager of Advanstar's East Coast Fashion Group, which ran the apparel and accessories trade show Industry (212). "It's important to talk to people, and get a feel for the show, before making a decision."
- Talk to previous exhibitors. Trade show management will provide you with a list of references, or you can examine prior year show brochures or websites, and make your own contacts.
- Call your competitors. This can be a touchy process, but assuming you have some line of communication open with your counterparts, it's worth probing for their experience at the trade show. Alternatively, have a look at their websites, where they may have announced their event calendars.

- Ask your sales people to sound out their networks of customers, competitors, and channel partners for information.
- Conduct a credit check on the show management company.
- Keep in mind that trade shows change and audiences change. Trade shows tend to have a natural life cycle. So keep an eye on the trends for the trade shows you are considering.

While the best source of trade show ideas will come from customers, prospects, and sales people, it also makes sense to comb through the industry directories to make sure some promising candidates are not overlooked. The leading trade show directories in the U.S. are listed in Exhibit 3.3.

Exhibit 3.3: Trade Show Listings and Directories

Directory	Distributor	Price	Phone	Website
American Tradeshow Directory	Trade Show Biz	$685	800-546-3976	www.tradeshowbiz.com
Tradeshow Week Data Book	ESP	$419	800-375-4212	www.espcomp.com
Trade Shows Worldwide	Gale	$355	800-877-4253	www.gale.com

There are also numerous industry-specific directories, including Healthcare Convention & Exhibitors Association and CEMA, The I.T. Event Marketing Community. In addition, many industry associations offer online directories of industry trade shows and events.

Keep in mind that no directory is completely comprehensive. Each has its areas of strength. So check as many as you can.

There are also several web-based trade show search resources available:

- ExhibitorNet.com
- ExpoCentral.com
- Expoworld.com
- TradeshowWeek.com
- TSNN.com

TROUBLE SPOTS IN SHOW SELECTION

Certain traps await trade show marketers as they make their show selection plans. Pay particular attention to the following.

- Choosing trade shows out of habit. It's prudent to take a zero-based approach to trade show selection. Companies—and especially marketing departments—tend to get into ruts, doing the same activities year after year, simply because "we always do it this way." So ask yourself the hard questions about each trade show that was on the calendar in the past. Were the results satisfactory? Do not reschedule it unless the trade show continues to perform to your standards and supports your current sales and marketing objectives.
- Choosing trade shows because the competition is there. Business marketing is a competitive world, and we are tempted to match our competitors' behavior in order to avoid appearing weak, or allowing our competitors unfettered access to prospects. But, when you think about it, selecting a trade show just because a competitor has may be attributing far too much credit to the competitor's marketing brilliance. Companies make unwise trade show selection decisions all the time. It is far more productive to select trade shows based on your own criteria than simply because a competitor has decided to attend. If the right prospects are there, fine. But if they are not, the competitor is just wasting its money anyway.
- Choosing trade shows based on personal appeal. It's not unusual for a sales executive or other senior manage to insist on exhibiting at a trade show scheduled for a favorite destination city. But "we like the town" is not a satisfactory justification for investing precious marketing dollars. If you gather the trade show credentials as described in this chapter, and the trade show does not pass muster, you will be able to make a strong case for resisting the siren song of a great sight-seeing or golf junket. Of course, you don't want to commit career suicide, either, so consider the source of the enthusiasm for the trade show in question.
- Exhibiting when another marketing tactic is called for. It's not always appropriate to exhibit at a trade show. If your target

audience is very narrow, and relatively small, a trade show may be less efficient than direct mail, telemarketing, or direct sales. Similarly, if your target audience is widely dispersed geographically, there may be too few prospects attending any given trade show to justify the investment. When a trade show attracts a reasonable number of targeted attendees, you may still be more effective using a non-booth strategy, like a hospitality suite, a client event in the evening, or a speaking engagement. So consider all options before slavishly deciding to invest in a booth.

Show Types by Markets

Trade shows come in many flavors, so be sure to consider a broad variety as you evaluate your marketing opportunity.

- Vertical trade shows, specific to a certain industry, like AccessoriesTheShow, for retailers, or the Society of Exploration Geophysicists, for oil searchers.
- Horizontal trade shows, which serves a product category, like the National Hardware Show, which covers hardware, home improvement, and lawn and garden, or Comdex, which covers all kinds of computing—hardware, software, services.
- Niche trade shows, like the Independent Liquid Terminals Association (ILTA), which caters to companies using above-ground storage tanks, or the Association of periOperative Registered Nurses.
- Regional trade shows, which cover several states, such as the OEM shows organized by Job Shop Shows in nine regions, including the southeast, southern New England, and northern California. Most attendees will come from a radius of a few hundred miles. These trade shows typically attract a qualified audience of influencers, specifiers, or end-users, whose objective is to learn about specific products.
- National trade shows, attracting visitors from across the country, and usually scheduled once a year, at around the same time.
- Local trade shows, attracting visitors from a municipality.
- International trade shows, based outside the U.S.
- Road shows, highly targeted series of local business events aimed at a particular industry or buyer type, such as NEXTTech, which targets technology buyers in small and medium businesses, and Emerging Interest, which reaches marketing professionals. Note: this stands in contrast to the proprietary corporate road show discussed in Chapter Seven, when a single company schedules a series of small events in various cities.
- "Controlled circulation" shows, like those managed by TechTarget, Inc., where both exhibitors and attendees must qualify to participate. Prices to exhibit are higher than normal, but so is the audience quality.
- Online trade shows, a concept that has never really gotten off the ground.

Tradeshow Week's September 2003 Executive Outlook survey asked respondents about the relative value of shows by size. Smaller shows are perceived of as more valuable than very large shows.

Exhibit 3.4: Event Types That Provide the Most Value

Show Size	Net Square Feet of Exhibit Space	Exhibitors' Assessment of Value
Mega	Over 250,000	14%
Large	100,000–250,000	36%
Mid-sized	50,000–100,000	32%
Small	Under 50,000	23%

Source: *Tradeshow Week's* 2003 Executive Outlook Survey, September 2003.

SHOW SELECTION CRITERIA

The number one criterion for selecting a trade show is the audience. Are the right people going to be attending? Are they the people whom you want to reach? If so, you are 90% of the way toward your decision. If not, none of the other criteria much matters.

The best way to investigate the quality and volume of the attendance is to get profile information from show management. It is the job of the exhibit hall space sales person to persuade you of the quality of the audience. You should be able to get considerable detail about their demographics, titles, industry classification and buying power from your sales rep. If you can't, consider this a major red flag.

Here is a checklist of the minimum data points you should seek from the show managers:

- ☐ Total attendance in three to five past years, and projected attendance next year.
- ☐ Net attendance. Sadly, the trade show world has a habit of inflating its audience numbers by adding in exhibitors, speakers, press, students, trade show staff, and even spouses, when reporting attendance. You must ask for a net number. Also asked how that number is audited or verified.

☐ Audience demographics, such as titles, industries, company size, buying authority, and product interest.

☐ Audience qualification. Some trade show organizers are applying the controlled-circulation publishing technique of limiting attendance to those who meet certain criteria, such as purchasing responsibility or job title.

☐ Number of exhibitors and total square footage of exhibit space. Gross space means the entire hall, including aisles, registration area and show offices. Net space, a more meaningful number, is the square footage expected to be sold.

☐ List of top ten exhibitors, to get a sense of product themes at the trade show.

☐ Indication of your competitors' participation at the trade show.

☐ Cost per square foot.

☐ Times and dates of exhibit hall opening, plus times and dates of program sessions. You need a sense of how much competition the hall will feel from the sessions.

☐ Trade show's promotional budget and plans.

☐ Sample of prior year's program and exhibit directory.

☐ Availability of prime space and booth locations for the next year.

Different show types will deliver your audience in different concentrations. As noted by Candy Adams, President of Trade Show Consulting, the more narrowly targeted the trade show, the deeper the interest. "If you are selling wide format color printers," she says, "Only 5% of the Comdex attendees will be interested. But at the Seybold show, 50% will be interested, and at the Society for Exploration Geophysicists, 100% will want to know about your product." Just keep in mind that 5% of Comdex may represent a larger number than 50% of a much smaller vertical show.

Some trade shows have experimented with auditing their attendance numbers. The Audit Bureau of Circulation, which audits magazine readership, made a run at trade show audits with its launch of Expomark in 1994, and by 1999 was auditing as many as 70 shows a year. However, Expomark found the demand for audits on the part of show management could not sustain the business, and they closed up shop in 2002.

More recently, a few technology shows have conducted audits. CeBIT America commissioned an audit from Exhibit Surveys for its debut show in the U.S., at the Jacob Javits Center in New York in June 2003. The audit reported a verified buying audience of 8,510 qualified attendees, 43% of whom were buyers from enterprises, government agencies or educational institutions, and 32% were resellers, systems integrators or other IT professionals, according to Crain's *BtoB* magazine. This kind of detail certainly improves exhibitors' ability to make sound decisions about show selection.

If the audience is attractive, there are other criteria to consider, among them:

- The larger audience. There is more to a trade show than the paid attendees. Consider also the speakers, the press representatives, and the other exhibitors as you analyze the trade show's potential.
- The location. Is the city likely to attract the attendees you want to reach? Does the geography fit your sales and marketing objectives?
- The timing. Make sure your sales and marketing teams are available during the trade show dates.
- The scope. Is this a national, international, or regional trade show?
- The facilities. Consider the layout of the exhibit hall and the amenities.
- The entrance criteria. Is show management allowing free entrance to the exhibit hall? If so, look for evidence of criteria in place to eliminate unqualified attendance, such as consumers.
- Show promotion plans, budget, and expected media coverage.
- Associated events. Are there additional opportunities for exposure or programs to attract a better audience, such as an awards banquet, special receptions, famous keynote speakers, or other ancillary activities, like golf outings.

At the end of this process, you should contact some prior year exhibitors to elicit their input. Were they happy with the quality and quantity of the attendance? How about their impressions of the show management's skill and responsiveness?

Tradeshow Week's September 2003 Executive Outlook survey asked exhibitors about the criteria they used in trade show selection.

Exhibit 3.5: Show Selection Criteria, Ranked by Importance

Criteria Used in Trade Show Selection	Percentage of Executives Who Ranked Criteria as Important
Lead gathering opportunity	63%
Perceived ROI or ROO opportunity	59%
Attendee demographics	52%
Whether competitors are exhibiting or sponsoring	52%
Attendance numbers, projections	44%
Event management experience, quality	18%
Other	7%

Source: *Tradeshow Week's* Executive Outlook Survey, September 2003.

EVALUATING COMPETING SHOWS

Skip Cox, President of Exhibit Surveys, Inc., believes that trade show selection can and should be a science. He has developed several methods that can assist you in selecting among competing trade show options. First, you calculate the size of the potential audience.

Your objective is to rank competing trade shows by how closely they map to your target audience. To begin, you compare what the show management says about its audience against your own target audience's profile. For example, if you are looking for engineers, you'll want to reduce the expected total audience to the engineer segment. Cox also points out that not all of the targeted attendees will be interested in your product, so your true potential "reach" at the trade show should be reduced again to account for product interest. Exhibit Surveys, Inc. has found that 52% is the right factor for companies that are exhibiting multiple products that are typical of the product categories featured at the show. If you are showing a single product, or if your products are out of the trade show's main stream, then 10% to 30% is a more realistic factor.

Once you have an estimate of the qualified audience you can realistically expect to reach at the trade show, rank the competing trade shows by the number of qualified attendees. You will find wide variances between gross attendee figures and the net number of people whom you really want to meet or can expect to meet.

You can take this method a step further if you compute the cost per qualified attendee. Reducing the comparison to the total cost to reach a qualified contact allows a value-based comparison of competing trade shows.

With these figures, you can then make trade show selection decisions based on volume of qualified attendees, or cost per qualified attendee, or a combination of the two.

Another data point that can help is the traffic density. This metric calculates how many qualified attendees will be milling around any given 100 square feet at the trade show. With this number, you'll get a sense of how active a show it is, and how difficult it will be to compete for the time and attention of visitors. More than 3.5 per 100 square feet is high, and less than 1.0 attendee per 100 square feet will be low. Overall, traffic density in the exhibition industry has been declining, since exhibit space has grown at a faster

Exhibit 3.6: Calculating Cost per Potential Qualified Contact: A Hypothetical Example

Gross attendance	4,000
Net attendance (subtract non-buyers like students, speakers, press, etc.)	3,500
Qualified attendees (net attendance x target segment factor, e.g., 75%)	2,625
Qualified attendees with product interest (Exhibit Surveys suggests 52%)	1,365
Total cost of exhibiting at the show	$50,000.00
Cost per potential qualified contact (total cost / # of qualified attendees with product interest)	$36.63

rate than attendance. Exhibit Surveys calculated the average in 2002 across all trade shows at 2.3.

To calculate density, you need to extract the following data points from show management:

- Net attendance.
- Average hours of hall activity.
- Net square feet of trade show space sold (or expected to be sold).
- Total number of hours exhibit hall is open.

Cox suggests that, if the show management does not have figures on the average hours visitors spend in the hall, you may use the national average of 8.3.

Perform the calculation as follows:

$$\frac{\text{Net attendance x average hall hours x 100}}{\text{Net square feet sold x total open hours}}$$

For example, if the net attendance is 3,500, the average hours is 8, the net square feet sold is 100,000, and the trade show is open for 12 hours, the average density will be 2.3 bodies per 100 square feet.

Traffic density can come in handy when comparing competing trade show options with similar audience characteristics.

REGIONAL SHOWS: THINK SMALL

A growing trend in the trade show industry is the emerging importance of regional and local trade shows. Regional means attracting an audience from a multi-state area; local refers to trade shows catering to a single city or business district. Regional shows offer attractive benefits:

- They are abundant, and still fast growing.
- They offer more focus, attracting under-served audiences that are unable to travel to national trade shows.
- They are much cheaper for exhibitors and attendees, not only in

the size of the investment, but also from the perspective of performance metrics such as cost to reach a qualified audience and cost per qualified lead generated.

Some tips for success at regional trade shows:

- Tighten up your product selection and signage to appeal more closely to the tighter audience. Janet Rapp of MTS Systems, for example, uses a message targeted to engineers when exhibiting sensors at national trade shows. But at the regional meeting of the Independent Liquid Terminals Association that meets in Houston, she uses graphics that speak specifically to the oil business.
- Deploy your field sales from that region to work the booth. This will keep costs low and likely improve the quality of the conversation, as well.
- Be prepared for active buyers. Lynne Parry of Apple Rubber Products attends the regional events organized by the Job Shop Shows, and finds that they attract engineers and purchasing people who come with blueprints in hand, ready to talk specifics.
- Consider your entire sales chain. Regional trade shows typically attract representatives from many tiers—distributors and wholesalers, as well as end-buyers.

CASE STUDY

IBM's Federal Command Center Shifts to Targeted Trade Shows

IBM's Federal Command Center targets government buyers all over the country and Europe, focusing on such big agencies as the Department of Defense and the CIA. Federal IT buyers appreciate face-to-face contact with their suppliers, but in recent years there has been a shift. The purchase decision is more highly placed in the organization than ever. So IBM's trade show strategy has changed as well. According to Cheval Force Opp, manager of the command center, IBM's new event strategy includes:

- Vastly fewer trade shows. Opp now attends a dozen trade shows a year, versus two to three a month in the past. "If it's a new or developing market for us, we'll send executives to the show as attendees, instead of exhibiting. We want the market to know we're listening to them."
- Fewer general and more specific trade shows.
- More appointments in advance. "We want to meet the right people. So we do our homework and set up meetings."
- Smaller booth and fewer staffers. The pre-appointed meetings mean less focus on driving booth traffic. "Monster booths are no longer necessary. We don't need a horde of sales people. We have some technical people on hand to do demos. But it's executive mind share that we're after."
- A strong website. "Customers and prospects need to be able to find what they're looking for. Our buyers are online. We need to be there, too."

Budgeting

Tradeshow Week reported that the average exhibitor's annual budget in 2003 was expected to be $410,300 for small to midsize companies, and $915,000 for large companies. Now of course these are just that—averages. You will set your annual spending level based on your marketing objectives. But there is no question that a typical trade show budget represents real money.

The care with which you set your trade show budgets will have much to do with your success in meeting your objectives. Similarly, your budget provides much opportunity for gaining leverage.

Over the past several decades, as exhibiting costs have risen dramatically, far outstripping inflation, exhibitors and show managers alike are facing increased pressure. Exhibitors are desperately seeking ways to do more with less. As represented by the Trade Show Exhibitors Association (TSEA), exhibitors are in regular negotiation with show managers to challenge various long-standing practices that benefit the organizers at the expense of exhibitors. Exhibitors also seek increased visibility into the source of the charges they incur. But it is slow going. For the time being, exhibitors must steel themselves to bear the brunt of various inefficiencies in the way things work.

Jeff Little, President of George Little Management, a leading gift show organizer, says that show managers are very concerned about rising costs. "As labor costs in the northeast and midwest continue to rise, organizers are voting with their feet. It's not a coincidence that Las Vegas and Orlando are growing their convention business while Boston and Chicago are struggling."

While exhibitors spent an average of $410,300 for trade shows during 2003, the largest group spent between $50,000 and $250,000.

Here follow the typical categories trade show marketers use for budgeting:

- Exhibit space (*Tradeshow Week* reported a 2002 average cost per square foot of $21.76).
- Booth design and construction (or rental).
- Show services (drayage, set up, electrical, phone, cleaning, and extras).
- Transportation (shipping).
- Staff (salaries, transportation).
- Hotel rooms.
- Staff training.
- Promotion and collateral material (pre-show, at show, post-show).
- Research (pre-show, at show, post-show).
- Hospitality.
- Miscellaneous.

Exhibit 3.7: How Much Exhibitors Spend at Trade Shows

Percent	Category of spending
16%	Over $1 million
5%	$750,001 to $1 million
9%	$500,001 to $750,000
14%	$250,001 to $500,000
38%	$50,000 to $250,000
18%	Under $50,000

Source: *Tradeshow Week,* March 24, 2003.

Tradeshow Week's September 2003 Executive Outlook survey reveals costs for a new booth at a North American trade show in 2003 (see Exhibit 3.8). Estimates do not include space cost, sponsorships, or employee travel. They do include new exhibit design and production, ground freight, audio-visual equipment, electrical or plumbing services, installation and dismantling, warehousing, furniture rental, general service contracting, and graphic production.

According to CEIR, the largest single item in the exhibit expense list is space rental, with travel and entertainment a close second. Here are the numbers from 2001, based on four years of Trade Show Exhibitors Association data. In total, companies spent nearly $21 billion annually on exhibiting.

Exhibit 3.8: Costs to Build, Transport, and Set Up a Booth

Respondents	Average	Median
All respondents	$108,036	$35,000
Technology and telecom only	$286,549	$80,000
Firms with over $1 billion in sales	$215,658	$100,000

Source: *Tradeshow Week's* Executive Outlook Survey, September 2003.

Exhibit 3.9: How the Exhibit Dollar is Spent

Expense Category	Percent Spent	Amount Spent (billions)
Exhibit space	28%	$5.8
Exhibit design	12%	$2.5
Show services	19%	$3.9
Shipping	9%	$1.9
Travel & entertainment	21%	$4.4
Promotion	6%	$1.1
Other	5%	$.9
Total		**$20.5**

Source: Center for Exhibition Industry Research.

TIPS FOR SUCCESSFUL BUDGETING

Treat your trade show plan as a profit center. If your budget looks like a P&L, your planning will follow suit, increasing the likelihood that you'll deliver a positive return on your company's investment in the event. So add expected revenues from all sources—the most straightforward being pipeline revenue associated with the leads generated—and demonstrate the connection between your activities and expected results. For example, if you must cut one demo station, you will show a concomitant reduction in qualified lead productivity.

Be sure to gather all the costs. Many trade show-related expenses are controlled outside of the exhibit budget, or even the marketing budget. Keeping track of these costs will give you a more accurate idea of the investment your company is really making. The fully loaded number will be of interest to senior management, and will also allow more accurate analysis of the associated ROI. Here are some line items that are trade show-related but likely to be absorbed by other people's budgets:

- Travel and entertainment for trade show staff and speakers.
- Press conferences, entertainment, and materials.
- Speaker support.
- Product inventory for display or demo at the booth.
- Pre-show promotions.
- Post-show fulfillment and lead follow-up.
- Agency fees.

It's also important to get a clear view of all event-related expenses so the company has a realistic data on the marketing communications options that are competing for resources. Once you fully load the business event budget, you may find that business events are a larger proportion of your marketing communications activities than previously understood.

Tie your budget items to your business event objectives. Make

---

Industry Benchmarks for Budgeting

You can get a quick reality check on your trade show budget by using industry rules of thumb. A number of industry benchmarks have emerged over the years, and these can serve as handy checkpoints to validate the logic of your budget. For one, see the industry averages published by the Center for Exhibition Industry Research (see Exhibit 3.9). Also, ask your show management whether they have figures to share from exhibitors who have participated in years past.

Another handy rule of thumb comes from Candy Adams, President of Trade Show Consulting, who says a trade show budget needs to be at least four times the cost of the space, plus a 10% cushion for add-ons, like video demos and other gadgets.

Edward A. Chapman, Jr., author of Exhibit Marketing, offers yet another formula. Space rent represents 20% of total out-of-pocket expense, not including expense for staff. To allow for personnel expense, add another 35%, he says.

Here is an example of how a Silicon Valley semiconductor company tracks its costs for exhibiting at one of its most important national trade shows. At this event, the company used a wide variety of promotions, comprising 13.4% of the budget, including pre-show email, show bag inserts, a lip-balm giveaway at the show, and prize drawings at the booth. During the trade show, the company co-operated with several hospitality events and demo suites organized by its business partners, contributing prizes, literature, signage, and logo napkins, which absorbed another 8.2% of the budget. The bulk of the spending went to booth space, services, theater, and signage. The total expense for the show came in at $288,325, against a budget of $300,000. The supplier names in this spreadsheet have been disguised.

sure you are spending the right amount to meet your measurable goals. For example, when you plan to include a party or dinner event, your budget will need to cover not only the event expense, but the cost of invitations as well. If your calculations show the need for extra demo stations, these will need to be covered in the budget.

Partnering with Show Management

There is a natural tendency toward friction between show organizers and show exhibitors. On the face of it, their interests are opposed. Show management is selling space, and exhibitors are buying.

But in the long term, the interests of the two parties coincide. If the trade show is unprofitable for the exhibitors, they will vote with their feet, and the trade show will fail. So, while some view show management to be the adversary of the exhibitor, treating management as a partner can actually yield very high dividends.

So, get personally acquainted with show management, not only the sales person managing your account, but that person's manager, the PR contact, and the customer service personnel.

Consider your account person to be your marketing advisor, a resource who can help you get the most out of your investment in the show. Explain your objectives and ask for advice on how to meet them successfully. You will get plenty of ideas, suggestions, and facts. Don't ignore this opportunity for an extra edge.

Here are some of the typical inputs you can expect from show management:

- Demographic data on past attendees.
- List of other exhibitors, now and in the past.
- Press list and help with press events.
- Trade show promotional plans.
- Explanation of the lead generation support and technology.
- Advice on booth size, traffic patterns, and likely number of qualified contacts.
- Advice on booth design, height, and signage.
- Advice on pre-show, at-show, and post-show promotions.

Exhibit 3.10: Sample Trade Show Budget Spreadsheet

Show XX Budget

Updated: current date

ITEM	Pay To	Notes	Forecast	Paid Q201	Paid Q301	Paid Q401	Paid Q102	Paid Q202	Actual	Date	Payment
Booth Expenses											
Conference Room Signs	Vendor	3 - 24 x36	$ 500	$ -	$ -	$ -	$ 631	$ -	$ 631	Date	PO
Partner Signs	Vendor	1 - 24 x 36	$ 200	$ -	$ -	$ -	$ 195	$ -	$ 195	Date	PO
Giveaways Signs	Vendor	2 - 11 x 14	$ 100	$ -	$ -	$ -	$ 80	$ -	$ 80	Date	PO
Power PC burst Signs	Vendor	7 total	$ 300	$ -	$ -	$ -	$ 310	$ -	$ 310	Date	PO
Deposit (Items 1-5)	Vendor	90%	$ -	$ -	$ -	$ -	$ 4,604	$ -	$ 4,604	Date	PO
Deposit (Item 6)	Vendor	90%	$ -	$ -	$ -	$ -	$ 2,743	$ -	$ 2,743	Date	PO
Final payment	Vendor		$ -	$ -	$ -	$ -	$ 5,788	$ -	$ 5,788	Date	PO
3. Product Easel (Emb)	Vendor		$ 577	$ -	$ -	$ -	$ -	$ -	$ -		
4. Setup Drawings	Vendor		$ 400	$ -	$ -	$ -	$ -	$ -	$ -		
5. Pull to ship	Vendor		$ 2,016	$ -	$ -	$ -	$ -	$ -	$ -		
6. Graphics Production	Vendor		$ 3,048	$ -	$ -	$ -	$ -	$ -	$ -		
7. Board Overlays	Vendor		$ 1,527	$ -	$ -	$ -	$ -	$ -	$ -		
Panels for Cases	Vendor		$ 1,000	$ -	$ -	$ -	$ -	$ -	$ -		
8. Layout panels with boards	Vendor		$ 300	$ -	$ -	$ -	$ -	$ -	$ -		
9. Mount boards on plexi	Vendor		$ 750	$ -	$ -	$ -	$ -	$ -	$ -		
3 Clear plexi covers	Vendor		$ 488	$ -	$ -	$ -	$ -	$ -	$ -		
11. Repair 2 light fixtures	Vendor		$ 125	$ -	$ -	$ -	$ -	$ -	$ -		
12. Patch 2 carpets	Vendor		$ 350	$ -	$ -	$ -	$ -	$ -	$ -		
Clean / shampoo carpets	Vendor		$ 660	$ -	$ -	$ -	$ -	$ 660	$ -	Date	PO
Additional items	Vendor		$ 2,000	$ -	$ -	$ -	$ -	$ -	$ -		
Dave Rue Supervise	Vendor		$ 800	$ -	$ -	$ -	$ -	$ 531	$ 531	Date	PO
Onsite Purchases	Vendor		$ 308	$ -	$ -	$ -	$ -	$ 536	$ 536	Date	PO
Tax on Job	Vendor		$ 1,200	$ -	$ -	$ -	$ -	$ -	$ -		
Inventory upon return	Vendor		$ 2,464	$ -	$ -	$ -	$ -	$ -	$ 2,464	Date	PO
		Subtotal	$ 19,113	$ -	$ -	$ -	$ 21,924	$ 1,727	$ 17,883		6.2%
	Initial Budget: $ 300,000	**Forecast:**	$ 317,084	$ 26,000	$ -	$ 97,767	$ 68,984	$ 69,093	$ 288,325		

This spreadsheet shows how a Silicon Valley semiconductor company tracks its costs for exhibiting at one of its most important annual shows. At this event, the company used a wide variety of promotions, comprising 13.4% of the budget, including pre-show email, show bag inserts, a lip-balm giveaway at the show, and prize drawings at the booth. The booth included a live theater and participation by business partners. The supplier names have been disguised. The total expense for the show came in at $288,325, against a budget of $300,000.

Show XX Budget

ITEM	Pay To	Notes	Forecast	Paid Q201	Paid Q301	Paid Q401	Paid Q102	Paid Q202	Actual	Date	Payment
Partner Programs											
Partner 1	They produce	3 lexan	$ 1,000	$ -	$ -	$ -	$ -	$ 1,000	$ 1,000	Date	
Partner 1 Party	Our shirts only		$	$	$	$	$	$	$		PO
Partner 1 Party	Venue Local		$ 30,000	$ -	$ -	$ -	$ -	$ 19,046	$ 19,046	Date	PO
Partner 2 Party Giveaways	Eye Retainers	Qty: 800	$ 1,918	$ -	$ -	$ -	$ -	$ 1,961	$ 1,961	Date	PO
Partner 2 Grand Prize	Jam Cams	3	$ 180	$ -	$ -	$ -	$ -	$ 180	$ 180	Date	Expense
Partner 2	800 entry forms	copy ctr	$ -	$	$	$	$	$	$ -		
Partner 3	party branding		$	$	$	$	$	$	$		
Partner 4	signage		$ 500	$	$	$	$	$	$ -		
Partner 5	Partner 5 creates		$	$	$	$	$	$	$		
Partner 5	Prizes - 3 Jam Cams		$ 180	$ -	$ -	$ -	$ -	$ 180	$ 180	Date	Expense
Partner 5	1000 entry forms	copy ctr	$	$	$	$	$	$	$		
Partner 5	Reprints	1000	$ 748	$ -	$ -	$ -	$ 913	$ -	$ 913	Date	PO
Partner 6 Party	photo frame X2 logo	cancelled	$ -	$ -	$ -	$ -	$ -	$ -	$ -		
Partner signs	Vendor	15 total	$ 560	$ -	$ -	$ -	$ 464	$ -	$ 464	Date	PO
		Subtotal	$ 35,086	$ -	$ -	$ -	$ 1,378	$ 22,367	$ 23,745		8.2%
Staff Expenses											
Staff Audit onsite	Vendor		$ 1,300	$	$	$	$	$ 1,300	$ 1,300	Date	PO
Staff Audit Travel	Vendor		$ 400	$	$	$	$	$ 261	$ 261	Date	PO
Hotel deposit	Vendor		$ 300	$	$	$	$ 300	$	$ 300	Date	Expense
Hotel deposit	IT Contact		$ 300	$	$	$	$ 300	$	$ 300	Date	Expense
Hotel deposit	Production Vendor		$ 1,200	$	$	$	$ 1,200	$	$ 1,200	Date	Expense
Tax on hotel deposits	Events Team		$	$	$	$	$ 185	$	$ 185	Date	Expense
Team Dinner	Software paid		$ -	$	$	$	$	$	$ -		
Bus to Team Dinner	Production Transport		$	$	$	$	$	$ 341	$ 341	Date	Expense
DAC supplies	Onsite	Bus Ctr	$ 100	$	$	$	$	$ 80	$ 80	Date	Expense
DAC supplies	Onsite	Bus Ctr	$	$	$	$	$	$ 41	$ 41	Date	Expense
DAC supplies	IT Contact	onsite	$	$	$	$	$	$ 49	$ 49	Date	Expense
Photo Developing	Vendor		$ 50	$	$	$	$	$ 37	$ 37	Date	Expense
Pre-Show Meeting	Onsite	no cost	$	$	$	$	$	$	$ -		
Survival Guides	Copy Center	50 people	$	$	$	$	$	$	$		
Staff shirts	Vendor	72@ 20.00	$ 1,424	$	$	$	$	$	$ -		
Partner shirts	Company Store	12 @ 34.50	$ 424	$	$	$	$ 424	$ -	$ 424	Date	Expense
Staff Nametags	Vendor	cancelled	$	$	$	$	$	$	$ -		
Pre-Show Dinner	Cancelled		$ -	$	$	$	$	$	$ -		
		Subtotal	$ 5,498	$ -	$ -	$ -	$ 2,409	$ 2,109	$ 4,517		1.6%

(continued)

Exhibit 3.10: *continued*

Show XX Budget

ITEM	Pay To	Notes	Forecast	Paid Q201	Paid Q301	Paid Q401	Paid Q102	Paid Q202	Actual	Date	Payment
Show Services											
Freight Transportation	Payment	To / Insur	$ -	$ -	$ -	$ -	$ -	$ 3,389	$ 3,389	Date	PO
	Final payment	Return	$ -	$ -	$ -	$ -	$ -	$ 3,091	$ 3,091	Date	PO
	Vendor	To show	$ 3,500	$ -	$ -	$ -	$ -	$ -	$ -		
	Vendor	Return	$ 3,500	$ -	$ -	$ -	$ -	$ -	$ -		
	Vendor	Unpack CD	$ 1,000	$ -	$ -	$ -	$ -	$ -	$ -		
Booth Insurance	Vendor	175K / 150 de	$ 650	$ -	$ -	$ -	$ -	$ 650	$ 650	Date	PO
Install & Dismantle	Vendor		$ 14,000	$ -	$ -	$ -	$ -	$ 9,260	$ 9,260	Date	PO
Truss Labor (I/D)	Vendor		$ 9,333	$ -	$ -	$ -	$ 9,333	$ -	$ 9,333	Date	Expense
Electrical	Vendor		$ 1,673	$ -	$ -	$ -	$ 1,673	$ -	$ 1,673	Date	Expense
Turn off lights overhead	up and down		$ -	$ -	$ -	$ -	$ -	$ -	$ -		
Cleaning	Vendor	3 days	$ 1,200	$ -	$ -	$ -	$ 1,200	$ -	$ 1,200	Date	Expense
Furniture	lft rack / chair/table		$ 232	$ -	$ -	$ -	$ 232	$ -	$ 232	Date	Expense
Special Furniture	Barstools/tble/chairs		$ 4,360	$ -	$ -	$ -	$ 4,360	$ -	$ 4,360	Date	Expense
Drayage/forklift	Vendor	15000	$ 8,913	$ -	$ -	$ -	$ 8,913	$ -	$ 8,913	Date	Expense
Marshalling Yard	Vendor	3	$ 45	$ -	$ -	$ -	$ -	$ -	$ -		
On-Site Charges	Vendor		$ 3,000	$ -	$ -	$ -	$ -	$ 35	$ 35	Date	Expense
Photography	Vendor	2 views	$ 220	$ -	$ -	$ -	$ 220	$ -	$ 220	Date	Check
Floral/plants	Vendor	1 arr/2 palms	$ 140	$ -	$ -	$ -	$ 137	$ -	$ 137	Date	Check
Onsite Floral/plants	Vendor	2 ficas	$ -	$ -	$ -	$ -	$ -	$ 140	$ 140	Date	Expense
Telephone	Vendor	1 line/Dep	$ 365	$ -	$ -	$ -	$ 365	$ -	$ 365	Date	Expense
Lead Reader	Vendor	7 total	$ 960	$ -	$ -	$ -	$ 960	$ -	$ 960	Date	Expense
Lead Reader	Vendor	7 disks	$ -	$ -	$ -	$ -	$ -	$ 560	$ 560	Date	Expense
Lead Reader	Vendor	1 for XUP	$ -	$ -	$ -	$ -	$ -	$ 160	$ 160	Date	Expense
Security for Booth	Vendor	45hrs@$17	$ 765	$ -	$ -	$ -	$ 757	$ -	$ 757	Date	Expense
Subtotal			$ 53,855	$ -	$ -	$ -	$ 28,149	$ 17,286	$ 45,435		15.8%

Show XX Budget

ITEM	Pay To	Notes	Forecast	Paid Q201	Paid Q301	Paid Q401	Paid Q102	Paid Q202	Actual	Date	Payment
Presentation Expenses											
Deposit	Vendor		$ -	$ -	$ -	$ 47,415	$ -	$ -	$ 47,415	Date	PO
final payment	Vendor		$ -	$ -	$ -	$ 24,352	$ -	$ -	$ 24,352	Date	PO
Production			$ 19,000	$ -	$ -	$ -	$ -	$ -	$ -		
Personnel	3 presenters/1 sup	Local	$ 11,648	$ -	$ -	$ -	$ -	$ -	$ -		
Lead Coordinators	3 people		$ 4,050	$ -	$ -	$ -	$ -	$ -	$ -		
promotions			$ -	$ -	$ -	$ -	$ -	$ -	$ -		
Video for stage Presento	w/video	7-10 min	$ 31,000	$ -	$ -	$ -	$ -	$ -	$ -		
Measurement	exit surveys		$ 7,800	$ -	$ -	$ -	$ -	$ -	$ -		
Lead Capture			$ -	$ -	$ -	$ -	$ -	$ -	$ -		
Travel Expenses			$ 8,500	$ -	$ -	$ -	$ -	$ 4,874	$ 4,874	Date	PO
		Subtotal	$ 81,998	$ -	$ -	$ 71,767	$ -	$ 4,874	$ 76,641		26.6%
AV Expenses											
Payment	100%		$ -	$ -	$ -	$ -	$ -	$ 26,606	$ 26,606	Date	PO
Plasmas w/poles			$ 2,832	$ -	$ -	$ -	$ -	$ -	$ -		
Main Theatre	6 - 2010's Flat		$ 6,844	$ -	$ -	$ -	$ -	$ -	$ -		
Demo Station Monitors			$ 4,248	$ -	$ -	$ -	$ -	$ -	$ -		
Technician's Time			$ 2,700	$ -	$ -	$ -	$ -	$ -	$ -		
Lighting Section			$ 7,170	$ -	$ -	$ -	$ -	$ -	$ -		
Lighting TechTime			$ 2,200	$ -	$ -	$ -	$ -	$ -	$ -		
Labor			$ 4,900	$ -	$ -	$ -	$ -	$ -	$ -		
Freight			$ 1,000	$ -	$ -	$ -	$ -	$ -	$ -		
Discount:	20% discount		$ (3,481)	$ -	$ -	$ -	$ -	$ -	$ -		
		Subtotal	$ 28,413	$ -	$ -	$ -	$ -	$ 26,606	$ 26,606		9.2%
Web Activities											
Internet Connections	T1 Internet Access		$ 1,000	$ -	$ -	$ -	$ 1,500	$ -	$ 1,500	Date	Check
Internet Connections	8 IP addresses		$ 1,500	$ -	$ -	$ -	$ 1,000	$ -	$ 1,000	Date	Check
Internet Cabling / labor	9(50ft) / 2 hrs		$ -	$ -	$ -	$ -	$ -	455	455	Date	Expense
		Subtotal	$ 2,500	$ -	$ -	$ -	$ 2,500	$ -	$ 2,965		1.0%

(continued)

Show XX Budget

Updated: current date

ITEM	Pay To	Notes	Forecast	Paid Q201	Paid Q301	Paid Q401	Paid Q102	Paid Q202	Actual	Date	Payment
Booth Space											
40 x 50 Booth Space	Show Mgmt	50% down	$ 52,000	$ 26,000	$ -	$ -	$ -	$ -	$ 26,000	Date	Check
Final Payment	Show Mgmt	50% final	$ -	-	-	26,000	-	-	$ 26,000	Date	PO
		Subtotal	$ 52,000	$ 26,000	$ -	26,000	$ -	$ -	$ 52,000		18.0%
Promotional Activities											
Show Guide Ad	Show Mgmt		$ 1,400	$ -	$ -	$ -	1,400	$ -	$ 1,400	Date	PO
DAC Web Banner	Show Mgmt		$ 2,000	-	-	-	2,000	-	$ 2,000	Date	PO
DAC Bag Inserts	Show Mgmt		$ 1,800	-	-	-	1,800	-	$ 1,800	Date	Expense
Bag Insert Production	Copy Center		$ 1,690	-	-	-		-	$ 1,690	Date	Other
Conference List	Show Mgmt	Emails	$ 600	-	-	-	600	-	$ 600	Date	PO
E News Bellyband	Publisher		$ 4,000	-	-	-		4,000	$ 4,000	Date	PO
E Business Bellyband	Publisher		$ 3,500	-	-	-		-	$ 3,500	Date	Other
EE Times Bellyband	Publisher		$ 5,200	-	-	-	5,100	-	$ 5,100	Date	PO
Bags	Vendor	1200 X 3.00	$ 3,600	-	-	-		3,827	$ 3,827	Date	PO
Bags Setup Charge	Vendor	1 time	$ 825	-	-	-		825	$ 825	Date	PO
Incentives	Lip Balm	5000 x 2.20	$ 11,000	-	-	-		11,111	$ 11,111	Date	PO
Incentives Setup Charge	Lip Balm	1 time	$ 750	-	-	-		750	$ 750	Date	PO
Grand Prizes	Replay TV	Qty: 1	$ 500	-	-	-	230	-	$ 230	Date	Expense
Conference Prizes	Jam Cam - 2 daily	Qty: 6	$ 360	-	-	-	360	-	$ 360	Date	Expense
Daily Prizes	Handspring - 1 daily	Qty: 3	$ 1,000	-	-	-	954	-	$ 954	Date	Expense
Daily Prizes	Handspring - 1 replace	Qty: 1 replace	$ 216	-	-	-		216	$ 216	Date	Expense
Daily Prizes	Jam Cam 1 daily	Qty: 3	$ 180	-	-	-	180	-	$ 180	Date	Expense
		Subtotal	$ 38,621	$ -	-	$ -	12,624	20,729	$ 38,543		13.4%

But, if you ask, you can elicit all kinds of other useful support, like:

- Better booth location as cancellations occur.
- Opportunities to join in the show organizers' promotions.
- Opportunities to leverage show PR, advertising, and sponsorships.
- Custom promotional programs to target key audiences.
- Meeting rooms.
- Introductions to other exhibitors—especially those slotted to be nearby—to share ideas and resources.
- Speaking opportunities.
- Special booth staff training seminars.
- Flexibility on terms, such as payment schedules or exhibit rules and regulations.
- Co-location of your corporate event.

In short, if you treat show management like an overall marketing resource, your trade show experience will be more productive and positive.

HOW TO BE A GREAT CLIENT OF SHOW MANAGEMENT

If you are serious about optimizing your relationship with show management, you'll want to know how they view a successful exhibitor. Carol Fojtik, Senior Vice President at the exposition management company Hall-Erickson, has provided her recommendations for how to be a great client.

- Read the rules, regulations, and display guidelines. This seems pretty obvious, but it's amazing how many questions arise from exhibitors who simply haven't read the trade show guide.
- Follow the rules, and ask questions about anything that is unclear.
- Make sure your booth staff is aware of the rules, the trade show schedules, and where to pick up their badges.
- Understand that the exhibit floor must be a fair environment for all and that, aside from safety issues, trade show rules are designed to be sure that fairness prevails.

- Submit all booth orders in enough time to take advantage of early-bird discounts. Early booking will also get you more recognition in pre-show promotions conducted by the organizer.
- If labor has been ordered for early morning, be ready for them. You may have to wait a long while before they can return.
- To handle problems or complaints, stay calm. Immediately alert show management via a floor manager or at the trade show office. If still unsatisfied, don't leave the trade show without asking for further explanation from show management.
- Address all on-site situations, like billing problems, union labor disputes, or theft, at the trade show site, not post-show.
- Secure all valuables at the close of the trade show each day. Valuable items such as laptops should not be left on the trade show floor or stored behind the drapes.
- Offer suggestions to show management that would help make the trade show better for your company.

And here are Fojtik's top three tips for what an exhibitor emphatically should avoid, in order to stay in the show management's good graces:

1. Do not promote yourself outside your booth, except for sponsorships. This means no distributing literature around the hall, no soliciting in the aisles, and no sending robots out to roam around.
2. Do not allow your live marketing programs, music, or any other types of noise to disturb your exhibiting neighbors.
3. Do not let sales people ignore an attendee just because his or her badge indicates someone outside of the sales person's sales territory.

COST-SAVING PLANNING TIPS

Candy Adams, President of Trade Show Consulting, has come up with myriad ways to reduce unnecessary expenses and get more value from exhibiting. Some of Adams's wisdom as it relates to the planning part of trade show marketing follows:

- Rule Number One: Plan ahead. Trade Show organizers—and everyone else—offer "early-bird" discounts to encourage commitment. The earlier you plan, the better your chance for getting deals from airlines, hotels, printers, and show management. Whatever you do, try to avoid missing deadlines and incurring rush charges. These are budget killers.
- Lay out your total event costs in one place. This will allow you to compare costs from trade show to trade show and year to year, and seek opportunities to reduce expenses systematically.
- Book your travel through show management, if they offer deals.
- Audit your final trade show invoice. Adams has seen over-billing for carpet padding by the square foot, when the stated price was for the square yard. Read your bill carefully, and take issue with any item that you don't recognize.
- Decide *not* to exhibit. Every trade show should be evaluated on its own merits every year. If you decide that it is no longer meeting your company's marketing and sales objectives, the quickest way to save costs is to kill it. Or walk the trade show as a visitor and re-evaluate. Or send a speaker, or sponsor an event instead of taking a booth.

EXHIBITOR'S TIMELINE

Anyone who has ever managed the details of exhibiting can tell you: there are myriad details to cover, and everything that can go wrong will go wrong. Experienced exhibitors know that sanity is preserved only through careful advance planning and attention to detail. This timeline, adapted from Marlys K. Arnold's excellent guide, *Build a Better Trade Show Image,* provides a helpful checklist of to-do's over the course of the year in advance of your participation in a show.

Exhibit 3.11 Exhibitor's Timeline

Ten–Twelve Months Before Trade Show
- Research and select trade shows.
- Set objectives and metrics.
- Define target audience.
- Establish budget.
- Reserve booth space.
- Book hotel, airlines.
- Plan booth strategy.

Six–Ten Months Before Trade Show
- Evaluate current display: reuse, revamp, or start over?
- Study trade show rules and regulations, before constructing booth.
- Design booth layout.
- Select staffers.
- Plan publicity and promotions.
- Order signage.
- Plan hospitality events.

Three–Six Months Before Trade Show
- Determine products to be displayed.
- Arrange for shipping.
- Finalize display and learn how to assemble it, even if it will actually be done by union labor.
- Order supplies and equipment needed—lead retrieval system, audio/visual, floral, computer, furniture, etc.
- Study the Exhibitor Manual.
- Order trade show services for early-bird savings—carpet, electrical, plumbing, booth cleaning, phone, security, etc.
- Develop and compile targeted mailing list.
- Design pre-show mailers and booth literature.
- Register all booth personnel.

Two–Three Months Before Trade Show
- Print pre-show mailers.
- Design press kits.
- Send press releases (you may need to do this earlier, depending on publication schedules).
- Plan follow-up communications.
- Order premiums.
- Design lead forms.
- Begin pre-show marketing and mailings.
- Train booth staff.
- Confirm all travel reservations.
- Make restaurant reservations for staff or hospitality events.
- Appoint person to oversee installation and dismantling.
- Appoint person to manage contact capture and delivery.

Exhibit 3.11 *continued*

One Month Before Show
- Verify trade show services.
- Assemble your display in-house and make last-minute adjustments.
- Confirm product samples and literature.
- Continue pre-show promotions—make appointments, send invitations to hospitality events.
- Finalize the booth staff schedule.
- Ship display and materials—exhibit display and graphics, product displays, literature, and premiums.
- Practice in-booth demonstrations.

Three Weeks Before Show
- Mail final pre-show promotions.
- Send last-minute reminders to media.

One Week Before Show
- Organize items to take to the trade show—tool kit, copies of all contracts, contact names and numbers for show management and services, exhibit emergency kit.
- Finalize follow-up plan.
- Do role-playing with staff—engaging, overcoming objections, disengaging.
- Confirm all shipments.

Set-Up Day
- Know your move-in schedule!
- Hold a staff briefing to review goals and techniques.
- Supervise setup of booth—have photos of the finished booth for reference.

During the Trade Show
- Hold daily team meetings to keep staff informed and to track progress.
- Keep booth neat and clean.
- Book space for next year.

After the Trade Show
- Supervise booth dismantling and move-out.
- Have a team meeting and evaluate trade show results.
- Distribute leads—begin follow-up immediately.
- Send customized follow-up materials.
- Report on show results.
- Send thank-you notes to staff.
- Begin planning next year's trade show

Source: From *Build a Better Trade Show Image* by Marlys K. Arnold, ©2002. Reproduced with permission.

Prior planning is truly the key to successful trade show marketing. If you have set measurable objectives, selected the right trade show, and developed a suitable budget, you are well on your way to optimizing the results of your investment.

4

All About the
Trade Show Booth

The booth—its design, construction and servicing—is the single element that will soak up the largest portion of your trade show marketing investment. It's the most obvious element, to be sure, and garners much management attention—probably too much.

The sad thing is that very little is known about what truly works in booth location, size, and design. No one has actually tested these variables in a controlled environment. So, it's difficult to evaluate the extent to which a 10 × 20 booth out-performs a 10 × 10 booth, not to mention which spot on the exhibit hall floor attracts the most traffic. Instead we have a myriad of opinions, observations, and preferences, many of which are directly contradictory.

Here's an example. Some exhibitors swear that the front of the exhibit hall is the ideal location. Your booth will be the first thing on view as attendees stream through the entrance doors, they say. But other exhibitors, with equally compelling logic, insist that the middle of the hall is the ideal spot. Attendees tend to rush by the first couple of booths, they say. You want to be in the thick of things.

Adding their voices to the chorus, of course, are the exhibit hall space sales people, who claim that all locations are good. From their point of view—no surprise—just being at the trade show is good. "There is no such thing as a bad location," says Affinity Expo Group's Marilyn Harrington, "Only bad use of the space. You can walk any show and see two booths side by side. One is having a great show, the other a lousy one. The exhibitors who develop an integrated promotion plan, and take advantage of the entire trade show package, are the ones who are successful."

Wise words. It is certainly true that planning and promotion are key levers in trade show marketing. But the booth comprises a number of variables that need to be considered. Let us examine each in turn.

Booth Location, Location, Location

While there may be plenty of conflicting opinions about the ideal location for your booth, the options are as follows:

- Near the entrance or exit. Often selected by leading companies on the theory that everyone in the hall will inevitably pass by, allowing a sheer volume advantage. Linda Nosko, who manages exhibits for Mayflower Transit, goes for the front door as often as she can get it. "Our company has many independent agents, and they come help us work the booth. Whenever I have a front-spot location, they always say, 'Great location!' That's what I want to hear. Their happiness is one of my objectives."
- To the right of the entrance. Psychologists often claim that people naturally turn to the right when entering a room, providing greater traffic volume than the left side.
- Smack in the middle of the show floor. A popular location among experienced exhibitors.
- Near the food. Some exhibitors find the traffic good near the café or cafeteria.
- Near a competitor. If you have a clear and compelling story to tell about how you compare favorably against a competitor, locating nearby can help draw qualified traffic from the competitor's promotions.
- Away from a competitor. At a recent show in Washington, DC, Sandra Lane, Exhibit Manager for Allied Van Lines, made her decision after Mayflower had already selected the front-door location. "Mayflower was ahead of me in the selection queue for

next year, so I moved over to dead center this time. This way, I am far from my competitor, and near the show host's booth, which is probably a good thing."
- Near others in similar businesses. Gang up with companies targeting the same niche audience so you can work off each other's attraction.

Although it makes your decision even tougher, keep in mind that the logic behind booth location varies by trade show. "Show floors are merchandised differently," says Marilyn Harrington. "You should discuss the pros and cons of various locations with your account manager and get a feel for the nature of each situation." At an apparel show where Harrington was general manager, the trade show floor was laid out by product category, such as Young Contemporary, Accessories, and Streetwear. Attendees at this show, primarily buyers from apparel retail establishments, are accustomed to shopping by category, so the trade show catered to their preferences.

And Skip Cox, President of the respected researcher Exhibit Surveys, Inc., has the last word on booth location. Exhibit Surveys studied hundreds of booths at dozens of trade shows at McCormick Place in Chicago and at the Houston Astrodome, and found no statistical correlation between booth location and either booth traffic or booth memorability. "There is absolutely no relationship between the location of your booth and the success of your show," he concludes.

Booth Types

Another decision to be made is the type of booth as it fits into the trade show floor grid. Here are the options:

- Standard booth in a row facing an aisle, with neighbors visible on two sides and a tall curtain or wall in the back. Can be standard 10 × 10, or linear 10 × 20 or 10 × 30 feet, or longer. Anything along an aisle longer than 10 × 10 is known as an "in-line" booth.
- Island booth, bordered by aisles on four sides. Island booths

often permit extra signage above the booth, which is visible
from great distances, and gives the booth more dimensionality.
- End of row booth, bordered by aisles on three sides, sometimes
  called a "peninsula" or an "end-cap."
- Corner booth, at the end of a row, and bordered by two aisles.
- Perimeter booth, along the outer edges of the exhibit hall floor.
  This location may offer you a backdrop space that is higher than
  normal.
- Cross aisle booths, where two booths are rented face-to-face,
  across the aisle from each other.

Trade show management often charges premiums for booths bordered by more than one aisle, on the theory that they benefit from
more traffic.

Booth Selection Process

All this discussion of booth location and type options may be irrele-
vant to the first-time exhibitor. Location selection is typically a function of seniority, so you may end up with little choice in the matter
anyway.

Most show managers have developed a fairly rigid hierarchical selection system over the years, often combining factors relating to
booth size, sponsorship, advertising or other dollars spent, association membership, plus the number of years of exhibiting. The choice
locations are snapped up, sometimes by lottery, on the first day of
the previous year's exhibition. For some show managers, the hierarchy is based on loyalty. Says Glenn Feder, Sales Director of National
Trade Productions, Inc., "We want to reward exhibitors who have
been with us year after year. Happily, 90% of our exhibitors renew."

But there is hope for new arrivals: Ask your account manager to
keep you in mind when space opens up. There are always cancellations. This is one of those times when a warm, cooperative relationship with your account rep can come in very handy. You might
improve your chances of getting to the head of the line for cancellations if you offer to support the trade show in other ways. Barbara

Axelson of Axelson Communications, notes, "Demonstrate that, although you are new, you are committed. Join the pre-show coop mailings. Sponsor something at the trade show. It can only help. "

The only wrinkle in waiting for cancellations is the constraint it puts on publicizing your booth number—you may want to keep the booth number out of your promotions until you are sure there will be no more changes.

Booth Size

The amount of space you take is an important decision, and represents the single largest factor in a typical trade show budget (see Exhibit 3.9). The best way to approach the booth size decision rationally is by working back from your trade show objectives.

If, as is common in trade show marketing, your key objective is generating qualified sales leads, then the number of qualified prospects and hours of active exhibit hall time will be key factors in the equation. Consider this example, built on the plastics industry situation mentioned in the previous chapter.

In that scenario, the pneumatic seals company wanted to reach as many of the 750 plastics industry attendees at the trade show as possible. Estimating that they could attract about half to the booth, they planned on a target of 375 demos during the 25 exhibit hall hours. If a rep can accomplish four demos per hour, then they would need 4 sales people in the booth. Here is how that math works:

375 prospects / 4 demos per hour / 25 hours of active hall
time = 3.75 sales people (which they round up to 4)

About 50 square feet is ideal for a single demo station and rep, so this company would want to plan on a 10 × 20 booth size to support the 4 reps. However, the amount of square feet needed is a function of the type of activity planned at the booth. If, for example, you intend nothing but standing conversation, then three or even four reps can comfortably operate in a 10 × 10, especially if it is furnished at a minimum. A very small theater presentation can be managed in half of a linear 10 × 20 space. No matter how you make the calculations, let them be driven by your show goals.

Objectives other than sales lead generation will impact the booth size decision in a similar manner. Exhibitors seeking to recruit channel partners may need enough space both to show off their wares and to conduct one-on-one meetings. Companies focused primarily on scoping out the competition may want to keep their booth space very modest, and use it as a launching ground for intelligence-gathering forays.

Another factor in the booth size decision is the depth of qualified attendees. If a relatively small percentage of trade show attendees represent your target audience, then you may want to reduce your booth footprint and increase your pre-show promotion to pull your specific targets out of the crowd.

According to *Tradeshow Week*'s September 2003 Executive Outlook survey, exhibitors planned similar booth footprint areas for their most important trade show between 2002 and 2003.

Exhibit 4.1: Average Booth Sizes

Respondents	2002 Average	2003 Average
All respondents	2,200 sq. ft.	2,396 sq. ft.
Technology and telecom industry only	2,638 sq. ft.	2,326 sq. ft.
Firms with over $1 billion in sales	4,891 sq. ft.	4,875 sq. ft.

Source: *Tradeshow Week's* 2003 Executive Outlook Survey, September 2003.

Booth Layout

There are three primary drivers of booth layout decision, the:

1. Attraction strategy.
2. Nature of your product or service.
3. Activities that are planned.

ATTRACTION STRATEGY

Essentially, a booth can be laid out to be open and inviting, closed and internally focused, or a combination of the two. Which strategy you choose is a function of the trade show attendee population and your objectives. For example, if you are exhibiting at a show where the bulk of the attendees are likely to be solid prospects, and your objective is generating qualified leads, then an open booth is the ticket. You'll lay it out to attract as much traffic as possible, eliminating barriers to entrance, and offering passers-by both a welcoming way in and a convenient way out. You'll take into account the likely traffic patterns that will result from your location on the show floor. This is the strategy chosen by the majority of marketers.

If, on the other hand, the trade show is more diverse, and only a small number of attendees are likely to be your prospects, then another layout may be called for. For example, in the apparel industry, exhibitors often create booths that mimic the experience of a private show room. They will set up appointments and only allow entry to registered guests.

Exhibit 4.2: Impact of the Attendee Profile on Booth Layout

Few Qualified Attendees	Many Qualified Attendees
Product displays facing inward Raised floors Registration table at entrance	Outward facing displays Thick carpet, same color as aisle carpet Warm colors, fabrics

You might also consider the psychology of your attendees. Deborah Goldstein, President of IDG List Services, has developed a sense over years of exhibiting with 10 × 10 booths of how her prospects feel as they walk up and down the aisles. "I always put a table at the front of my booth, and I stand behind it. This makes me less threatening. People don't want to be accosted. Neither do they really want to enter my space. They want to stay in the aisle, which is their space. So I lay out the booth to make myself accessible, but also make them comfortable."

Some situations will call for a hybrid booth model. A software company introducing a hot new product, for example, might have an open area to attract passers-by, plus an enclosed theater where only qualified buyers are allowed to see the detailed demonstration. This allows maximal traffic attraction, but controls for exposure about product details to competitors.

These activities are, of course, a function of the trade show objectives. Notice how everything ties back to objectives? Without clearly defined objectives, you'll be sunk.

Exhibit 4.3: Booth Layouts

An example of an open booth layout.

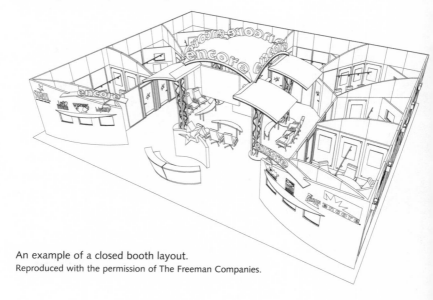

An example of a closed booth layout.
Reproduced with the permission of The Freeman Companies.

THE PRODUCT OR SERVICE BEING PROMOTED

The nature of your products or services will have a major impact on your booth design. When choosing which products to promote at your booth, remember the old adage: less is more. Trade show visitors have a limited capacity to absorb product information. If you overwhelm them, they are less likely to stop. It is always better to introduce a few products well than many poorly.

Here are some guidelines for effective booth design by product type:

- A large variety of small products can be well displayed on shelving covering the back wall of the booth.
- Small to medium sized products that require a demonstration suggest stations positioned at suitable intervals within the booth. For comfortable over-the-shoulder viewing, use pedestals at chest height or eye level.
- Large products that can be viewed but not demonstrated, like machine tools or printing presses, should be placed toward the back of the booth. Aid the explanation of their benefits and features with large photos, illustrations, and signage on the back wall. If you have a large product that can be demonstrated, put it out front.
- Intangible services can be explained with large graphics and copy points on a back wall.

As an example of effective booth design, *Exhibitor* magazine reported in December 2003 that Mattel decided to increase the meeting space from three to 14 rooms, and reduce the products on display from 500 to 120, from 2002 levels for its 2003 booth design at the Licensing International show. Why? Because Mattel's main objective for the show was to conduct meetings with licensors. The new layout allowed an estimated 300% increase in client meetings for the company. Year after year, the show attendance rose by 7.5%, but Mattel's daily traffic at the 50 × 60 booth rose by 257%, from 700 to 1,800 visitors.

THE ACTIVITIES PLANNED FOR THE BOOTH

Typical activities in trade show booths involve:

- Product demonstrations. Depending on the product type, you can demo an actual product or working model, offering a hands-on opportunity to touch and examine it. Industrial products with moving parts can provide a fascinating attraction to visitors. Companies whose products are intangible, such as services companies, will strive to convert their service features into more tangible customer benefits that can be illustrated.
- Video monitors. Moving images are dynamic and eye-catching, so video loops can make a compelling element of the show booth. Some exhibitors find that placing a video monitor with a 60-second loop next to the aisle is an effective way to stop traffic and grab the attention of passers-by.
- Computer stations. A powerful way to demonstrate software products, or to deliver vivid presentations about intangible products. Key issues to consider are the space allowed around the computer demo stand and the monitor's height. If the demo is intended to be delivered to small groups, make sure there is enough space and that the screen is at eye level or higher. It's also a good idea to design the demo to be short, no more than a few minutes, reserving additional details for a follow-up interaction.
- Theater. Complex products benefit from a theatrical demonstration or explanation. A theater setting also allows more time to gather qualifying information and give attendees a welcome chance to rest their legs.
- Meeting space. Dedicated space for private meetings is important in certain situations, such as closing transactions on the show floor. Some exhibitors go so far as to build enclosed meeting space on the second floor of their booths, to ensure an inviting meeting environment. Open meeting space can also be effective for certain kinds of business discussions—those that require little privacy and are not imperiled by frequent interruptions from passers-by.
- Photo wall. An array of photographs showing people using your

Exhibit 4.4: Presentation Options:
Delivering Your Message to Groups and Individuals

Presentation Type	Strengths	Weaknesses	Best Applications
One-on-one Individual kiosks or pedestals	Simple, low-cost Possible in all booth sizes A personal connection helps generate qualified leads	Inefficient	When product demo or required explanation is short, e.g., 2–3 minutes
Small group Demos set up to serve several standing prospects	Maintains intimacy Possible in 10 x 20 space	Can be uncomfortable for participants	When the demo is simple and can be absorbed effectively from 4 feet away
Theater	Efficient coverage of multiple prospects People like to sit	Difficult to coordinate demo times Expensive to set up Requires minimum 20 x 20 booth size Requires a professional program and experienced presenters Anonymity impedes a one-to-one conversation, making it harder to capture detailed prospect information	When product requires a complex demonstration, e.g., 5–15 minutes For new product or new category launch

product or service can be an effective attention-grabber, and especially powerful in adding a human element to a highly technical category.

- Refreshments. Some exhibitors attract visitors by appealing to their appetites. An espresso bar, a cookie-baking oven, or a popcorn machine attract based on both smell and taste.

LIVE PRESENTATIONS

Live theater presentations can communicate ideas, or information, or images that are difficult to get across otherwise. But, they must be done well. There are many suppliers available to help you create a professional theater experience for your prospects. Here are some general guidelines for live theater:

- Make sure your theater strategy supports your trade show objectives.
- Integrate the theater experience into your trade show marketing plan, from the booth look and feel, to the pre-show promotion plan, to staff training.
- In order to hold people's attention, combine three elements: information, selling, and entertainment.
- The theater experience must suit the audience, meeting their expectations for tone and manner, and aimed at their level of technical product sophistication.
- Use professional script developers.
- Use professional theater designers for technological elements such as lighting, audio, animation, and video walls.
- Keep the presentation focused on two-three key messages, maximum.
- Keep the theater presentation as short as possible.
- Consider how you will capture contact information from the hordes who sit down for your presentation. Many companies have a sheet waiting on each chair for visitors to fill out. Whatever you do, you need to compensate for the possible lack of one-to-one conversation with a booth worker.

Booth Design and Accoutrements

Because it is the most visible evidence of trade show marketing, booth design attracts a lot of attention and opinion. Unfortunately, booth design and graphics tend to suffer from the same fuzzy thinking that goes into some business-to-business marketing communications programs. The marketers will say, "We want to build brand awareness," or "We want to break through the clutter," without giving much thought to the needs of their prospects and customers.

Like any variable discussed in this book, booth design is the best approached by starting with your objectives for the trade show, in combination with an analysis of the attendee population. Are you trying to generate qualified leads? In that case, the booth look and feel should be maximally appealing to the kind of buyer you seek—and possibly even repellant to the unqualified passer-by. Don't let your agency talk you into ideas intended to create a pretty image. Booth design isn't about beauty. It's about sales and about building relationships.

Think of the booth as a three-dimensional ad. Not an awareness ad, but a direct response ad. You want people—the right people—to grasp your message and take action, namely, to come into your booth and engage in a discussion. So, ensure that the look and feel of the booth motivate that action.

Great direct response advertising has the following characteristics:

- Its message is simple, clear, and easy to grasp quickly.
- It focuses on benefits versus features.
- Its graphic environment is inviting, and does everything it can to support, and not get in the way, of the message.
- It is personable, warm, and friendly.
- It calls for an action, deliberately and compellingly.

Consider how these characteristics can drive a superior design for your booth. The objective of motivating an action will impact every detail of booth design, from layout, to materials, to signage. What materials and fabrics will attract the visitors you seek? What colors, what images, are most appealing?

Match the look and feel of your booth with the audience you have in mind. Focus on that targeted buyer. What kind of person is it? What motivates that person? What are the pain points, the peeves? If you understand the mind of your prospect, your booth design has a stronger chance of success.

Above all, keep your booth strategy simple. An overly elaborate booth can actually get in the way of your objectives. Says Marilyn Harrington of Affinity Expo Group, "If customers can't get a clear feel for what you're selling, a whiz-bang booth can be a disadvantage."

Carrie Freeman-Parsons, Vice President of Marketing at The Freeman Companies, suggests that you consider consolidating all the "booth properties" around your company, and build up a portfolio of flexible components that can be assembled for a variety of show types as needed. "Sometimes the problem is about corporate silos," she notes. "In a large company, each division is likely to have its own booth, which it might use three times a year. It's much more cost effective to consolidate."

COMPETITIVE DIFFERENTIATION

Your booth must grab attention and attract an action from your target audience, but it must also serve to differentiate you from the competition. In a commoditized category, booth design can be an effective weapon in the competitive wars. How will your widget stand out in a sea of widgets? If the show is filled with your competitors, and they are all saying the same thing, then you can use your booth image to set yourself apart successfully.

Study your competitors' designs and graphics at every trade show you can attend. Keep a record—possibly snapshots—of their booths. As you discuss your plans with your designers, consider differentiation as one of your design objectives.

Consider how you differentiate your company from your competition in the wider marketplace. Those points of competitive differentiation can provide a theme or strategic approach to your booth design. For example, if you compete on service and offer service levels that are superior to those of your competition, your booth might communicate this theme by providing easy chairs or massages to visitors. If your reputation is for technical excellence, your booth might display your hottest new product, with specs and technical drawings as the graphic theme of the environment.

BRAND IMAGE

Nothing you do at the trade show should conflict with the image your company is creating for its brand identity. Booth design, as one of the most visible image-builders, needs to be consistent—or at the very least not inconsistent—with your brand image. The reasons are obvious: your company is likely to be spending heavily on its brand image, and the trade show is a natural place to reinforce that investment. Possibly even more important, your customers and prospects have—one hopes—a clear idea of who you are. It's imperative that their experience at the trade show do nothing to tamper with the power of that idea.

Booth designs and images will vary widely by company type. An "image" company, for example, whose brand is an important part of its competitive position in the marketplace, will want to focus heavily on the look and feel of the booth. An industrial company may get away with a more utilitarian approach.

According to the brand image professionals, messaging should flow hierarchically, from top to bottom. For example, the corporate brand name should appear at the very top. With a large, or island booth, this identity would be hanging from the ceiling, visible from afar, so customers can navigate their way through the show floor to find you.

Below the brand should appear the theme, or tag line, that communicates the company's key message. Below that are the divisions, or product categories or solutions areas, and finally, at the level of a kiosk or demo station, is the product itself, preferably described with a benefit statement.

This is the way the corporate identity people think about messaging in an exhibit context. How are exhibit designers and builders thinking? More likely from the bottom up, according to John Guthrie, who evaluates the brand experience at trade shows for technology and pharmaceutical clients. Planning from the demo pedestal up is the logistical approach to booth design. "This is the number one problem I see with the exhibits I am asked to inspect," says Guthrie. "The design doesn't reflect how visitors interact with the brand. The booth needs to do a better job of helping the prospect understand why they should come in and talk."

BOOTH DESIGN TYPES

There is infinite variety in booth design options, and there are plenty of exhibit houses and design professionals ready to help you come up with elaborate new structures. Large enterprises are known to invest literally millions of dollars in eye-catching booth design and construction. But one questions the long-term—even short-term—value of an investment in glitzy booths. These examples are closer in philosophy to brand advertising than to hard objectives like sales lead generation. Perhaps these marketers are not being asked to make clear ROI arguments for their trade show budgets.

A results-oriented marketing strategy would argue that throwing more dollars at booth design is not an effective approach. Image is important, but sales results are more so—by far. The booth design must fit effectively into the ROI equation, in both the short and the long term. Each trade show must pay its way.

So consider carefully the various options in booth design and construction. Here are the types of booth designs you'll encounter:

- Table, plus draped back wall and side rails, and a small stenciled sign. This much equipment typically comes included with the price of floor space, provided by show management. On a tight budget, this basic design can work, with a few modifications. Enhance this basic layout with some lighting, modular graphics, and plants. A few inexpensive additions can make a huge difference in the look, the appeal, and the professional atmosphere of your space.
- Portable, modular elements. A wide variety of new space-age materials have emerged in recent years to allow exhibitors the flexibility of modular portability, but with the good looks and design interest of more expensive solutions. Collapsible web-like tubular structures, cloth materials that can be printed and stretched over light-weight frames, retractable systems—known as banner stands—that can be carried over the shoulder and scroll up like a window shade to create a large sign—there are numerous low-cost options available today. These systems save not only on construction costs, but also on transportation, set-up, and storage.

• Custom exhibits. Here's where the budget gets interesting. Custom booths must be professionally designed, built, stored, transported, set up, dismantled, and maintained. A full service exhibit house will handle all these functions for you, or you can pick and choose from a variety of suppliers. A custom booth should last five to seven years if designed to allow change and multiple configurations, as well as new graphics and lighting effects, according to Carrie Freeman-Parsons of The Freeman Companies. Managing a custom booth will require at least one trained and experienced exhibit manager in house to oversee the logistics, handle budgets, and keep things on track. When a certain product or service requires a unique design, a custom exhibit may be the only option.

Heritage Exhibits, a national exhibit house, has estimated a range of prices you can expect to pay for new booths of various sizes. The estimates include the cost of design, development, construction, and carpeting, and provide a custom container for shipping. They do not include costs for space, graphics, furniture, and trade show services. According to Mike Seymour, Vice President of Sales for Heritage, budgets can vary widely by industry and marketing objectives. So exhibitors would do well to consult a professional builder to develop an accurate estimate to meet their needs.

Exhibit 4.5: Cost of Building a New Booth

Booth Size	Sq Ft.	Low $	Med $	High $
20 x 20	400	67,000	85,000	96,000
20 x 30	600	87,000	105,000	114,000
30 x 30	900	124,500	155,500	185,500
30 x 40	1200	161,000	199,000	225,000
30 x 50	1500	216,500	245,500	280,500
40 x 50	2000	265,000	305,000	350,000
50 x 50	2500	310,500	375,500	437,500
50 x 60	3000	345,000	435,000	525,000
50 x 70	3500	440,000	507,500	612,500
50 x 100	5000	575,000& up	725,000 & up	875,000 & up

Source: Michael R. Seymour, CME—Heritage Exhibits-Chicago.

HOW TO BE A GREAT DESIGN CLIENT

Booth design is a high art. A professional exhibit designer can save you time and headaches, and—in the long run—money. Naturally, you want a booth design that supports your trade show objectives. But there's another reason to use a pro: the myriad regulations dictated by show managements. You'll also rely on a professional to consider efficiencies relating to shipping, durability, installation, and dismantling.

Your relationship with a professional designer will be enhanced if you follow these guidelines.

- Select a designer with whom you feel comfortable, professionally and personally. This relationship can be rocky, and it pays to start off with a solid base. Get references and check them.
- Come to the planning meeting prepared. Bring your trade show schedule for the next 12 months, including location and size, show rules, and your marketing objectives for each trade show. Be clear about your budget and your preferences as they relate to portability and modularity. Share details about your competitors' trade show plans and booth strategies. Also explain the nature of your company, and your target audience. As Carrie Freeman-Parsons points out, "You wouldn't hire an architect and simply give him a budget and tell him to go build a house for you. You need to provide strategic information about the image and the culture of your company, as well as your tactical requirements."

Exhibit 4.6: Link Your Booth Design to Your Show Goals

Show Objective	Booth Strategy
Prospecting	Open, inviting, easy movement in and out
Sales	Room for face-to-face interaction, meeting spaces
Demonstrations	Plenty of pedestals and staff; theater
Current customer marketing	Easy chairs, tables for small meetings; refreshments

- Don't make your selection based on what you like. Think about the audience, and what will motivate them.
- Plan ahead. Time crunches reduce quality and raise costs—and stress levels.
- Don't change your plans midstream.

BOOTH DESIGN ELEMENTS

Other than tables, chairs and signage, consider the following elements as you plan your booth design.

- Lighting. This is the secret weapon of booth design. Relatively inexpensive, lighting has a powerful impact on the image and clarity of the booth's look. Try a table lamp to warm up the booth environment. Use lighting to highlight key features and benefits in your signage. It's a smart way to differentiate a small booth or tabletop exhibit. And it has the added attraction of keeping booth staff motivated during a long day.
- Storage space. Often forgotten, locked storage space in the booth is a boon to both staff and managers. It also promotes a clean, professional look at the booth.
- Carpets. A quality carpet contributes to the professional look of your booth, allows some differentiation by color, and most of all, can improve the energy of booth staff and visitors alike. Worth the investment.
- Plants. What better way to improve a booth's image and appeal? Houseplants and flowers are a low-cost but welcome addition to any booth. Just be sure not to position the plants in a way that interferes with traffic flow.
- Telephones. Trade show management will offer you a phone rental option, but these days cell phones have rendered this service unnecessary. That said, cell phone use should be limited to the aisles or lobbies. A staff worker talking on a cell phone is an immediate turn-off to booth visitors.

THEMES ARE POPULAR—AND DANGEROUS

Exhibitors tend to be enamored of booth themes, ranging from the very kitschy to the relatively dignified. Here are some of the more popular themes seen around trade shows in the business world:

- Hawaii.
- Mardi Gras.
- The Fifties.
- Sports.
- Broadway.
- Doctor's office.

Use of a theme can create a memorable experience for visitors and provide an effective point of differentiation in a highly competitive category.

But themes can be risky. At a recent TS2, the trade show produced by the Trade Show Exhibitors Association, one exhibit house created a "kitchen" theme to differentiate itself from the myriad other exhibit houses on the trade show floor. The booth was certainly eye-catching. It contained an industrial stove, a gigantic refrigerator, and plenty of colorful plastic fruits and vegetables strewn around on countertops. However, passers-by who were not previously familiar with the company were just as likely to get the impression that the booth was promoting cookware or kitchen construction. One visitor was compelled to approach and ask the dreaded question, "What do you guys do, anyway?" Any booth design that shifts the burden of communication from the booth to the visitor is missing an opportunity to sell. The problem with a memorable gimmick is that, often, the gimmick is all that's remembered.

> **Where Can You Cut?**
>
> *Exhibitor* magazine (August 2003: 33–35) offers suggestion for areas where you can save budget dollars with minimum impact on your booth's effectiveness. Consider reductions in the following:
>
> - Premiums.
> - Booth-cleaning services, especially in smaller booths.
> - Lead retrieval systems (use paper or your own electronic forms).
> - Plant rental.
> - Landline telephone.

Booth Sourcing Options

Your first booth sourcing decision is whether to rent a booth or buy one. In fact, you have three options to consider: rent, buy or rent-to-buy. Some rules of thumb:

- If a booth will be used more than three to four times a year, buy.
- If you are just starting out or only exhibit occasionally, rent.
- If you are committed to several shows, but the longer term is uncertain, rent to buy.
- If you have bought a booth and occasionally need expanded space, you can supplement the purchased property with rented property, such as a conference room.

The next question is the sources, the suppliers, and resources that will help you pull together the right booth. Your options include:

- For rentals, check rental and display resources online or through the Yellow Pages. Another source is the show decorator selected by show management, although this is generally viewed as a pricier solution than using an outside resource.
- Exhibit houses, also known as custom shops, offer a wide range of services, from booth design and layout, to fabrication, storage, crating, and shipping. They will even supervise the installation and dismantling, and then manage any repairs or refurbishing needed between shows. Exhibit houses typically will submit proposed designs on spec.
- Design companies handle only booth design and layout, but may also offer to manage the booth manufacturing by contracting out to a custom shop.
- Independent exhibit design professionals with lower overhead can offer a competitively priced alternative to design companies. In both cases, however, you will pay for the design, even if the booth is not eventually built.
- Graphics companies, essentially printers who have diversified into additional services, can handle many of the same functions

as a design company and exhibit house, but are best used for smaller, less ambitious booth configurations.

- Business event agencies offer a full range of business event-management services, handling everything that an exhibit house offers, plus audio/visual production and complete marketing services, like marketing plans, collateral materials, sales training, promotional campaigns, and sales lead tracking. There will be variations. For example, some business event agencies—those with a communications bent—do not build booths. And others will not offer promotional campaign services.

Booth-Building on a Budget

Candy Adams, President of Trade Show Consulting, suggests the following ways to save on the costs of booth building:

- Get competitive bids on booth design and construction from a variety of exhibit houses. Do the same for shipping companies.
- Consider a modular booth instead of a custom exhibit. This will save you on shipping and drayage, as well as installation.
- Buy and refurbish used exhibit property, and save as much as 75% versus purchase of a new one. An Internet search will turn up plenty of suppliers.
- Expand your budget's reach by teaming up with business partners and getting a larger booth than you could afford by yourself.
- Redesign your booth to be as effective in a smaller footprint. One way to do this is to eliminate older products and only show your newest ones.
- Update your custom booth with new laminate affixed on top of the old laminated surfaces.
- Cooperating on pre-show promotions, too, will enhance your ability to make an impact. Another way to cooperate with a business partner is to do mutual promotions at each other's booth. A small sign at each booth referring visitors to the other's booth—with a reason why they should stop by—can be effective, and inexpensive.
- Only use one-color handouts at the booth, and save your four-color collateral to send to qualified visitors after the show.
- Buy furnishings instead of renting them—and that includes the carpet.
- Select the most lightweight and durable signage possible.
- Don't skimp on the cost of building sturdy crates for your new exhibit. You will save much in the way of damage repairs, not to mention extra labor costs for padding and wrapping.

Signage and Literature

After design and layout, signage is the second most visible element of the booth, but tends to get too little attention from marketing professionals.

It is true that the booth size, look, and feel deliver strong, often unconscious messages about your company and your offering. But, in fact, the words you choose to attract qualified prospects, and the skill with which you display these words, are the most powerful driver of success on the show floor itself. So don't skimp on developing your signage.

There are two key drivers of signage success:

1. The message must be short, clear, and easy to grasp.
2. The typeface must be legible enough to read easily at 30 feet.

This is easy to say, but not as easy to execute. Here are some tips that will help:

- Select a message that expresses your unique selling proposition. This is the key benefit of value to your customers, the benefit that differentiates you from the competition. Remember: go for the benefit, not the feature. Think the customer, not youself.
- As you craft the words, keep in mind what you want visitors to *think*, to *know*, and to *do*.
- Choose benefit-oriented words, like "new," and "proven."
- Get rid of any buzzwords, acronyms, and jargon.
- Beware of using your PR or ad agency to create your signage. As Mim Goldberg of Marketech points out, "Communications agencies are good at writing printed collateral, but when it comes to the succinct messages needed in booth graphics, they have trouble grabbing the key benefits and using the words the audience can understand."
- If you have identified a winning subject line in your emails, it will probably make a powerful message for your booth sign, as well.
- Test different messages. You can bring several message treatments with you to a trade show, alternate them during the day or from day to day, and evaluate which bring in the best traffic, both in terms of quality and in terms of quantity.

- Don't knock your competition. As wisely observed by Marlys K. Arnold, author of *Build a Better Trade Show Image,* signage that trashes your competition is in poor taste and reflects badly on you and your judgment. "It is far better to demonstrate how good you are, and let your audience draw its own comparative conclusion," she notes.
- Only hype your company name and logo if it's already a well-regarded brand. If you are a lesser known among this audience, focus instead on the benefits you offer to the customer. Remember, it's about them, not you.
- Creating booth signage is like creating a billboard, which must be read and absorbed by people in cars whizzing by. Use the same logic. A simple message, a call to action, light-colored background, an easy-to-read font, and large type.
- Rule of thumb for type size: use one inch of type for every three feet away your visitors will be standing. And don't forget good lighting—it will make a huge difference.
- Consider how your signage can pre-qualify visitors. You want to attract the right visitors and repel the ones who will waste your time. So, if you are looking to attract pediatricians in a sea of doctors, your signage can help: "The best widgets for pediatricians."
- If you have detailed messages to communicate via signage, use a combination of methods. A large, simply worded sign in a high position for distance viewing, plus additional signs with more detail inside the booth, either on the walls, or on countertops.

Exhibit 4.7: Powerful Headline Words that Drive Action

Advice	Introducing	Smart
Announcing	Limited-time	Special invitation
At last	New	Success
Because	Now	Wanted
Confidential	Proven	Which
Congratulations	Revolutionary	Who else
Free	Save	Why
Guaranteed	Secrets	Yes
How to		

Signage That Makes Visitors Do All the Work

I am a direct and database marketer by training, and one way I keep up with my profession is by attending trade shows and conferences. As I visited the exhibit hall of the National Center for Database Marketing show recently, I was struck by the varying levels of skill with which the exhibitors made use of signage to attract visitors and get their messages across. My conclusion: most of the booths were making me—the visitor—do all the work.

As I walked the aisles, I noticed how my eye would scan the signs, in an effort to decide which booth to visit and which to pass by. When the signs made sense, I was fine. But many of them left me clueless.

So what does a clueless aisle walker do? They have two choices. Either go up to the booth and pose the big question, "What do you guys do, anyway?" Or, they move on, mumbling to oneself, "Why don't they just tell me what they do? Why do I have to do all the work?"

Let me provide an example. Here's a sizable booth, nicely populated with good-looking people, obviously a prosperous business. And the signage? Three headline words, "Innovative, Experienced, Dedicated," plus the name of the company.

So what do I make of that? Nothing. I have no clue. I am forced to go up and ask the big question. And when I do, I get a pretty compelling answer. "We're a direct marketing agency, handling everything from soup to nuts. We do creative, we do databases, we have millions of email names for sale. We do production. We do outbound telemarketing."

Sounds good. Sounds like a company I'd like to know about. So why didn't they say so on the signage in the first place?

Then I notice a smaller sign at the side of their booth, which does list a menu of services. But the list contains their cutesy trademarked product names for the services. If I don't already know these product names, I am still clueless. I still have to ask the question. They're still making me do the work.

Here's another example: A booth whose signage said "Connecting the eGeneration." What does that mean? Is it a telemarketing shop specializing in the youth market? Is it an Internet service provider? Nope. Turns out it is enterprise-level software product that creates personalized communications in multiple media, like paper and email. It's used by companies like Fidelity and Merrill Lynch to create monthly statements for customers. Again, an interesting product, and worth knowing about, but why does it have to be so hard to figure out what they do?

At another booth, I found an answer. The guy manning the booth summed up his product succinctly: "It's a tool that prevents you from key-entering an incorrect address." So, I asked him why his signage didn't say that. "Because I'm not in marketing," he said. Hmmm.

But all is not lost. I did come across some excellent signs. Consider this one, from InfoUSA. The signage literally said, "We Have the *Best* Database of 14 Million Businesses." And "Our Database of 266 Million Consumers Can Help You." I get it. I want to know more, so I go up to the booth and start a conversation.

Source: Ruth P. Stevens

WHERE CAN YOU PUT A SIGN?

- Back and side walls.
- Table tops, fronts, and sides.
- Demo pods, kiosks, or monitors.
- Tower or hanging banner.
- Theater marquee and seat backs.
- Video wall and photo wall.
- Product display.
- Archways.
- Hospitality suites or demo suites.
- Attendee badges, as a sticker or pin.
- Sponsorships.

SALES COLLATERAL

Use literature sparingly. For some reason, sales collateral has evolved into a crutch for booth workers. Staffers will hide behind literature as a way to avoid the real engagement that face-to-face contact allows. By handing out literature, they somehow feel that they have accomplished something. But the handout is more than likely to end up in a hotel room wastebasket, if it even gets that far.

Your staff training session should include instructions on how to use literature. The best use of staff at a trade show is to engage in conversation. Once a prospect is qualified, and there's a true need for additional product information, then the staffer should offer to mail the literature as a follow-up. This ensures that the material will actually arrive, and it becomes an effective beginning to the longer-term relationship-building process. The collateral request becomes, in effect, a qualifying point. Janet Rapp of MTS Systems Corporation says she makes an ongoing effort to persuade visitors who request literature to receive it by mail. "You don't want to carry that," she says. "Let us send it to you and save you the trouble."

Rather than taking a full complement of brochures, catalogs, and annual reports to a show, a better strategy is to limit collateral at the booth to a single sheet that covers key features and benefits of your company or your product line. Don't bother with four-color designs.

This approach will save plenty of money in printing, shipping, and storage costs. And it's more likely to be used effectively by booth workers. In fact, the best use of literature is for ending unproductive conversations politely: "Very nice of you to stop by. Here, please take one of our brochures."

Tabletop Shows

Smaller conferences—which often attract a narrowly defined and highly qualified audience—may limit their exhibitors to use of so-called tabletop space. Simply a series of free-standing draped tables set up in rows in a carpeted ballroom, the tabletop exhibit space is inexpensive to rent and requires much less in the way of booth material. Most exhibitors will set up a portable sign at the back of the table, drape a banner over the front, perhaps set up a single computer monitor with a demo, and stand expectantly at the side of the table awaiting visitors.

According to Deb Goldstein of IDG, the key advantage of the tabletop show is the intimacy. "Visitors can be seen moving around the entire floor," she notes. "In contrast to the walled aisles of the typical exhibit hall, the open feeling is very welcome and encourages conversation."

Not only are attendees at these conferences likely to be more qualified, they tend to be eager to learn new ideas. Janet Rapp, of MTS Systems Corporation, advises that tabletop shows call for a different strategy in trade show selling, fulfillment and follow-up. "These attendees are there to learn, to meet colleagues, and to network, not necessarily to look for new products. At a tabletop exhibit, I concentrate on making sure I am gathering names, rather than engaging in 20-minute conversations. I will then follow up with materials that are more educational, than heavily sales-oriented in nature. And, I will nurture the relationship. If I run across a visitor who is very interested in learning more about my products at the show, I will make an appointment for breakfast or drinks, rather than engaging right on the show floor."

Some tips for success with tabletop shows:

- Take the trade show seriously. Tabletop shows feel less formal than regular exhibits, but they still provide a valuable opportunity for customer interaction. Make sure someone is covering the space during the entire period the exhibit hall is open. Most tabletop shows run limited exhibit hall hours, often between program sessions.
- Less is more. Don't cram your space with collateral material and trinkets.
- Keep your signage to a minimum. Stick with one key message and deliver it clearly.
- Don't try to turn it into a regular exhibit. Your standard booth material—signage, lighting, backdrops—will only get in the way of the intimate, informal feel of the space.
- Make your tabletop materials available to your business partners, who are likely to be exhibiting at a variety of local trade shows and conferences.
- Follow the process. Don't forget the pre-show promotion, the inquiry capture methods, and the ROI calculations. This thing is simpler than usual, but it's still a worthy part of your trade show program.

Judy Studenski, formerly Executive Vice President of American Slide Chart, finds tabletop shows particularly suited to her product line, which benefits from hands-on touch and interaction. "Our lines of paper slide charts, wheel charts and pop-ups simply call out to visitors to play with them. So, we appreciate the opportunity to show a number of samples at counter height, and invite passers by to fiddle with the merchandise."

In order to make the flat tabletop more inviting, Studenski created a portable display she calls a "tilt-top." It consists of two hinged panels, 30 inches wide, which open front-wise like a book. The insides are covered with a nubby fabric, where the samples can be affixed with Velcro. "The big advantage of the tilt-top is that it elevates the interactive space," notes Studenski. "The product is now at eye and hand height. I stand behind the table, available to chat. With the tilt-top, the visitor feels comfortable interacting, as if they were at a cosmetics counter or a bar. It warms up the tabletop environment, and also differentiates us from the rest of the exhibits. Also, the tilt-top is small enough to travel as checked luggage. Our sales people take them to vendor days at companies all over."

Final Booth Considerations

Some additional items to consider when planning and budgeting for your booth include:

- The booth is a highly visible representation of your company's objectives at the trade show, but avoid the temptation of spending too much attention on it, to the detriment of the less visible but much more powerful elements of the trade show program.
- Think of the booth as the "hardware" of your trade show marketing execution. The "software," namely the pre-show promotion and the post-show follow-up should not be neglected. You'll get more leverage from excellent "software" than from a razzle-dazzle booth.
- Resist the temptation to pay a premium for a choice booth location. Spend the money on targeted traffic-driving promotions instead.
- Booth size provides more leverage than booth design and construction. You are very likely to find that you can get as much done in a simple, but sizable space, with next to no booth accoutrements at all.
- Clear signage, good lighting, and a couple of houseplants will get you 90% of the way to your goals.
- Keep a close eye on reducing your fixed exhibiting costs, like booth transportation, drayage, installation, and dismantling, by selecting lightweight structures and modular elements. Those dollars will work a lot harder if they are devoted to promotional activity.

5 Trade Show Booth Management

Staffing and Recruiting

The quality of your booth staff is arguably the single most important variable in your trade show marketing program. Events are a people business. Huge leverage can be gained with a knowledgeable, engaged, and energetic staff. The right people, and the right training, can mean double the normal quantity of sales or sales leads you produce—for the same amount of investment. There is no better place to improve your show ROI than by selecting the best staff and giving them proper preparation.

STAFF SELECTION

The ideal booth worker has the following characteristics:

- Outgoing, personable, and polite.
- Well informed about the products.
- Professionally matched to the interests and level of the audience.

But finding such a person within your organization is not necessarily easy. Here are some tips for selecting the best possible booth staffers:

- Look at your call center personnel. Some experts believe that telephone reps are superior to field sales people at booth work, because they know how to engage with strangers, and solve problems in short, sequential manner. This includes both inside sales reps and customer service reps.

- Consider the audience profile. You'll want to select booth workers who have similar characteristics, in terms of organizational level, technical skill, ethnic mix, gender, and age.
- For a regional show, include the sales team that covers that territory. But be sure to get them trained on booth selling skills. Booth work is a very different animal from most face-to-face selling.
- For a national show, however, you may or may not want to staff the booth with field sales people. The sales organization has traditionally been the source of booth worker supply, but in fact many field reps have difficulty adjusting to the rapid-fire nature of booth selling. Also, they tend to be distracted by their regular jobs—helping customers, solving problems back in the field. If you do decide to use field sales people, be sure they are well trained in booth selling techniques. Also, schedule plenty of down time for them to handle their own business.
- Consider involving your business partners, resellers, distributors, and vendors.
- When selecting sales people, choose neither the most seasoned nor the rookies. The best bet is someone in the middle who has enough product and company knowledge to represent you properly, but it not so jaded as to see trade show work as an inconvenience.
- Strive for a mix of specialized product knowledge and technical skill. This way, the staff can call each other over for help, if the conversation requires particular expertise.
- Consider outsourcing. Polite, professional temp staff can be pulled in locally to help at your booth. Just be sure you include sufficient training for them.

Barry Gold, a seasoned sales executive in the database marketing industry points out that trade show duty is at the bottom of a sales rep's list of preferred activities, "When I am working a booth, I tend to meet only three kinds of people: either they are so young they don't know any better, or they are freebie hunters grabbing souvenirs for their kids, or they are conference attendees just stretching their legs between sessions." Clearly, Gold is jaded on this subject.

But he offers sound advice for how he does extract value from working a show. "I figure I am shelling out $1,000 a day in expenses, not to mention the opportunity cost of being out of the field. The only way to make this worthwhile is to set up a series of meetings in and around the show—in advance—with target customers and prospects. You simply can't depend on qualified people happening by your booth, unless your company has a major presence, or you have big news or big buzz."

STAFF RECRUITMENT

Working a booth is no picnic, so you must make a persuasive case to your company employees, and to others, for taking on booth duty at a show. Here are some tactics that might make the internal selling easier:

- Educate top management on the goals and expected ROI of the trade show marketing program. Explain to them the critical leverage that can be gained from having the right staffers participate. Ask for their support in recruiting staff members from across the company.
- Offer an incentive. Comp time off, cash bonuses, and gifts or prizes are common rewards. Tie the incentives to clear, measurable objectives for each staff person.
- Make the logistics and schedules as painless as possible. Consider perks like a private bus to ferry staffers from the hotel, or a private concierge to help them with dinner reservations and other details. Arrange for a catered lunch in a private room for booth staff every day.
- Hold the accounting for the travel budget for booth workers. If staffers, and their managers, know the expense is not going to hit their own T&E budgets, they'll be happier. As an aside, there is another good reason for consolidating the travel budget under

the trade show budgetary umbrella: It increases your ability to analyze the true cost of the trade show marketing program.

- Don't use sales people as cheap labor. You want them fresh and excited to meet with customers and prospects. Assign other resources to handle booth set-up and all the details before the exhibit hall opens.
- A trade show is not the place to break in new employees. Remember, the booth staff is the variable with the most leverage for success. Don't squander that opportunity on someone who does not have the right personality, or the industry, product, or technical skills required.
- Take the staff recruitment process seriously. Plan ahead.
- Send thank you notes to the booth staff, and their managers, after the show. Include highlights of the positive contribution the event made to the company, and congratulate the staffers on helping drive the results.

Once you have your staff candidates identified, send them a package introducing the trade show and how it fits into your company's sales and marketing strategy. The package might contain the following elements:

- A welcome letter congratulating them on becoming part of the booth staff team.
- A statement of your specific objectives for the show.
- Last year's show brochure.
- Pre-show and at-show promotional plans.
- Basic information about the schedule, dates, and locations.
- List of booth staff.
- An audience analysis.
- Benefits to the staff of attending (e.g., attendance at sessions, industry visibility, competitive intelligence gathering, bragging rights, sales leads for their territory, bonuses, or incentives).

Posting the materials to an Internet or Extranet site can be a low-cost substitute for distributing hard copies.

MOTIVATING SALES PEOPLE TO WORK AN EVENT

Mim Goldberg of Marketech shares some insights about sales people's attitudes to booth duty. "Sales people often don't take trade show marketing seriously. Sometimes they won't even show up. Or you'll only be able to recruit the new ones, who don't know enough to say no, or the sales people who live closest to the show city. You are at risk of staffing your booth with the wrong people." Goldberg offers these tips for overcoming sales reluctance:

- Take advantage of sales people's natural competitiveness.
- Reward lead generation at the show with a percentage of the commission on the later sale.
- Convert booth duty into a reward. Invite the top sales people in the quarter to work the event. Pick them up at the airport and give them VIP treatment.
- Allow sales people to follow up their own trade show leads, or at least several of the hot leads from the trade show, regardless of territory.
- Set up teams, and give prizes to the team that generates the most—or best—leads in the morning or afternoon, each day of the show.

GOAL SETTING

Booth staff work better if you assign them specific, attainable goals, on an individual level. Consider the pneumatic seals example in Chapter Three. That company set a goal of giving 375 demos to visitors from the plastics industry throughout the trade show. But, you don't want to discourage your booth staff by simply announcing that your goal is to give 375 demos. Instead, break it down to the rep level. Say you want each booth staffer to accomplish 4 demos per hour during their shifts. The staff will find this kind of specificity to be highly motivating.

Training

An investment in training is one of the best uses of your trade show budget, for two reasons:

1. The booth staff has an enormous impact on your ability to meet your trade show goals. Anything you can do to make them more productive is money well spent. Consider this: a Deloitte & Touche study for the Center for Exhibition Industry Research (CEIR) found that staff training increased the conversion of booth visitors to qualified leads by 68%.
2. Trade show selling is a unique skill, and very different from traditional face-to-face selling. The skill can be taught. A small amount of training can vastly improve your results.

The ideal approach is to hire a professional trainer. An Internet search will turn up scads of qualified experts. Or ask your account person from show management for recommendations. Sometimes, show management will even provide complimentary training by a professional, as a value-added service to exhibitors.

Few marketers have figured out the importance of staff training. According to CEIR, only 30% of exhibitors use training regularly, and only 2% use outside trainers. Of course, given this state of affairs, the company that does invest in training is likely to gain considerable competitive advantage.

Whether you use an outside professional or an internal trainer, allow about two to three hours for the training session. Since it can be difficult to coordinate people's schedules for a session in advance of the show, exhibitors often conduct the training just before the trade show, in the trade show city. This also allows the trainer to stick around to observe the staff's performance, and offer coaching and fine-tuning during the show itself.

Another solution is suggested by Mim Goldberg. "We have had great success with distance training," she says. "An hour's webinar can work wonders."

The cost of training can vary widely, depending on the staff headcount and their skill level. But as a percentage of the trade show budget, the investment is minor—especially when you consider the leverage training provides.

While it is most timely to conduct staff training immediately in advance of a trade show, you might also consider trade show training a regular part of your employee education program. "The annual sales meeting is a good time for training in trade show selling skills," says Goldberg. "Trade show selling is different from field selling. It's helpful for sales people to receive training in both."

"The best programs have ongoing training throughout the year," concurs George L. Vanik, Marketing Communications Manager at Northrop Grumman's electronic systems division. "Then the marketing teams can provide a quick refresher for the booth staff before each show." Vanik finds that an outside trainer brings expert credibility that goes over better than he and his colleagues can achieve.

If you are looking for evidence that training works, listen to Bob Burk, who manages exhibit marketing for King Industries, a chemicals manufacturer. When Burk started with King, there was no staff training scheduled. Once training was instituted, the company's trade show performance improved dramatically. "We know training works," says Burk. "We have gone from above the industry average for 'poor' ratings for our booth staff—which was 6% at the time—to virtually zero 'poor' ratings."

THE BENEFITS OF STAFF TRAINING

Doug MacLean of MacLean Marketing, a seasoned exhibit staff trainer, identifies several key benefits to training:

- Staffers will feel as if they are on the same team after training. This is significant, because exhibit staffing is very much a team activity. Equally significant is the impact on booth staffers who come from the sales ranks—sales people being notorious for working independently. In such a situation, team-building can be very helpful.
- Staffers will know what is expected. Professional training will make clear the specific goals and objectives for the trade show,

reducing the chance of misunderstandings or too personal an interpretation of what the trade show results should be.

- Staffers will understand that the rules of engagement are different at a trade show. They will grasp the impact of shortened time frames, of different audience expectations and different business objectives. They will realize that this is not a typical sales event but an opportunity for marketing, branding, education, research, and personal communications.

STAFF TRAINING AGENDA

Here are the topics that can usefully be covered in a staff training session:

- Self-introductions.
- Welcome by senior management. An appearance by a senior executive will illustrate the importance of the trade show investment, as well as pump up the team.
- A trade show overview (trade show objectives, history, program).
- Attendee analysis (audience profile, badge color code listing).
- Product information and operations, including competitive comparisons.
- Booth work schedule and assigned tasks, including daily meeting schedule, dress code, and other instructions.
- Specific goals, with quantifiable daily objectives for team members.
- Guidelines for speaking with the press.
- A booth selling skills workshop, including role play and preparing answers to tough questions.
- How to work the demo, including scripting and hands-on experience with the technology.
- The information capture and lead management process.
- A visit to the booth, if the training is on-site.
- A social event to bond and reward the team, whether it's a lunch, a dinner, or an outing.

Some of these items can be covered through other methods, like webinars, audiotapes, teleconferences, or newsletters in advance. Some topics you may want to save for the pre-show staff meeting described below.

CASE STUDY

Handling Problems at the Booth: Murphy Was Here

Jane Lorimer, President of Lorimer Consulting, recalls the time when she was exhibit manager for Coors Brewing Company, and her booth crates never arrived at the trade show. So, a few hours before the exhibit hall was to open, she rented some emergency tables and chairs, and went out to a graphics store and created a sign that read, "Our booth didn't make it, but we did, so please come in and talk to us." Lorimer propped the sign up on a mop standing in a bucket, and placed it at the front of the 10 × 30 booth. The show was a success for Coors, thanks to her quick thinking and her recognition of the key characteristic of a trade show: it's a place where business conversations are launched. As Lorimer notes, "People do business with people."

Scheduling

The quantity of your booth staff will be a function of the size of the booth, the activities planned at the booth, and the number of hours you decide each worker should be on call. Of course, the size and activities, like everything else, are driven by the goals you set for the trade show. But the number of hours is a new wrinkle. Experts say that the ideal maximum number of hours for booth duty is four per day, in two-hour shifts. This kind of schedule will keep workers consistently fresh and at the top of their games.

However, many companies consider this a luxury they cannot afford, and they ask their booth staff to be on the trade show floor during the entire exhibit hall day, with short breaks. Pat Jaglowitz, manager of North American trade shows for Open Text Corporation in Canada, feels strongly about the responsibility of the booth staff: "When they are at the show, I own them" she says. Pat expects her staff to be available all day, whether for booth duty or any other activities she assigns.

Here is a formula for calculating the number of booth workers you will need:

$$\frac{\text{Prospects (e.g., attendees interested in your product)}}{\text{active show hours (subtract hours that overlap with distractions like keynote speakers)}} = \text{prospects per hour}$$

$$\frac{\text{Prospects per hour}}{\text{\# discussions per rep per hour (5–15 minutes, depending on the amount of detail required)}} = \text{\# staff required}$$

For the pneumatic seal company, the staff requirements would work out as follows:

$$\frac{375 \text{ prospects}}{25 \text{ show hours}} = 15 \text{ prospects per hour}$$

$$\frac{15 \text{ prospects per hour}}{4 \text{ demos per hour (15 minutes per demo)}} = 4 \text{ reps (rounded up from 3.75)}$$

MANAGING A ONE-PERSON BOOTH

The exhibit day can be long, and if a single person is assigned to staff the booth for the whole trade show, you need to take some extra steps to avoid burnout and meet your marketing objectives. Some tips from Marc Goldberg, partner in Marketech:

- Allow plenty of extra time to set up and dismantle the booth.
- Use prepared demos, like video loops or self-managed computer visuals.
- Design your contact sheet so it can be partially filled in by the visitor.
- Hire a local temp to fill in during lunch breaks—but only if you can arrange for the person to be thoroughly trained.
- Make friends with neighboring booth staff.
- Bring signage that instructs visitors about what to do when you are away from the booth.

THE SHOW HANDBOOK

Prepare a handbook for each booth staff member that contains the following:

- Schedules for booth duty and daily staff meetings.
- Client meeting schedule.
- Trade show floor plan and city maps.
- Team contact information (hotel rooms, cell phone numbers).
- Product information.
- Sample answers to objections and difficult questions.

SPECIAL BOOTH ROLES

There are a number of special functions that need to be covered at the booth. Save time and increase productivity by naming a point person in charge of each of the following:

- Lead management. This role involves trouble-shooting and decision-making relating to the information capture process, and the data handling. This person will be responsible for timely delivery of contact data and qualified leads back to the office.
- Ombudsman. One person should be trained in handling any angry visitors who may turn up.
- Press relations. If a trained media relations specialist is on hand, all staffers may refer press inquires to that person, reducing the

amount of preparation and training needed for the rest of the staff. But make sure at least one press relations person is scheduled to be at the booth at all times.

Pre-Show Preparation

Like many trade show-related activities, setting up and taking down the booth is a logistical challenge that absorbs much of the exhibit manager's time and attention. It is at such points in the process that the rest of the company—especially marketing management—needs to be supportive and grateful, but stay out of the way.

However, for anyone who will be representing the company at the trade show, here are some points relating to booth set-up and take-down to keep in mind:

- Introduce yourself to the exhibitors adjacent to you. The companionship will be welcome during slow times, and especially helpful in emergencies.
- Don't succumb to the temptation to knock off early on the last day of the trade show. Serious buyers are often cruising the show floor at the last minute. According to CEIR, 68% of sales people surveyed said they had met a qualified prospect in the last half hour of the exhibit day. So be ready for them.

PRE-SHOW STAFF MEETING

It's imperative to meet in advance with the team that will be working the booth. You also should invite company employees who do not have booth duty specifically, but will be attending the show for other reasons. This way, they will better be able to represent the company's marketing goals at the trade show. They will also be prepared in case they need to be pressed into emergency booth duty.

This meeting is primarily about logistics, and should not be confused with a true staff training session. Your results will be much improved with a modest investment in training. Don't neglect it.

The staff meeting agenda might cover the following categories:

- Review company objectives for the trade show.
- Assign individual goals for the trade show, and for each day.
- Review the products that will be promoted, and their key selling points (this may best be done by teaming up a sales person and a technical person).
- Review the appointment schedule, and any key customers who are expected to drop by.
- Assign booth work schedule, and daily staff meeting schedule.
- Give out competitive sleuthing assignments.
- Practice product demos.
- Review collateral literature and give instructions on how to use it.
- Go to dinner together and relax.

Particularly effective in a pre-show staff meeting is an appearance by a senior company executive, who can raise enthusiasm and impress upon the staff the importance of the trade show in the company's sales and marketing plans. Matt Hill, of The Hill Group, suggests that you prep the senior executive with a calculation that illustrates the investment that the trade show incurs. Take the entire trade show budget, including salaries and travel expense, and divide it by the number of staff people and again by the number of exhibit hall hours. The result will be an eye-catching amount representing the cost per person-hour the company is investing in the booth. This number helps focus everyone's attention on the importance working the booth and generating the conversations that will result in substantial sales. This number also, notes Hill, can impress upon the senior sales reps the value of their people's arriving on time for booth duty.

Great Boothmanship

While working a booth can be exhausting, it can also be exhilarating. Making new contacts, representing your company's products and services, being part of a vibrant show floor—these aspects tend to appeal to the natural extrovert.

But whatever is the essential personality of your booth staff, it's important that they follow the time-honored rules that have emerged from years of trade show selling experience. Great booth workers may be born, but they can also be made. This section reviews the essentials of great boothmanship.

BOOTH BEHAVIOR: DO'S AND DON'TS

Working a booth is just that: work. It's not a time to relax and enjoy yourself. Your behavior is the number one variable that will make an exhibition successful for your company. Don't blow the opportunity. Over the years, experienced booth workers have identified plenty of behaviors that work, and plenty that don't. Here's a fairly long list of rules that have been proven important.

Do	Don't
Arrive 15 minutes in advance	Eat or drink
Keep the booth neat and clean	Chew gum
	Slouch
Put your badge on your right shoulder	Look bored
	Smoke
Dress comfortably	Sit down
Change your shoes frequently	Wear new shoes
Look expectant and interested	Use your laptop or handheld computer
Eat right	Turn your back
Avoid alcohol, spicy foods, and garlic	Fold your arms in front of your chest
Keep to the booth staffing schedule	Put your hands in your pockets
Greet everyone who comes by the booth	Chat with colleagues
	Tell jokes
Speak clearly (shows are noisy)	Talk on your cell phone
Take notes on your conversations	Hand out literature indiscriminately
Be alert even during quiet periods	Leave the booth

WHY BOOTH SELLING IS DIFFERENT

Engaging with customers and prospects at a trade show booth is a unique experience. The booth worker is expected to be upbeat, energetic, and open to an ongoing series of conversations—many of them probably fruitless—with strangers. The entire process is exhausting.

Booth selling is also a different process from typical face-to-face selling. Some of the key differences are:

- It's a noisy and distracting environment for both buyer and seller. Attention spans are short, and competition for the visitor's time is high.
- In direct contradiction to traditional sales strategy, the booth worker's objective is to spend as *little* time as possible with a prospect.
- The prospect is on your turf—the booth.
- The visitors arrive at the booth at random, and there is no chance to prepare specifically for them.
- Everyone is a potential buyer. You don't want to make assumptions. Instead, you want to engage with everyone who comes by, and qualify them.
- Rarely are you offered the opportunity to close the sale.

Identify Problems and Make Changes Mid-Course

Keep an eye on how things are going, and proactively make changed during the show, advises Doug MacLean of MacLean Marketing. Here are some areas to observe carefully:

- Booth layout. Stand back and watch how traffic is flowing. Adjust your signage, product displays and furniture accordingly.
- Lead capture. Review lead forms as they are filled out, and make changes at a local copy shop if needed.
- Staff motivation. Get regular feedback and assess their energy and skill levels. Don't wait until the end of the show to learn about problems—or opportunities.

In short, booth selling is a series of opening conversations, the kick off to many—one hopes—profitable business relationships. To avoid frustration, make sure your classically trained sales people are made aware of the differences.

HOW TO ENGAGE AND DISENGAGE

As booth-based selling is a series of opening conversations, the secret to success is in fine-tuning the conversational process and making each minute with each prospect as productive as possible. The process can be broken into the following components, each with its own technique and appropriate time allotted.

1. Engage.
2. Qualify.
3. Discuss or demonstrate.
4. Capture information.
5. Disengage.

If the prospect is unqualified, then you will move directly from Step Two to Step Five, by-passing Steps Three and Four altogether, as in Exhibit 5.1. Similarly, you may decide to eliminate the deeper discussion with some qualified prospects, and schedule a demonstration for a later date. The entire process should be completed in five to six minutes, or two minutes if the prospect is unqualified.

Exhibit 5.1: How to Engage and Disengage

Engage ⇨ Qualify
- If unqualified, disengage
- If qualified, discuss or demonstrate ⇨ capture ⇨ disengage

THE FIVE-STEP ENGAGEMENT PROCESS

Step One: Engage. At engagement, you want to stand open and tall, looking alert and interested. Stand at the edge of the aisle, and make eye contact with passers-by. Greet them by name, reading from their badges. Pay attention to who is walking up and down the aisles. Scan the badges to eliminate unqualified prospects by color, where available.

Some opening gambits are better than others. Avoid yes-no questions, like "Are you familiar with our company?" Instead, try open-ended questions like "What do you know about our company?"

Some great conversational openers are:

- What are you looking for at the show today?
- Tell me about your business.
- What are your needs regarding [product category]?
- How are you enjoying the show?
- What products or services are you looking for?

Also have handy your elevator speech. This is the 30-second summary of your business, one that you might be able to deliver in an elevator, in response to the inevitable question, "What do you do?" The speech must be short enough to be delivered before the inquirer gets off the elevator, but compelling enough to stimulate the next step in the engagement. A superb elevator speech contains the following:

- A description of your product or service.
- How it is different from (better than) the next guy's.
- Some evidence of its credibility.
- The target audience for your product or service.
- The key benefit of the product or service to the target audience (or the listener, more specifically).
- A call to action or indication of opportunity to continue the conversation.

And all that in 30 seconds. It can be done. The secret is preparation, in advance. One way to prepare the speech is by inviting all

Elevator Speech Examples

Rich Simms of DialAmerica Marketing keeps his elevator speech handy at all times: *I work for DialAmerica Marketing. We're the nation's largest privately owned telemarketing agency. We do inbound and outbound telemarketing programs for companies like AOL Time Warner, Citibank, AT&T, Microsoft, and Sears. Altogether, we have over 400 clients and generate about 150,000 orders a week. If you've ever bought or renewed a magazine subscription over the phone, we probably made the call.*

Carol Myers of Unica Corporation has a prepared elevator speech, but alters it in response to signals from the recipient. "Based on whether the person in front of me is nodding his head or looking bewildered, I will provide more or less detail," she says. *Unica Corporation provides Enterprise Marketing Management solutions used to acquire and build customer relationships for maximum loyalty and value. Our EMM Suite, Affinium—which includes modules for customer analysis and predictive modeling, cross channel campaign management, emarketing, real-time recommendation, planning and collaboration, lead management, and marketing resource management—is the most complete marketing solution available. Over 300 customers around the globe rely on Affinium to achieve "right-time" marketing and drive higher ROI and marketing success.*

customer-facing employees into the process of elevator speech development. Ask your CEO and sales management, but also ask your inside and outside sales teams, your customer service teams, and your receptionists. That way, you'll find some useful turns of phrase and concise elements that can refine and improve the speech.

Everyone in the booth should be drilled on the speech and able to deliver it smoothly and energetically, on call. The speech may need to be modified to fit the target audience at the event.

Other tips for successful engagement:

- Assess the visitors and adjust the flow by their level of involvement. For an active visitor, who walks up and initiates the discussion, answer the question, and move to qualify. For a more passive visitor, you'll need to establish rapport with some small talk before moving to qualify.
- Keep control of the conversation. Very quickly, you'll want to move to the qualifying stage, so try turning a question around as follows: "Great question, but let me ask *you* a question." Or, "Before I answer that, let me ask you. . . . "
- Don't forget to introduce yourself, too.
- While you must focus on the prospect at hand, don't take that to mean that you ignore others. When engaged with one visitor, if you see another visitor enter the booth, acknowledge that person's arrival with a wave, a smile, and a quick comment ("I'll be right with you!").
- Avoid private conversations in the booth. Everyone there is on duty, comissioned with engaging the people who walk by.
- Treat the booth like your own home. Don't let anyone walk through anonymously. Go up and say hello.

> **Where's the Leverage?**
>
> Your ability to engage visitors at the booth is the constrained resource that offers opportunity for leverage in trade show marketing. Consider this: Say the exhibit hall is operational for 24 hours, and you have five staffers each of whom can interact with five visitors an hour, for a total of twenty-five visitors an hour. This promises a maximum potential contact base of 600. But what if there are 5,000 visitors at the show, all of them potential customers? You are missing 88% of your opportunity. There are several things you can do:
>
> 1. Add more capacity to your booth presence. Larger booth, more staff.
> 2. Train your staff to improve their productivity. If each staff member can talk to one more visitor an hour, in this example, you can increase your contact rate by 20%.

Step Two: Qualify. This is the critical stage of the conversation. Your objective is to discover, as crass as this may sound, whether this prospect is worth your time. The exhibit floor hours are limited, you have a finite number of staff people at the booth, and there are—one hopes—plenty of qualified prospective buyers in the aisles. Your job is to identify them.

Consider these numbers: if the show comprises 18 hours of exhibit hall time, and you spend five minutes with two unqualified people in an hour, that adds up to three hours of wasted prospecting time over the 18 hours, reducing your productivity by 16%. So, it is important that everyone in the booth keep focused on qualifying prospects, and reducing the time spent on people who will never buy.

The qualification criteria you use will vary by your business, and your trade show objectives. Are you looking for senior financial officers at large corporations? Is your best prospect a database administrator who is looking to upgrade his software in the next quarter? Perhaps you want to talk to anyone with an interest in your product. Whatever your criteria, they need to be clearly identified in advance, and everyone at the booth must be aware of them.

Most businesses will develop their criteria around the following categories:

- Product interest.
- Industry.
- Company size.
- Job function.

Ideally, you may want to qualify even further, using the kinds of criteria typical in sales lead qualification:

- Budget. Is the purchase budgeted, and what size of budget does the prospect have available?
- Authority. Does the prospect have the authority to make the purchase decision?
- Need. How important is the product or solution to the company?
- Timeframe. What is their readiness to buy? When is the purchase likely to be?

- Potential sales volume. How much of, or how often, might they need the product?
- Account characteristics. Company size, whether number of employees or revenue volume. Industry. Parent company.

Here are some sample questions that might be used to get at these qualifications, in a polite way:

- What company are you with? What do you do there?
- What are your business objectives?
- What products or services do you use today?
- What challenges do you find?
- When do you plan on making a decision?
- Is there a budget available to solve this problem?
- What alternative solutions are you considering?

For more details on at-show qualification strategies, please see Chapter Eight.

The critical issue your booth staff must keep in mind is: don't waste time. You are not at the trade show to chat and make friends. You are there to meet your trade show goals.

At the same time, a certain amount of subtlety is welcome. If the answers to your qualifying questions suggest the person at hand is not worth pursuing, then disengage politely. Your objective is to use your time efficiently, but not to the point of rudeness.

If the prospect is with the press, you may want to hand the person off to a trained media relations person in the booth. If not, all booth personnel should be trained in what to say—and not say—to press representatives.

Step Three: Discuss or Demonstrate. If the prospect is qualified, the next step involves a brief discussion. At this stage, the objective is to convey information about your products, find out more about the prospects' needs, and generally move the relationship along.

> **Keep a Lookout for Buying Teams**
>
> Buying decisions for complex products and solutions are usually the province of buying teams, a cross-functional group of employees from such areas as finance, engineering, purchasing, and IT. Ask visitors if they are part of a buying team for their company. If so, offer to set up a private demo for all the team members at the show, or back at the office later. Put your most experienced salespeople on the case, and bring your most senior management representatives into the discussions.

If this stage involves a product demonstration, here are a few guidelines that will help:

- Don't present too early in the process. You'll waste your time and annoy your prospect.
- Practice your demonstration in advance. Make sure everyone in the booth is comfortable with the technology and the patter. Test the technology to reduce snafus.
- Focus on product benefits as you illustrate the features. Remember, this is about *them*, not you.
- Keep it simple, and keep it short. No more than two to four minutes.
- Include plenty of repetition, to reinforce your key points.
- If the prospect shows serious interest in deeper product information, suggest moving to an alternate location for the ongoing discussion. This will keep the booth free to welcome new prospects, and allow the conversation to continue in an environment more conducive to sales.

Step Four: Capture Information. Once the prospect has been qualified, it is time for the most important stage, when contact information is captured. This information is essential to the possibility of continuing the relationship in a proactive manner.

The information captured typically includes the following:

- Contact information (name, title, company, address, phone, fax, email).
- Preferred contact channel (phone, email, visit).
- Next steps, such as sending collateral material or calling to set up an appointment.

In some cases, you may want to capture contact information immediately upon qualification, postponing the discussion or demo stage for a later appointment. There are numerous options for information capture. For a further discussion of information capture strategies, please see Chapter Eight.

Step Five: Disengage. With the information safely captured and follow-up steps decided, it is time to disengage. Remember, time at the booth costs you money, and it is important to keep things moving.

In order to disengage politely, a combination of body signals and spoken phrases is most effective. Look the prospect in the eye, and shake hands. Use such closing comments as "Thank you for stopping by. Enjoy the show." Collateral material is also helpful at this stage: "Why not take this with you." You may at this time decide to "cross-sell" the prospect by referring him or her to another area of the booth, by making an introduction to another booth staff member.

The tactics described here will also be effective when you are trying to disengage early on with unqualified visitors, such as students or competitors.

Receiving International Visitors

Visitors to your booth who come from outside the United States and Canada should be treated with special care. For one thing, they are more likely than the average local attendee to be a senior decision-maker. They are also just as likely to be engaged in competitive intelligence gathering. In dealing with international visitors, keep in mind the following:

- Treat their business cards with respect. Use two hands to receive the card, and examine it politely.
- Avoid using American colloquialisms and jokes, which may be misunderstood or found offensive.

DAILY STAFF MEETING

A daily staff meeting is critical to your success. Schedule it either for the end of the day or at breakfast the following day. Keep it short. Follow a clear agenda, and stay focused.

The daily meeting will allow you to identify problems and opportunities, and make any interim course corrections needed. Ask your booth staff to bring up issues so they can be addressed.

The daily meeting agenda might cover the following topics:

- Review daily sales and/or lead production.
- Compare experiences.
- Review key customers who came by the booth.
- Revise work schedules as needed.
- Surface and resolve any problems.
- Review staff feedback survey results.
- Award a "sales person of the day" prize.

Booth-Based Sales

For some companies, the key objective for working a trade show is to transact business, actually closing sales on the show floor. This strategy makes sense for business situations with any of the following characteristics:

- The target audience is so perfectly matched that you are likely to find substantial numbers of buyers ready and authorized to commit on the spot.
- Your product is simple enough to explain or demonstrate that the buyer can quickly gain all the information needed to make a decision.
- The price is within the range of the budgetary authority of many attendees.

Most business shows forbid cash or credit card transactions on the show floor, because of tax and liability issues. According to Carol Fojtik of Hall-Erickson, any show organizer allowing direct sales at the trade show becomes responsible for state sales tax and for product liability problems. "We show organizers have no control over individual exhibitors' sales—how much they sold, how much tax was collected. The state tax people would be on the floor monitoring sales, and we, the organizer, would be liable. Or we'd be held to blame if an exhibitor were selling a product banned in that state, like perhaps a medicine from abroad. We simply can't take on that responsibility."

Marilyn Harrington of Affinity Expo Group points out that some trade shows rec-

---

How to Manage Angry Visitors

It is inevitable that, at some point, your booth will receive a visit from a disgruntled person, probably a customer. Be prepared. Designate one booth staffer to be the ombudsman at each show, and train that person in advance. Here are some steps that can defuse the situation:

1. Listen patiently. Move the discussion to another location, like the show cafeteria or lobby.
2. Do not get angry back.
3. Express a desire to work it out. Empathize.
4. Ask for a suggested solution from the angry visitor.
5. Promise to follow up, and do so.

Doug MacLean of MacLean Marketing recommends an additional, proactive step: Prepare a unique form with an eye catching title, something like SPECIAL CUSTOMER ATTENTION FORM, in large type across the top. Leave space in the middle of the form for the staff person to record the details of the complaint. The bottom of the form should be perforated, allowing the staffer to write his or her name and contact information. Then, the staffer tears off the bottom, hands it to the unhappy customer, and says something like, "If you don't hear from us within ten days, please call me."

ognize the need for "cash and carry" transactions, and will make it possible, usually by setting up a special area of the show floor that can be monitored efficiently. "In the apparel industry, several shows will have one area for order writing and another for cash and carry. But if the show does not allow transactions, exhibitors must comply. Trade show management needs to maintain the integrity of the show and not turn it into a flea market."

Fortunately, for most business-to-business transactions, the deal is closed with a handshake, a signature on a contract, or a purchase order. So issues of tax liability do not come up. If your product or service is suited to closing transactions on the trade show floor, then take advantage.

The key thing to keep in mind is that booth-based selling is different from the "selling" typically required at trade shows, which is essentially lead generation. If you are seeking to close business on the trade show floor, then revert back to the same sales process you use in the field, with a few variations.

According to Jacques Werth, author of *High Probability Selling*, and a leading sales consultant, the secret of booth-based selling is prospect elimination. Unlike lead generation strategies, which focus on qualification, Werth recommends a strategy of *disqualification*.

This strategy recognizes that the most important resource on the trade show floor is your time. You want to sift through all the available prospects, looking for the ones that are most likely to convert to a sale. So, Werth lays out a series of steps to follow:

1. Greet everyone.
2. State what you have to offer.
3. Ask if that is something the prospect wants or needs.
4. If you get a no, then capture the name for follow-up marketing. Move on to the next prospect.
5. If you get a yes, then ask why. This move identifies the prospect's requirements.
6. Then ask when. If the answer is later, then capture the name for follow-up sales.

7. If the answer is now, then move to a sales discussion, preferably in a different, quieter, location.

Werth points out that most visitors to a trade show are out looking, not necessarily buying. The exhibitor, on the other hand, is not there to make friends, but to sell. So the secret to success is eliminating the non-buyers as quickly as possible and engaging with the high-potential buyers. "It's like phone prospecting," says Werth. "We can't waste time with tire kickers. Only one of 30 will be the right targets."

Working with a company that sold capital equipment to the electronics industry, Werth would say to a booth visitor, "We have an automatic component placement system for surface-mounted circuits. Is that something you want?" After countless such conversations, he came upon a vice president of manufacturing engineering for Digital Equipment who was setting up three new plants and needed about a dozen such systems. The encounter turned into a $6 million sale.

STAFF THE BOOTH WITH CLOSERS

In contrast to the staff profile for lead-generation activity in the booth, your booth should be staffed with sales people who know how to close. In many cases, these will be experienced sales reps from field or phone-based teams.

In the early 1990s, at the height of the personal computer boom, Paul O'Brien was Vice President of Sales and Marketing for Computer Select, a division of Ziff-Davis that sold computer industry information delivered monthly on CD-ROM for a $1,000 annual subscription price. Recognizing that the attendees at shows like Comdex and Network + Interop were hungry for this information and that most were empowered to make a $1,000 purchase decision, O'Brien revised his trade show strategy to focus on direct selling. He redesigned the booth to feature a half dozen demo stations, and populated the booth with inside sales reps who normally managed geographical sales territories.

In rapid order, O'Brien's team was closing 30 or 40 deals a day at the larger shows. O'Brien put in place incentive plans to keep the excitement high. "I'd constantly set measurable checkpoints throughout the day," he says. "The reps who reached the daily goal could look forward to an evening at a Vegas show. Or I'd give cash handouts on the spot, to reward a nice sale. When the reps are standing on concrete all day, and the food is lousy, you have to do something to keep the adrenaline going."

One of O'Brien's biggest lessons was the importance of buzz. "The crowd mentality is critical at trade shows," he observes. "If there's just one person hanging around the booth, no one will buy. The first sale of the day was always the toughest. But if we could create a small mob scene to slow traffic down and bring people into the booth, to look at demos, and build excitement, then we can motivate a feeding frenzy of sales."

Sales compensation can be an issue when territory reps are working a trade show, selling to prospects outside of their territories. The way O'Brien handled that is by setting a 30-day window for trade-show sales to close, before the account is passed back to the territory rep. Sales completed within the window produced a split commission for the rep working the deal and the rep whose territory included the account.

How to Annoy Your Prospects

The frightening thing about trade show marketing is the inherent fragility of customer good will. For all your careful planning and good intentions, a single snafu can destroy years of relationship building in an instant. Some snafus will be out of your control, but with a bit of foresight, you can reduce their frequency.

The following are some recommendations from business people from a variety of industries who attend shows regularly.

- Keep one eye out for prospects. Gloria Kurant, a consultant in the teleservices industry, relates this tale from her experience at an industry show: *There were three people working the booth. I was chatting informally with the senior executive—it was a general conversation, not need-specific. The other two sales people were hanging off to the side, engaged in a conversation among themselves, one with his back to the aisle. I noticed a prospect approaching, but she was ignored by the two reps. I mentioned to the senior executive that we could talk later, motioning to the prospect. But he scowled and said that's the reps' job—not that they were doing it. The prospect wandered off.*

- Your badge is not some hip accessory. Gloria Kurant also wonders why badges these days are allowed to dangle down around the exhibitor's navel: *Why don't badges come with a clip and a pin any more? These badges on long hanging ropes make me bend over to places I don't want to be bending, and then they are usually flipped upside down anyway. Badges need to be place on the upper right shoulder, where they can be easily read when shaking hands or saying hello.*

- Love the one you're with. Carol Myers, Vice President of Marketing at Unica, wants the booth staff's respect during a demo: *I was getting a demo of a product I was very interested in from a booth staffer. Another of the company's staffers kept interrupting to tell the individual who was demonstrating for me to hurry up because he had another prospect to demo to. How rude!*

- Don't force it. Carol Myers also recommends that exhibitors take "no" for an answer: *Once I tell you I am not interested in your product or service, don't continue to accost me or try to get me to enter your sweepstakes. I am not a good prospect, and you will just be wasting your time. You'll enter my name and address and continue to market to me when I have no use for your product.*

- Keep the weight off. Carol Myers cautions that bulky collateral material is ineffective: *Don't bother giving me lots of collateral or thick reports. I never have time to look at those materials while I am at the trade show, and when it's time to pack, they are going to get tossed.*

- Keep it professional. Anne Vargo of CDW Computer Centers, reminds us: *Lose the scantily clad women or men. The sexy stuff might work at the consumer shows, but not with business buyers. And make sure your booth people know their product or can put me in touch with someone who does. And, while I'm at it, I hate it when I trip on an exhibitor's carpet. Make sure the thing is glued down properly.*

- Don't run out of business cards. Rich Simms of DialAmerica Marketing gets annoyed by lack of exhibitor preparation: *Remember to bring enough business cards. And if you do run out, don't ask your prospect for one so you can write your info on the back. This is beyond annoying your prospect—this is insulting.*

- Stick with it. Rich Simms deplores an empty booth: *It's so dumb to leave the booth unattended. Prospects are walking by. What are they supposed to think about your company? Nothing good! Make sure you have a relief worker scheduled, and if that person doesn't show up, don't leave—even if your feet are killing you.*

- Get a new attitude. Rich Simms says that body language is key: *If you look like you are tired, hungry, thirsty, exhausted, and angry at the world, I am going to keep walking. Don't be sitting at the table in your booth with sandwich and coffee. Don't be talking on the phone in a loud voice. I am going to get the message you don't want to be interrupted with anything like a question about your company.*

- Don't lose the gimmicks. Grace Chan, Director of Marketing at RBC in Canada, has a contrarian view on premiums: *As for gimmicks: even though everyone claims they don't work, I notice that they do end up getting me to stop by and spend some time at the booth. A while back I got the cutest stuffed green frog with a little t-shirt on. The company sent me a pre-show teaser mailing with the frog smiling at me, telling me he was at the booth and I could come pick him up. I made a bee-line for it. Of course, the fact that I can't remember the company's name now tells you something.*

- Train your booth staff. Ted Seward, Vice President of Marketing for BCC Software, shares some of his pet peeves: *I expect the booth staff to know the products. So why hire dumb blondes or talking heads? I also have seen sales people playing cards, or eating, and ignoring the passers-by. Why are they at the show? And what about the booth with no exhibitor, just a fish bowl? What's that all about? They should remove their signage before they do something that stupid.*

Event Promotions: Before, During, and After

If there's a constant theme in this book, it's a focus on the areas where you can gain extra leverage for your business event marketing program. Areas where a small shift in resource or attention will drive a substantial increase in results. Promotion is one of those critical leverage points. By applying a modest effort in planning and executing promotional strategies, you can double, triple, even quadruple the results of your trade show investment.

Trade show marketers often get so preoccupied with designing and building their booths, they can forget to concentrate on driving qualified traffic. There are a number of important reasons why an investment in promotion is critical to your success:

- You cannot expect show management to do all your recruiting for you. Despite what they say, show management's real job is to get plenty of attendees to the event. It is still your job to get the *best* prospects to visit your booth. If you wait for them to drop by randomly, you'll miss major business opportunity.
- Business buyers generally plan their trade show time in advance. The Center for Exhibition Industry Research (CEIR) found that 76% of attendees use pre-show information for this purpose.

You are competing with conference sessions, and with other exhibitors, and with outside attractions (especially in destination cities like Las Vegas and San Francisco), so you must get on your prospects' calendars early.

- A fabulous booth is not an end in itself. The end is only reached by attracting qualified traffic. You'll do well to divert some dollars from the booth itself, and increase your investment in promotion.

- Front-end and back-end promotions extend the impact of the event over a longer period of time and deepen the resulting connections with customers and prospects. Don't think of the event's scope as lying within the one to five days of the show. Think of it as beginning with the first communication and ending with a sale—and then continuing on throughout a long-term profitable relationship.

- CEIR commissioned a study by Deloitte & Touche that proves the case. Those exhibitors who conducted a pre-show advertising or email campaign raised by 46% their "attraction efficiency," meaning the quality of the audience they were able to attract to their booths. Similarly, the conversion of booth visitors to qualified leads rose 50% when a pre-show promotion was used.

- Promotions will improve results of your trade show investment, but they also generate the "halo effect" of targeted marketing communications among recipients who do not attend the trade show itself. While this effect is difficult to measure, it is likely to be more productive than general advertising due to its targeted nature.

Business Event Promotion Strategy

A trade show marketing plan must include an integrated strategy for communications to support your objectives. All parts of the strategy should reinforce one another. The whole will be greater than the sum of its parts. And no part—pre-show, at-show, or post-show—should be neglected.

The strategic planning process is actually easier than you might think. Let the optimal promotions emerge naturally from your show objectives. Consider the strategies outlined in Exhibit 6.1. It lists several possible trade show objectives, and the metrics associated with them, picked up from Chapter Three, on planning. It then develops a promotional strategy or two associated with each objective. The promotional strategy is then converted into a set of tactics specific to pre-show promotion that will drive the strategies, and in turn, the metrics. These are only hypothetical plans, and not to suggest that these tactics are necessarily ideal for any given business situation. Furthermore, this table only considers the pre-show promotion. A complete plan will add columns for at-show and post-show promotions as well.

So, in this example, if your objective at the trade show is sales lead generation, and you will declare success based on the number of qualified leads, then you want to select promotional strategies and pre-show tactics that support them. This table suggests some hypothetical pre-show promotional tactics that might emerge. Notice how the promotional tactic is specifically selected to support measurable objectives. The neat thing about this approach is that it narrows the tactical field to the elements that will be most effective in meeting your goals. And it provides useful ammunition against the random tactical ideas that inevitably come up during the marketing process.

TARGET AUDIENCES

You can refine your strategy by considering the types of audiences the trade show will target. Here are some of the audiences you may want to drive to the trade show:

- Current customers.
- Lapsed or inactive customers.
- At-risk customers.

Exhibit 6.1: Sample Business Event Promotion Strategic Planning Grid

Event Objective	Associated Metrics	Promotion Strategy	Pre-Show Promotion Tactic
Generate sales leads	• Number of qualified leads • Cost per qualified lead	• Drive qualified prospects to the booth or the event	• Pre-show mailing to show attendees • Pre-show email to house file of customers and prospects
Recruit channel partners	• Number of partners recruited • Cost per recruited partner • Geographic penetration of recruited partners	• Drive potential channel partners to our booth or event • Create good will among partner candidates	• Set up show appointments with qualified partner candidates • Pre-show mailing to prospective partners • Cocktail event for partner candidates with speech by CEO • Outbound telemarketing to set up appointments with channel recruitment executives
Retain current customers	• Number of customer appointments • Number of new product demos to current customers • Revenue closed from current customers	• Maximize appointments with current customers • Show appreciation for their business	• Outbound contact by account teams to set up appointments at the booth • Golf outing and customer appreciation dinner

- Known prospects, such as inquirers.
- Unknown prospects, from list rental.
- Influencers, like industry consultants and thought leaders.
- Journalists.
- Potential employees.
- Business partners.
- Potential business partners.

You may want to develop tactics specifically targeted to each audience. Your message to lapsed customers, for example, will differ greatly from what you say to current customers.

BUDGETING FOR PROMOTIONS

According to the CEIR, exhibition marketers spend a mere 6% of their entire trade show budgets on promotion. This makes no sense. How have marketers lost sight of the essential principle underlying everything they do? We have learned time and again how deluded is the attitude of "If we build it, they will come."

To counteract this 6% promotional spending average, Jefferson Davis, President of Competitive Edge, an event training company, advises his clients to budget 15% for promotion. "Exhibitors' single biggest frustration when they get to a show is that they don't get enough visitors, or they don't get enough of the right visitors. That says that the current average spending you see reported in the industry is *not working*. So, my conclusion is, if you spend more than average, you'll do better. To find the money, you can manage your costs better in other areas." Davis includes both pre-show and post-show promotions, including lead fulfillment and follow-up in his 15% recommendation.

Bob Burk, Marketing Communications Manager at the chemical additives manufacturer King Industries, points out that the percentage method needs to be viewed with a dose of common sense. When the denominator is the entire show budget, the promotion percent can shift based what you're doing with the rest of the program. If you are planning a large splash at a trade show, but expect to meet a relatively small number of high-value prospects, your promotion budget will be a small percentage of the entire spend.

Judy Baker-Neufeld, president of her own trade show promotions firm, concurs. She recommends that exhibitors build their budgets from the top down, taking the macro view. How many pre-show targets do you want to reach, and what will it cost to make the case to them for visiting your booth? How many leads will you expect to generate, and what does it cost to follow up on them? "Exhibitors tend to build budgets from the bottom up," she observes. "They'll fund the booth and the space, and if there's any money left over they'll allocate it to promotions. But promotions need to be set according to your objectives."

Budgeting for promotions is best done on a zero base, versus a percent of total trade show budget. Select the promotions that will best support your objectives, cost them out, and fund them *first*. If you leave promotional planning for later, it is likely to be squeezed financially. Consider the entire expense incurred in a trade show. As a percentage your promotion investment may be relatively small, but it provides an excellent lift in results.

A number of factors can influence your decision about the necessary level of promotional investment:

- The size of the trade show. In a large trade show, you are competing with a lot of other noise.
- The value of a sale. A multi-million-dollar equipment seller can afford to spend more on identifying qualified prospects than can an office-products dealer with an average order size of $500.
- The percentage of qualified prospects and customers among the attendee population. A higher percentage will support a broader reach for your communications. A lower percentage demands narrower targeting.
- The size of your booth, number of demo stations, and staff availability. There is no point in driving more traffic to your booth than you can handle. Of course, this is a chicken and egg problem. With the capability of driving more quality traffic, you

should consider taking a larger booth space and doing more business at the trade show.

While you don't want to under-budget your promotions, neither should you over-budget. Consider this example: if you are trying to reach the key 100 buyers out of the 1,000 total attendees expected at the show, why spend the money for a pre-mailing to the entire attendee list? Similarly, it makes no sense in this situation to put a 50-cent trinket out on your tabletop for all passers-by. Better to keep a two dollar gift behind the curtain to give to qualified visitors as a thank-you.

Do not succumb to the temptation to keep up with the Joneses in trade show promotions. Your competitors may hold lavish parties open to the entire attendee base. Other exhibitors may hand out the hottest new premium of the season. But who says they are smarter marketers than you? More likely, they are simply less disciplined and have a weaker understanding of how to drive value for their shareholders. So budget against your sales and marketing objectives, and stick to it.

Pre-Show Promotions

The most-cited goal of a pre-show promotion is to drive traffic to your booth. But not just any traffic. You want qualified prospects only. Think of it this way: You are front-loading the sales qualification process.

An effective pre-show strategy employs two prongs:

1. Targeted communications to registered attendees. Extract high-potential visitors from among the trade show attendee population and encourage them to visit your booth or set up an appointment. The secret here is qualification. Not everyone at the trade show is worth your attention—with the one exception of highly targeted, niche trade shows where nearly all attendees are likely prospects. So, a blanket mailing inviting all attendees to stop by usually contains a lot of waste. Instead, begin the qualification process with the first outbound communication. Explain who you are looking for, and why these

buyers should come to your booth. Implicitly, you are discouraging everyone else. The first step: cull the pre-registration list you receive from the show organizer to eliminate non-prospects and competitors.

2. Communications to your house file. Invite your own customers, inquirers, and prospects to the show. These people are already interested in doing business with you. If they are not planning to attend the trade show, your invitation might encourage them to change their minds. At the very least, it will remind them you are exhibiting, and serve as a useful part of an ongoing relationship-building communications stream.

The point here is: If you are investing a considerable sum in exhibiting at a show, you should do everything possible to maximize the value of that investment. If you simply rely on the show organizer to deliver you the best audience, your investment will be sub-optimized. Be sure you merge the show organizer's list with your own, to eliminate duplicates.

MULTI-TOUCH PROMOTIONS

Ideal pre-show promotions use a series of contacts, leveraging multiple media channels. While it's impossible to make recommendations for every possible scenario, here are common pre-show multi-touch contact strategies that have been proven to work.

To drive qualified traffic to the booth, using the trade show attendee list:

1. Outbound postcard to the registered attendee list. Show organizers typically do not offer detailed selections based on such qualifying criteria as job title, industry, or company size. When you cannot target the list as narrowly as you'd like, the best solution is to craft your direct mail copy to attract the qualified and repel the unqualified. An example of such a headline might be: "Attention, purchasing managers! Come find out how you can save time and money in your search for the best widgets." The creative thrust of the message should be around

Exhibit 6.2: Pre-Show Postcard

Stop by our booth and receive a **FREE** Data Management White Paper!

The Mission: Achieve consistent, accurate, reliable data.
The Method: Data Management solutions from DataFlux.
The Hero: Mike Ames, DataFlux user.

DataFlux, a data management services company, has done everything right with this pre-show promotional postcard to pre-registered attendees at the NCDM conference in Long Beach, CA. With a photo of an actual DataFlux customer, they both personalize their product and communicate an implied endorsement. The offer of a free white paper gives recipients a good reason to visit the booth.

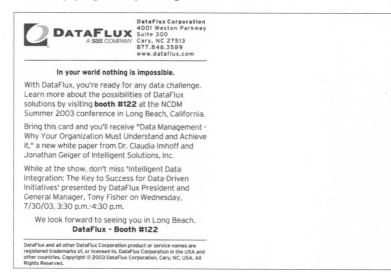

DataFlux Corporation
4001 Weston Parkway
Suite 300
Cary, NC 27513
877.846.3589
www.dataflux.com

In your world nothing is impossible.

With DataFlux, you're ready for any data challenge. Learn more about the possibilities of DataFlux solutions by visiting **booth #122** at the NCDM Summer 2003 conference in Long Beach, California.

Bring this card and you'll receive "Data Management - Why Your Organization Must Understand and Achieve It," a new white paper from Dr. Claudia Imhoff and Jonathan Geiger of Intelligent Solutions, Inc.

While at the show, don't miss 'Intelligent Data Integration: The Key to Success for Data-Driven Initiatives' presented by DataFlux President and General Manager, Tony Fisher on Wednesday, 7/30/03, 3:30 p.m.-4:30 p.m.

We look forward to seeing you in Long Beach.
DataFlux - Booth #122

Within a very small space, DataFlux makes a persuasive case to recipients for visiting them at their booth, and manages to cross sell a conference session being conducted by a DataFlux executive. The right-hand space is used for a mailing label and first-class stamp.

Source: Courtesy, DataFlux Corporation.

why the prospect would benefit from a visit to the booth. The postcard should go via first-class mail, and be scheduled to arrive a week to ten days before the trade show. Note: Plan ahead. There is nothing more wasteful than a pre-show mailing that arrives after the prospect has left town for the event.

2. Follow-up email reminder to the same list. The email should be equally targeted in its message, and include links to a landing page from your company website. The landing page should describe in detail your plans for the event, such as the new products you plan to introduce at the trade show, any parties you will host, and sessions where your executives will be speaking.

To set up appointments with past inquirers:

1. An outbound postcard announcing that your company will be at the trade show, and explaining why this is important to the prospect. Is a useful new product being introduced? Is this a chance to meet with the product designer? You must give some reason why the prospect will benefit from the fact that you are exhibiting.
2. A follow-up phone call seeking to set up an appointment to meet a sales rep at the booth at a specified time. You might include mention of other attractions, like an executive panel session or a party you are hosting. The point is to gain an appointment so that prior inquirers can have a face-to-face meeting and, one hopes, move them further down the buying cycle.
3. A confirming letter or email, or both in succession, to remind the prospect about the appointment, and resell the prospect on the reasons why it is going to be worthwhile. You might include a pass to the show floor, with the sales rep's business card attached.

PRE-SHOW PROMOTIONAL TACTIC CHECKLIST

Business marketers have used all kinds of tactics in pre-show marketing communications. You can use this checklist as a jumping off

Maximizing the Power of Your Pre-Show Campaign

How would you like to double, even triple, the results of your pre-show promotional campaign? It's easier than you think. Try applying the techniques of direct response creative strategy. These techniques have been developed, tested and refined over decades, and they really work.

Direct response creative principles have but one goal in mind: to drive an action. How convenient. That's exactly your objective with a pre-show promotion. You want the prospect to visit your booth, or enter a drawing, or take a demo. Whatever your goal with the promotion, the art and copy must work to support it.

So let's review the key principles of direct response creative strategy. Your communications will show dramatic improvements if you apply these techniques.

GET PERSONAL

Direct response communications strive to create a personal relationship between the marketer and the recipient. So make your copy sound the way a real person talks to another real person: friendly and warm, not clinical and objective. You're not talking to the world; you're talking one on one, to an individual.

The easiest way to do this is to make liberal use of the most powerful word in the English language: "you." Take a look at your opening sentence, and turn the copy around. Instead of starting with something like "Our company is exhibiting . . . ," try "When you come to our booth . . . "

Another way to get personal is to use personalization technology wherever it's available. In direct mail and email, it's a snap. You can address the recipient by name ("Dear Ruth,"), and tailor the message based on what you know about the prospect's preferences and needs. Some media—print advertising, for example—don't allow personalization. In these cases, work extra hard to make the copy warm and engaging.

Direct response copywriters often tell stories, to create an emotional bond with the reader. Your goal is to grab them, and compel them to keep reading.

Here's an idea: once the copy is finished, read it out loud to a colleague. You'll know right away whether it's appealing—or boring.

TALK BENEFITS, INSTEAD OF FEATURES

Engineers concentrate on features, but marketers focus on benefits. Direct response copy is most effective when product features have been converted to benefits that have value to the reader. So avoid talking about the how great your product is. Talk about what it is going to do to help the customer. Put yourself in the place of the prospect, and ask, "What's in it for me?"

Benefits come in many forms. You can focus on business benefits (save time, save money), or personal benefits (be a hero, get a raise).

Here's an example. Instead of saying "Our tech support center is staffed round the clock by highly skilled specialists," try "You'll rest easy, knowing our tech center is available 24 by 7 to help you avoid downtime."

CHOOSE DESIGN ELEMENTS THAT SUPPORT YOUR OFFER

Here's where some art directors get aggravated when they migrate from general advertising to direct response. Direct response design is less about creativity, and more about delivering the message clearly. When the objective is to motivate an action, the benefits must be easy to absorb quickly. The reader has to be able to grasp the reason to act, and not hesitate.

So the first rule of direct response design is this: Don't get in the way.

Here are some design tips that will enhance the clarity of your message:

- Use serif typefaces in body copy. (Serifs are the little hooks that hang off the letters, as in the type style in this column.) Serif-style type is easier to read. But watch out: Sans-serif type is modern looking and is often favored by art directors, so you may have some persuading to do.
- Avoid drop-out type, where the words are light-colored on a dark background. Drop-out type is much harder to read, except in very large font sizes.
- Use underlining to draw the reader's eye to your key benefits or your incentive offer. It's attention getting and facilitates scanning. But don't go overboard or the effect will be lost.
- Apply bursts, call-outs, and other devices to highlight your most important messages.
- Do nothing that harms your brand image. All this attention-grabbing will be effective in driving action, but be sure it is not done in a way that is inconsistent with your brand.

ASK FOR THE ORDER

Don't forget to tell the prospect what you want him or her to do. Say it clearly, and say it often. It's amazing how often we forget this simple maxim, especially as we concentrate on the benefits, and the offer, and the design elements. Go back and make sure the call to action is obvious. Make it big!

If you are using a letter in your promotion, remember that the second most-scanned spot is the P.S. So this is a good place to repeat your call to action. (Are you wondering what the most-read position in a letter is? It's the salutation.)

MAKE IT EASY TO RESPOND

You know what you want the prospect to do. You've given him a good reason to do it. You've clearly asked him to take action. Now remove the obstacles.

If your goal is to drive booth traffic, and you want the prospect to find you easily, then provide a reason—like an incentive offer—to hold on to the mailer and bring it to the booth. And, when the prospect arrives at the booth, make sure you've planned for the visitor's experience to be speedy and satisfying.

Ease of response is not only about convenience; it's also about risk reduction. Think about what might make your prospect hesitate to take the action, and try to fix it. You might try a guarantee, or a testimonial, to remove any concerns the prospect has about your value.

Apply these principles, and you'll drive more attendance at your booth without spending an extra dime.

point. Just be sure you don't get enamored of the fun and creativity of all this, and forget that your objective will be optimally supported by a set of tactics that grab prospects' attention and persuade them of the value of following your suggestions. Your objective is not simply to gain awareness; it's to drive an *action*.

Also keep in mind that you only want qualified visitors to come to your booth. An aggressive offer should only go to very targeted audiences. With lists that are less qualified, use a message and offer designed simultaneously to attract the wheat and to repel the chaff.

☐ Print up stickers with your booth number and the name, date, and city of the trade show. In the months before the event, affix the stickers to all kinds of communications—invoices, letters, packages, whatever you can think of. Provide each sales person with a batch of stickers, too.

☐ As a supplement to, or substitute for, the stickers, create a small flyer about your trade show plans that can be inserted in outgoing letters, collateral, invoices, and packages.

☐ Create an electronic ad or tagline that can be dropped into your regular electronic communications (your website, e-newsletters, solo email).

☐ Add a starburst, similar to the sticker, to trade advertising programs.

☐ Create a mini-site off of your company website that describes your activities at the upcoming trade show. Populate it with your press releases, product announcements, exhibit hall hours, contact information for staff working the show, speaking engagement schedule—whatever will inform or excite your customers and prospects. Mention the URL in all your correspondence before the show.

☐ Send out free passes to the exhibit hall, or discount registration offers to the trade show. This tactic requires cooperation of show management. But since it is in the interest of both parties, arrangements can usually be made.

☐ Send part of a two-part item, inviting recipients to pick up the other part at the booth. Walky-talkies are the classic example of this strategy at work. It is best used with a limited number of valuable targets.

☐ Send a letter plus a map of the exhibit hall, with your booth location highlighted.

☐ Advertise in pre-show issues of your leading industry trade publications.

☐ Produce a show appointment book. Set up appointments with your key customers. Send each book as your confirmation with that appointment hand-written inside.

☐ Do what everyone else does: send a coupon, puzzle piece, or key that can be redeemed for a gift at the booth. But also do what only a few do: narrow your target for this promotion to attendees who are likely to convert to qualified leads—and not every name on the list.

☐ Offer a time-limited incentive, to create a sense of urgency. "The first 30 people to visit our booth will get a special prize!"

☐ Use testimonials from last year's attendees.

☐ To get past gatekeepers at the executive suite, try a dimensional mail package.

☐ When you rent the list of pre-registered attendees, review it carefully to eliminate competitors, students, and other exhibitors, as appropriate. Keep an eye out for obvious duplicates, as well.

☐ Include the show's logo in your pre-show promotions, for an eye-catching brand impression.

☐ Never use less than first-class mail. Don't be among the pre-show mail pieces that attendees will inevitably find in their inboxes on returning from a trade show.

☐ Personalize your communications. Trade shows are a highly personal medium. Get the relationship off to the right start with a letter or phone call that acknowledges the name of the recipient and explains the particular benefits to that person of visiting your booth.

☐ Try these attention-getting formats:

   —An invitation card instead of a letter.

   —An outer envelope from an overnight or 2-day carrier.

   —Dimensional mail, like a box or a cylinder.

   —A telegram.

☐ Develop a series of contacts using all the media options available to you: letter, fax, postcard, telephone, email, personal visit from a sales rep.

☐ For a stronger impact than the mail: have your sales people drop off invitations to customers and prospects by hand.

☐ Stress the benefit. Don't say "Visit us at booth number x." Say *why*. Why should recipients take the time to visit you? Are you offering a show special? Launching a new product? What's in it for them? Give them a good reason to take the action.

☐ Send your targeted list a coupon for a free gift that they can pick up at the booth.

☐ Promote your trade show special offer.

☐ Try mailing to the list of the trade show's prior year attendees.

☐ Send a personal letter from a senior executive at your firm. Include the dates and locations of your trade show activities, and explain why they should come. Use the executive's personal letterhead stationery, and mail it first-class.

☐ About five weeks in advance, have your sales people call their clients to set up appointments at the trade show. Try to make the meetings coincide with the least-trafficked time periods on the trade show floor. Create a master schedule of expected visitors, and make sure you don't overbook in relation to the booth space and demo stations available. If prospects are unwilling to commit to a specific time, ask them to name an afternoon or a morning period when they'll come by. Follow up appointment-setting calls with a confirmation letter, and then an email reminder a few days before the trade show.

☐ Make sure that appropriate staff will be ready and available to meet with the customers and prospects you invite. Match the seniority and technical level of your staff to the customer wherever possible. You don't want the CEO of your prospective new account meeting with a junior marketing assistant.

A PRE-SHOW PROMOTIONS DATABASE STRATEGY

The objective of pre-show promotions is to target the highest quality prospects and invite them to visit the booth, make an appointment or otherwise establish contact with you at the trade show. Your data sources for pre-show promotions include:

- The pre-registration list provided by show management.
- Your own house files of customers and prospects.
- Other rental lists.

Consider the example of King Industries, a chemical manufacturer. Bob Burke, Marketing Communications Manager for King Industries, uses a three-pronged approach for his pre-show mailings:

1. Pre-registered attendees, the list rented from show management.
2. Customer database, contacts who have purchased from King or requested their technical newsletter.
3. Show database, six years of booth visitors who qualified as prospects for King.

According to *Tradeshow Week*'s September 2003 Executive Outlook Survey, most exhibitors conduct their pre-show communications via the sales team and direct mail channels.

Exhibit 6.3: Pre-Show Communications Media Mix

Communication Channel	Percent of Respondents
Personal contact (sales force)	75%
Direct mail	44%
Advertisements	42%
Internet (self-sought by attendees)	29%
Internet (outgoing to attendees)	21%
Other	14%

Source: *Tradeshow Week's* Executive Outlook Survey, September 2003.

Burk practices a merge/purge process of the house files against the pre-registration list, then adds past visitors located in the city where the trade show is to be held, plus customers within a 300-mile radius of the trade show.

If you want to know the most effective media for reaching prospects pre-show, look no further than Exhibit 6.4.

Exhibit 6.4 How Attendees Learn about Exhibitions

Communication Channel	Percent Identified by Prospects
Direct mail	52%
Attended previous exhibition	31%
Trade publication ad	28%
Word of mouth	24%
Invited by an exhibitor	22%
Member	22%
Internet	18%
Article or editorial	12%
Newspaper	7%

Source: Center for Exhibition Industry Research, 2000 study.

At-Show Promotions

Trade shows are bright, noisy, and very distracting. The simpler your message, the more attractive it will be; too complicated, and visitors will give up and move along. Trade shows are a prime example of the old adage, "less is more." So keep your at-booth promotions simple.

THE BOTTOM LINE ON PREMIUMS

Why have trade shows devolved into a mad rush of tschochke-grabbing? Much money is squandered on handing out "trinkets and trash" to all passers-by, whether or not there is any possibility that they would ever become a prospective buyer. This practice not only soaks up budget, it becomes a crutch. The use of premiums, however strategically sound, should not get in the way of the primary mission of your marketing at the show: active engagement with customers and prospects. Premiums are no substitute for quality face time.

Be disciplined about your use of premiums. Best uses:

- Display the item prominently only at shows where a large percentage of the passers-by are expected to be qualified prospects for you, such as at a niche trade show or a vertical trade show.
- Otherwise, save the premium as a thank-you gift, and bring it out after conducting a meaningful conversation and kicking off a business relationship.

Exhibit 6.5: Premium-for-Survey Form

"Parade of Performance Products" Survey Form

Fill Out Or Staple Business Card

Name:_____
Title:_____
Company:_____
Address:_____

SYSTEMS	Current Business %	Future Business Please Place √ In Appropriate Column		
		Increasing	Decreasing	Same
Conventional Coatings				
High Solids Coatings				
Waterborne Coatings				
Powder Coatings				
UV Coatings				
Other: (Please Specify)				

Describe an additive related problem (or product need) you have been unable to solve (fulfill):

ADDITIVE USE	Currently Use	Future Use Trends Please Place √ In Appropriate Column		
		Increasing	Decreasing	Same
Acid Catalysts				
Catalysts for Urethanes				
Corrosion Inhibitors				
Defoamers				
Dispersants				
Epoxy Curing Agents				
Leveling Agents				
Photoinitiators				
Resin Modifiers				
Rheology Modifiers				
Surface Control Agents				
Thickeners (PUR & Other)				

What is the most significant trend you see in our industry:

King Industries handed out a Mardi Gras bead string as a premium in exchange for market data from visitors who came by their exhibit at the 2002 International Coatings Exposition in New Orleans. Show attendees were primarily PhD chemists who formulate coatings and inks—the perfect target audience for King's chemical additives products.

Source: Bob Burk, CTSM—King Industries, Inc.

- Only give the gift to someone whose contact information you've collected. Make it an incentive to provide complete answers to the qualifying questions.
- Only give the gift to visitors who agree to answer market research questions.

If you do decide to give away a premium, consider the following guidelines:

- The best choice is genuinely useful items, particularly those with some business application.
- Information products tend to be valued beyond their cost, and they also can help move your prospect further along the buying process. Consider books, white papers, executive briefings, case studies, guides (e.g., "Ten Tips"), checklists, and surveys.
- Be sure the item displays your logo and contact information, if only your website and phone number.
- Let the premium not conflict with your company's brand image. The best choice is a premium that reinforces the key messages you are trying to convey at the trade show.

Marlys Arnold, President of ImageSpecialist and author of *Build a Better Trade Show Image* offers a helpful formula for selecting a premium item. Your premium must be:

1. Logical. It fits with your booth theme or your company's marketing message.
2. Memorable. They'll remember the association with you.
3. Practical. Something they will keep and actually use.

PROMOTIONS AT THE BOOTH

Forget the fish bowl. If you need random names for your database, you'll get them much more cheaply through list rental. The purpose of exhibiting at a trade show is to have conversations, to assess the prospects' likelihood to become buyers or influencers, and to kick off a relationship. Don't squander the opportunity by implying that you simply want to gather business cards. Bottom line: keep your fish bowl for fish.

Checklist of good ideas for at-show promotions:

- ☐ Conduct a contest. Just make sure it is designed to support your objectives. Create a winning prize based on another qualifier, such as a free trial or an extended warranty.
- ☐ Ask for referrals. If a visitor turns out to be unqualified, take advantage of the conversation and ask who else might be interested in your products or services. Reward the referring visitor with a small premium. Follow up with these names via phone or email, making reference to the referring party in the communication.
- ☐ Advertise in the at-show media, such as the show daily, the trade show editions of your leading trade publications, and the trade show program.
- ☐ At a large trade show, hire hosts to hand out flyers near the exhibit hall entrance, directing traffic to your booth. Craft the copy to appeal to the highest potential buyers and screen out the unqualified.

Keep in mind that some tactics are ready for the dustbin:

- Beware of using celebrities, magicians, sports figures, comedians, and other attractions. Attractions can over-attract. Unless you truly want to interact with all passers-by, such tactics will waste the time of your sales people. At a niche trade show, when the entire attendee base is suited to your product, then go for it. Just make sure the attraction projects an image that does not conflict with your brand. And promote the special appearance to the press as well as in your pre-show mailings.
- Beware of themes. Hawaii, deep sea fishing, the kitchen, the Fifties, sports—you've seen it all. Themes can certainly be memorable, reinforce the brand image, and attract an audience. But they can also come off as trite, unprofessional, and dumb. Tread carefully.
- Avoid staffing your booth with models. The notorious "booth

bimbo" phenomenon has no place in modern business communications. Your booth workers should be attractive, to be sure,
but also well-informed and professional.

What Not to do at the Booth

Did you know there are trade shows about trade shows?
One of the larger of these is the Exhibitor Show, produced by *Exhibitor* magazine every March in Las Vegas.
The attendees targeted at this trade show are corporate
exhibit managers, and the exhibitors are the vendors who
serve them—the booth designers, the lead capture technology companies, the shippers who transport exhibit
material around the world. One would expect exhibitors
at the Exhibitor Show to know their craft cold. But it ain't
necessarily so.

At the Exhibitor Show of 2003, one hapless exhibitor
hired The Amazing Kreskin, a legendary television "men-
talist," as an attraction. The exhibitor promoted the time
slots for the Kreskin appearance with a photocopied flyer
distributed around the trade show. Kreskin is a charming
and skilled magician, and he is remembered fondly by
generations of TV watchers. He had been well coached
on delivering the vendor's message as part of his magic
show. His session at the booth attracted a large crowd,
and the aisle quickly became impassable.

But here's the rub: as this delightful performer did his
act, the booth workers stood in the crowd enjoying the
show. When the show ended, the crowd dispersed, and the
booth staff simply hung around in the aisles. No attempt
was made to capture the names of the crowd attracted by
The Amazing Kreskin, not to mention qualifying them, or
beginning a business conversation. Kreskin was offering

free autographed photos, and not even then were visitors asked for their contact information.

So why did the exhibitor hire Kreskin? As a good-will gesture? They certainly generated some awareness among the visitors clogging the aisle during Kreskin's act. But consider the business opportunity squandered. This is a very targeted, niche show. All the Kreskin watchers were likely prospects. But the exhibitor failed to take advantage of the key value of trade show marketing: an opportunity to initiate an ongoing business relationship.

PROMOTIONS AROUND THE SHOW

Show organizers spare no effort to create opportunities for exhibitors to advertise throughout the trade show environment. Your exhibitor manual is likely to contain a menu of options for sponsoring events, plastering your logo on chair backs, or advertising in the trade show directory. What should your sponsorship strategy be? Again, let it emerge from your objectives. If your company is trying to build awareness among the bulk of the show attendees, then sponsorships can be a low-cost and effective way to build a positive brand image. If, however, you are only trying to influence a segment of the population, you will incur a lot of waste by paying to reach everyone.

There may be other promotional options around the trade show and the trade show city that are not managed by the show organizer or the convention center. Again, these are best applied to situations where the bulk of the attendee audience represents qualified prospective buyers. Business marketers have made good use of such advertising vehicles as:

- Airport terminal displays.
- Taxis, buses, shuttle buses.
- Taxi drivers. Microsoft is famous at Comdex for offering a $100 bonus to Las Vegas cab drivers who were overheard mentioning Microsoft's new product to their passengers.

Exhibit 6.6: Example of Promotional Opportunities Made Available by the Show Organizer

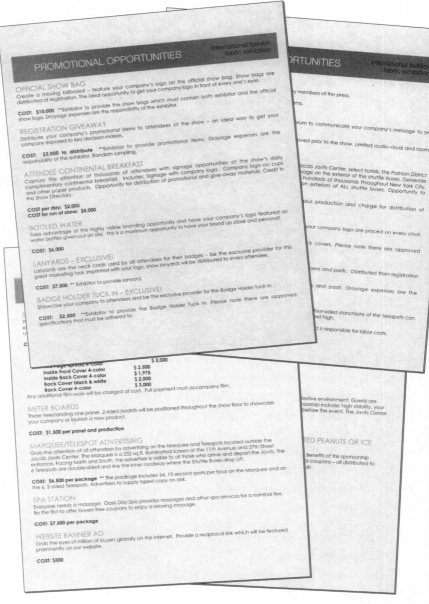

List of promotional opportunities available to exhibitors at a large fashion industry show at the Jacob Javits Center in 2003.

Source: Reproduced with permission of International Fashion Fabric Exposition, Oct. 2003.

- Hotel marquees.
- Hotel drops, under room doors, or on pillows.
- Local television advertising.
- Mobile billboards.
- Local city billboards.
- Portable electronic billboards.

Some tips for getting value from promotions around the show:

- First, find out what show management is offering in terms of paid opportunities. Then, explain your objectives to your account person and ask for suggestions on how to reach your goals. You can rely on show management to come up with plenty of ideas, especially if it means additional dollars invested with them.
- Rent a block of rooms on behalf of top customers. Provide them with limo service from the airport and around the city.
- Hold a golf outing for top customers the day before the show.
- Drop off a gift for top prospects at their hotels. A small box of chocolates, or a pillow might be welcome. Don't forget to have the item display your logo.
- Rent a hospitality suite, and invite your customers and prospects to use it for relaxation and refreshment.
- Use roving attractions, like robots, costumed characters, or celebrities. This strategy only works when the majority of attendees fit your prospect profile. Check with show management for any restrictions before making your arrangements.
- Submit samples of your new products if show management is running a special display area.
- Don't neglect the press room. Journalists are just as susceptible to promotions as anyone else.

For other ideas about activity options around the show, please see Chapter Seven.

Post-Event Follow-Up

An ongoing series of messages after the trade show can extend the value of the trade show investment indefinitely. Your objective is to build on the relationship with contacts made at the trade show. If your objective at the trade show is developing sales leads, please see Chapter Ten for a fuller discussion of lead follow-up strategies. If you have other objectives for the trade show, your post-event program can be simpler, perhaps limited to a thank-you note.

Whatever you decide let your follow-up strategy and tactics emerge from your show objectives. Here follow a number of options companies have found productive for post-show follow-up.

- ☐ A personal email thank-you note from the individual staffer who met with the contact at the business event. If your staff has any energy left, the email can go out the evening of the meeting.
- ☐ A personalized letter with the further information requested at the show.
- ☐ An invitation to subscribe to the corporate e-newsletter.
- ☐ A personal thank-you letter from a senior executive, on his or her own letterhead stationery.
- ☐ A reprint of your press coverage or another article relating to the trade show.
- ☐ Reminder of the final expiration date for the trade show special offer.
- ☐ A series of communications. If you have invested hundreds of dollars in generating the initial connection with a customer or prospect, you certainly want to keep the relationship going.
- ☐ Consider promoting to the attendees who did not make it to your booth. The mailing list will be available from show management.
- ☐ An update to your website thanking visitors to your trade booth and adding a contact form for website visitors who did not attend the trade show.

Arguably the most important point in follow-up communications is this: if a company representative promises some kind of follow-up, that promise must be kept. You must either train and motivate your staff to do the follow-ups themselves, or put in place a process that allows the follow-up to be conducted centrally. A broken promise is worse than no contact at all.

7

Business Event Marketing Beyond the Trade Show Booth

Exhibiting at a trade show can provide many benefits, but it is not the only way to take advantage of the power of events. For one thing, selling goes on everywhere at a trade show. Everyone in attendance is representing a company. Don't think that because you're away from your trade show booth—or not exhibiting at all—that you're not on duty.

Similarly, trade shows are not the only efficient venue for face-to-face contact with customers and prospects. Many companies are actively organizing their own proprietary business events, in order to get even more quality face time, in a less competitive atmosphere.

Optimizing the Trade Show without Exhibiting

There are numerous ways to get value from participating in a trade show that go beyond renting booth space. In fact, in some business situations you may not want to exhibit at all. While this strategy does not necessarily warm the hearts of the show organizers, they are sensitive to the facts, and recognize that they need to find ways to serve a variety of needs.

Whatever activities you decide to pursue, be sure you manage them with the same discipline you apply to your business event marketing program as a whole. Set measurable objectives, target your highest potential audience segments, schedule appointments, follow up quickly—you know the drill by now. Each of these events will have its own ROI. Make sure you know what it is.

The Non-Booth Booth

Who says you have to install a booth at every trade show? Take a nice space at a well-targeted trade show and do something different to attract your audience. Bob Burk of King Industries did just that in May 2002, for an automotive industry show in Detroit, when he took a 20 x 20 space for his Lubricant Additive Division. Instead of a booth, he parked a 1931 Packard in the middle of his carpeted space. He added two counters and two old-fashioned signs that talked about King's "long-standing love affair with the automobile." The result? Burk increased his normal level of qualified leads by 35%, and he found that renting the Packard cost less than installing his regular booth.

Exhibit 7.1: King Industries' Non-Booth Booth

Source: Bob Burk, CTSM—King Industries, Inc.

THE BARE-BONES EXHIBIT

Some companies have found success by eliminating the booth structure, and simply using the rented square footage on the trade show floor for meeting space. A few plants, a simple standing sign, a few

---

"Outboarding" and "Suitcasing": The Show Organizer's Dilemma

The show organizer's mission is to create a market for exhibitors by delivering a qualified audience at a reasonable price. Whenever a market is created, however, the entrepreneurial spirit kicks in, and ancillary markets arise. For example, competitive trade shows will co-locate in the same town during the same time period. Or non-exhibitors will find clever opportunities for meeting attendees outside of the sanctioned trade show events.

The exhibit industry has come up with colorful terms for some of these practices. According to the International Association of Exhibition Management (IAEM), outboarding means "marketing, sales, and hospitality events conducted by exhibitors and others without the sanction and/or knowledge of show management." Suitcasing is when "a non-exhibiting seller engages a visitor in a marketing/selling activity at a place not sanctioned by the rules of the exhibition, such as in the aisles or off the show floor." Both practices threaten the show organizer's revenues and are viewed as unfair and unethical.

As trade shows become more competitive, show organizers recognize that they must exercise a dual strategy: both to fight 'em and to join 'em. Whether by persuasion or contractual language, show organizers often attempt to control, or at least get a piece of, ancillary selling opportunities. They may offer to exhibitors the extended service of managed ancillary events such as hospitality suites, dinners and parties, and transportation from the trade show floor.

In these matters, frankly, the interests of show management and business marketers are diametrically opposed. For a thoughtful discussion of the arguments on both sides of this issue, see the IAEM's white paper, called *Outboarding*, available at http://www.iaem.org.

---

rented chairs, plenty of sales reps—and you have a productive environment for conducting business conversations. You will still need to follow the other rules of successful exhibiting: pre-show promotions, careful qualification of visitors, and post-show follow-up.

HOSPITALITY SUITE

Renting a suite at a nearby hotel can be a convenient way to entertain and conduct meetings at a show. One advantage is that the suite can effectively extend your active business hours at the event. Suites also give you extra control over who gains access to your material, which makes suites particularly suited to sneak previews of a hot new product.

On the other hand, suites are expensive and can be wasteful if not managed properly. Tips for getting the most value include:

- Set specific hours when the suite will be open.
- Promote the suite the same way you would your booth or any other event. Make appointments in advance. Give people a reason to drop by.
- Stock the suite with enough clear, accessible signage to get your point across at a glance.
- Don't confuse an open hospitality suite with private meeting space. If you need both, designate a certain room for meetings and use the living room for welcoming visitors.
- If you are not exhibiting, there may be restrictions on your reservation at an official show hotel. According to Angela L. Eastin, Group Show Director at Primedia Business Exhibitions, show organizers may veto a suite reservation by a non-exhibitor. "We will try offering the non-exhibitors a sponsorship, to at least bring them into the show fold. Of course, we have no say over what takes place at non-show hotels," she notes.

Competitive Reconnaissance

Whether you exhibit or not, trade shows can be a valuable source of competitive intelligence. As your competitors are selling on the floor, their marketing strategies and tactics are on display for your perusal. Here are some of the intelligence-gathering techniques business marketers find effective at shows:

- Keep an ongoing notebook about competitors' presence at trade shows and include a competitive discussion in your trade show post-mortem discussions and reports.
- Visit your competitors' booths, and ask questions about their products, pricing, sales strategies, and target audiences. The booth workers may not be trained to know when to dodge your questions. Some marketers will borrow a friend's badge, to disguise their status when visiting a competitor—but this subterfuge may have its consequences.
- Wrangle invitations to your competitors' parties and hospitality events.
- Take photos of their booths, and pick up their literature.

For techniques in measuring competitive activity, please see Chapter Eleven.

DEMONSTRATION ROOM

Similar to a hospitality suite, in that it involves renting space off the exhibit hall floor, typically in a nearby hotel, the demo room gives you more space and time to show your wares to customers and prospects. Demonstration rooms are particularly well-suited to complex products for which the sales process benefits from hands-on interaction. Follow the same rules as with hospitality suites in terms of cross-promotion, setting specific hours, and clear signage.

ENTERTAINING AT MEALS

Taking clients and prospects out to a meal can give you extra face time and generate abundant good will. Book top restaurants far in advance. At some major trade shows, the best tables during prime dinner hours can be reserved as much as a year ahead. Also get invitations out early, since your clients no doubt have plenty of other options for enjoying themselves.

Breakfast may be the most productive opportunity for a serious business meeting, since no alcohol is involved. You won't have trouble getting a table, the room will be quieter, and the tab is more affordable. Best of all, your prospect is fresh and focused. You can be in and out in under an hour.

As to evening events, a dinner affords much more quality face time than a cocktail party. Consider the experience of Andy Hallock, Vice President of Marketing, and Carlin Stamm, Vice President of Sales, at the food industry supply company Hubert. "We tried having cocktail parties at some of the smaller niche shows, where there's a highly qualified audience. But we found the event was not personal enough. People just roam in, drink, eat, and leave. We couldn't establish enough interaction with them. So now we concentrate on dinners, where we get more time to converse with qualified prospects."

PARTIES

When many clients and prospects are physically converging on a single city, entertaining becomes all the more efficient. Many marketers find that parties are a good way to give sales people and executive management access to customers in a relaxed setting.

Some tips on successful party planning at trade shows:

- It's wise to check with show management before scheduling a party. They will discourage you from planning something that overlaps with regularly scheduled trade show events. You may also get a feel for what your competitors are doing.
- Ask your customers in advance about their preferences.
- Consider unique venues or themes that might help you secure your desired level of attendance in the face of competitive party options. There may be a museum, an aquarium, a lovely mansion, or a celebrity home available.
- Avoid planning parties on boats that leave the dock. This requires an unwelcome commitment on the part of your guests and will likely have an impact on attendance. This problem can be alleviated by arranging for frequent return visits to the dock during the event, to pick up and unload passengers.
- Whatever fascinating theme or venue you engineer, make sure it doesn't get in the way of your business objectives.
- Set clear goals. If your objective is simply to thank your clients for their business, you'll wind up with a very different kind of party from one intended to give sales people plenty of conversation one-on-one with prospects.

FOCUS GROUPS

Industry events are the perfect location for conducting focus groups or round-table discussions with customers, prospects, distributors, or even competitors. Your targets are assembling in a single location, so take advantage. Be sure to arrange the session well in advance, since attendee calendars get quite full. Check with show management about room availability or use a nearby hotel conference room. It's a good idea to offer some kind of incentive, whether a nice meal or a gift. Some of the topics you might use the groups to explore include:

- Insights about your activities at the show, your booth, your promotions, your sponsorships, your staff.
- Product development.
- Customer needs and concerns.

TRADE SHOW EVENT SPONSORSHIP

Instead of hosting your own party or event, consider letting show management do the work. Whether you exhibit or not, you can sponsor ancillary events, such as cocktail parties, golf outings, and refreshment breaks connected with the trade show. With sponsorships, what you lose in control and exclusivity you gain in convenience and low cost. Show organizers will permit non-exhibitors to sponsor business events but will likely charge a premium for the privilege. For more examples of show sponsorship options, please see Chapter Five.

Rock-Bottom Trade Show Tactics: Participating on the VERY Cheap

If you are a start-up, or you've burned through your marketing budget for the year, or you're simply a cheapskate, there are still plenty of ways you can take advantage of a trade show. When you consider that a trade show offers a concentrated opportunity to interact with many potential buyers over a few days, you'll recognize the need to be there, budget or no budget.

- Register as an attendee, and use the trade show as a networking opportunity. You can do plenty of business by wandering around.
- If you're really cheap, buy only an exhibit hall ticket. Make appointments with your current customers and prowl around the hall together.
- Apply for a speaking opportunity on the trade show program, which will get you into the trade show for free.
- Host an off-site breakfast: the cheapest, and possibly most productive, meal of the day. The event will give you concentrated face time and the chance to pitch your wares.
- Crash parties. Ask your friends and colleagues what parties or business events they've heard about. Stop by those booths in advance and wrangle an invitation. As long as you're polite and not a competitor, you'll stand a good chance of making useful new contacts—and conserving your meal budget.
- Treat your attendance as a trade show marketing campaign. Review all the possible target audiences—attendees, exhibitors, and speakers. Set up appointments in advance, qualify prospects as you meet them around the show, nurture leads on your return to the office, track and report on business closed. This campaign has to demonstrate an ROI like any other.

Corporate Events

In recent years, business marketers have gradually shifted portions of their trade show budgets into the arena of corporate events. A number of factors are driving this trend:

- Frustration over the quality and quantity of attendees trade shows are able to deliver.
- Concern that the multi-vendor trade show environment includes too much competitive pressure.
- Desire for more control over the customer or prospect experience.
- The importance of an intimate environment for education, product introductions, and face-to-face conversations as part of the sales process.
- The availability of multiple competing media—the Internet being only the most recent—that dilute the trade show's hold on the ability to convey product information and generate connections with prospects.

According to *Tradeshow Week*'s March 2003 Executive Outlook survey, 57% of respondents said they either hold their own private events with exhibits or participate in their partner's exhibit events.

Trade show organizers are well aware of these trends. Many of them have concluded that they'd rather embrace the enemy than fight, so they are actively looking for ways to get a piece of the corporate event action. Some are teaming up with corporate event marketing companies. Others are encouraging exhibiting companies to co-locate their corporate events with the show. "Our exhibitors often conduct user group meetings," says Angela L. Eastin, of Primedia Business Exhibitions. "My challenge is to figure out how to capitalize on this. I am thinking they could run their seminar or user group the day before my event, and they can extend an invitation to their customers to attend the show. The content match is a good fit."

Corporate events tend to be applied to current customer marketing, versus prospecting, for the simple reason of efficiency. For one thing, it's easier to persuade a person with whom you already have a business relationship to come to your corporate event. For another, the future value of a current customer or inquirer is much higher than that of the average unwashed prospect, which justifies the expense of creating and running a dedicated event.

But corporate events can be cost-effective versus trade shows, depending on how you structure them. Dennis Frahmann, formerly Director of Global Event Marketing at Xerox, expects a continuing, steady shift toward proprietary events. Xerox centrally coordinates around 300 to 400 customer events annually—not including the myriad sales events organized on the local level. Because Xerox's sales management tracking system is used consistently across the corporation, Frahmann can compare costs by category. Events run Xerox about $30 per contact versus $70 per contact at trade shows, he notes.

According to Dan Belmont, President of the Specialist Communications Group at Carat, companies rushed into proprietary events to the point of overkill. "Private events have sprung up all over, but companies need a better understanding of what these events can do and what they can't. Many corporate events were set up for prospecting, and were unsuccessful. It's hard to deliver the right volume of qualified attendees, especially when you're competing with 11,000 trade shows and all the other corporate events out there. But now the pendulum is swinging back, and companies are focusing on events for enhancing their relationships with their current customers."

Trade shows are unlikely to ever go away. But they can be supplemented with other business events that serve different marketing objectives, such as seminars, VIP breakfasts, channel partner conferences, and even smaller, regional trade shows.

The ideal event marketing program contains a mix of both corporate events and trade shows, with the latter focused more heavily on prospecting. As pointed out by Stephen Hacker, President of the IAEM, an exhibition management trade group, even the most avid users of proprietary events, such as Microsoft and Coca-Cola, recognize that they are supplementary. "Industry-sponsored events are still the most important venues for prospecting," he says. "Corporate events are best for retention and penetration."

This section will focus on the major types of corporate events in use today. Keep in mind that events are a very fluid, flexible marketing activity, so there is inevitably overlap. For example, much education takes place at user group meetings. Some partner events feel more like a trade show than a private meeting. Hospitality, sponsorship, exhibits, educational programs, product demonstrations, VIP sessions, entertainment, sports outings—all can be mixed together with customers, prospects and business partners in myriad ways. While this chapter brings some systematization to the mix, it is only a stab at classification, and subject to rearrangement for any sales and marketing purpose (see Exhibit 7.3 at the end of this chapter).

Additionally, there are countless other corporate event options that you may want to consider, among them:

- Company tours, which are particularly suitable if you have a manufacturing process, laboratories, or assembly plants that would appeal to visitors.
- Executive breakfast or luncheon, with a speech by the CEO or an outside expert or thought leader.
- Advisory councils, made up of key customers or business partners, who meet several times a year to air problems and provide insight into customer needs.
- Executive briefing centers, a dedicated space at your site where products are on display and key customers can visit for education and information.
- Mobile marketing, when a tractor-trailer is decked out with demo stations and exhibits, and driven to the parking lots of key customers and prospects—a targeted strategy that is increasingly used by business marketers.
- Very high-end hospitality, such as a trip to the Olympics, for senior executives at top accounts.
- Executive forums organized by third party firms, such as analyst groups or business publications, where attendees are there by invitation only, and corporate sponsors gain special access to them.

General principles of corporate event optimization:

- Consult with your target audience. In order to attract and influence them, you must first find out what works. Let their preferences and needs guide your planning.

- Seek opportunities to defray your costs. You can ask your business partners to take sponsorships, or ask your clients to pay their own travel and hotel expenses. Some conferences even charge attendees a fee, which both qualifies their serious interest and supports the budget.
- Apply each corporate event to its best use in the marketing mix. There are innumerable options available. Make sure each is optimized to your sales and marketing objectives.
- Corporate event management is complicated, and requires expertise and resources from multiple parties, inside and outside the company. So a focus on project management and team-building will enhance your likelihood of success.
- Proprietary corporate events share many characteristics of trade shows, when it comes to marketing strategy, planning, and execution. The same rules apply about setting objectives, promotions, post-event follow-up, and so forth. Treat the corporate event like a full-fledged marketing campaign, not a one-off.

Tradeshow Week's June 2003 Executive Outlook Survey reported on the other business events used by trade show exhibitors. In addition, 21% of respondents said they planned to participate in more non-show events over the next 2 years (see Exhibit 7.2).

Prospecting Events

Most corporate event marketing focuses on maximizing the relationship with current customers. When prospects get together in a room, it can be hard to control the conversation, so some companies limit their corporate events to the already committed. But in some cases it makes sense to conduct corporate proprietary events for prospects. A common example of a prospecting event is the road show.

ROAD SHOWS

Road shows consist of a multi-city series of meetings designed to deliver richer product information than is possible through mail or phone, but to be more efficient than solo sales calls. The road show

Exhibit 7.2: Business Events Used by Trade Show Exhibitors

Business Events	Percentage of Respondents Selecting the Business Event
Sales meetings	67%
Training programs	44%
Conferences	35%
Private corporate events with exhibits	34%
Road shows	31%
Employee recognition programs	26%
Community events	23%
Client appreciation events	22%
Corporate sponsorship programs	21%
Product introduction programs	20%
Press events	19%
Incentive programs	18%
Local corporate events	18%
Chamber of Commerce events	14%
Opening receptions	12%
Concerts	1%
Other events	4%
None of the above	9%

Source: *Tradeshow Week's* Executive Outlook Survey, June 2003.

takes the event to the market—sparing customers and prospects the need to travel. Typically, the marketer bears all the expense, and no fee is charged to attendees.

The road show venue is usually a hotel meeting room, with a half-day session that includes breakfast or lunch. Please note: this meaning of the term road show is not to be confused with mobile marketing, wherein a large tractor-trailer is outfitted and driven from site to site, also sometimes called a "road show."

Because the cost per contact is fairly high, ranging from $25 to $100 or more, road shows are typically reserved for clients or prospects who are fairly far along the buying cycle. However, occasionally they may be appropriate for cold prospecting. Most road shows target a customer based within driving distance from the venue. A road show is essentially a local event.

Like any face-to-face event, road shows must be planned and executed methodically to improve the likelihood of a strong ROI. Tips for road show success include:

- Plan multi-city road shows at the same time, and then arrange for the sales and marketing team to move from city to city in the afternoon of each event.
- Set clear goals and metrics. Some typical metrics might include the number and quality of prospects attending and the cost per contact.
- Make sure that the road show tactic is being put to its best use. Road shows are generally not efficient for cold prospecting. But they can be very effective at later stages in the sales cycle, or for introducing new product lines to current customers.
- Road shows are at their best when used to accelerate the sales process by providing the subject matter expertise and rich product information that will help the customer make a purchase decision.
- Balance your sales message with plenty of educational content. Where possible, bring in an authoritative third party to attract more attendees and increase the credibility of your message. Hand out white papers, case studies, and other valuable takeaways.
- Enhance your sales pitch with real case studies, and research reports that explain how your solution will help attendees do their jobs better.
- If you are doing a demo, make sure it can be moved in and out quickly and that the technology is tested.
- Road shows are as much sales events as they are marketing events. You'll be most successful if you involve the sales force.

Get them to help invite the attendees. Invite them to work the room. Get their buy-in.

- Keep the event to three or four hours, tops. You won't get senior managers to commit much more time than that.

Like many technology companies, Microsoft is an avid user of the road show format, an example being its DevDays 2004 program for independent software developers. For the last 10 years, Microsoft has conducted DevDays in cities around the U.S., now up to 32 per year. The program runs from 8:00 to 5:00 p.m., and features a series of product updates and educational sessions where developers can receive continuing education units to maintain their certification in various Microsoft products.

The Freeman Companies serve as Microsoft's preferred event marketing supplier. According to David Gauthreaux, Freeman's National Director of Corporate Events, the secret to keeping the developers happy is providing not only good education but also plenty of goodies. "To keep the attendees in the building for the day, we lay on enormous catering, freebies, and, at night, brand-name entertainment," Gauthreaux observes.

The developers are recruited through direct mail and email invitations, based on their geography, and each pays around $100 to attend. Depending on the city, a DevDays event attracts around 200 to 800 attendees. Microsoft business partners also participate as event sponsors.

Customer Events

Most corporate events are focused on the current customer, in an effort to penetrate the account more deeply, gain insight into customer needs, and deepen the customer relationship.

The number one strategy for success in customer events is to create experiences that the customers value. This deepens the relationship and keeps them coming back for more. And the best way to create perceived value is by designing the event in response to customer needs. Be proactive about gathering input from customers—

not just at the event, but throughout the year. Ask them about their preferences and their needs—for education, for business support, for entertainment, food and drink—and design the event accordingly.

USER GROUPS

The user group meeting has taken center stage in the information technology arena, but is also in wide use in other industries. Typically the company's objective with a user group is multi-fold:

- Education about the current products in use at the account.
- Surfacing problems and trouble shooting solutions.
- Identifying customer needs for additional products or features.
- Deepening the relationship with the customer.

Most companies find that the opportunity to network with other product users is one of the key benefits appreciated by attendees.

RightNow Technologies, a call center software service company based in Bozeman, Montana, runs a successful user group conference over three days, every summer out in Big Sky. The event attracts hundreds of customers, who enjoy learning from RightNow and other customers about what's working and what's not. Customers share case studies of best practices they have developed with the software. Product management gets together with 20 top customers for a day-long input session to help them set product development priorities.

RightNow's Vice President of Marketing and Business Development, Sean Forbes, points out one unusual aspect of the RightNow user group meeting. "We also invite prospects to our user group conference. They walk around freely and mingle with our customers. The reason we feel so comfortable with this set-up is that our customers are so deeply satisfied with our product. We have more referenceable customers than any of our competitors."

RightNow's overall business event marketing program combines the annual user conference, customer roundtable meetings in various cities throughout the year, and a monthly series of webcasts that attract as many as 700 attendees. Says Forbes, "The customer roundtables and webcasts act like very frequent, mini-versions of our user conference, which we only run once a year in the U.S. and Europe. They also attract more prospects, and as the prospects mature, they are fed into the annual event. We like to let our current customers help us persuade prospects to try our solution."

Forbes is considering adding road shows to the mix as the company grows. But he shies away from trade shows. "Our business solution is too specific in its prospective customer base to work at a trade show. Also, I am concerned about the misalignment between us and the show organizers. Their job is to drive the highest number of visitors. I need more targeting. For us, the ROI is better at a corporate event."

Tips for success with user groups include:

- Maniacally investigate user needs. Everyone in your company will have an opinion about what users want, but it's best to go to the source. Gather input from users via all options available—surveys, advisory board, advice from sales people, and business partners. And include users from various levels in their companies, to get as broad a picture as possible.
- Promote the event inside and out. You will invite users directly, but if everyone around your company knows about the event, they can help pass along the message.
- Keep an ongoing marketing database dedicated to the event. Record promotion history, attendance history, and survey feedback about all qualified users, whether they attended or not.
- Have a process in place for speedy follow up and resolution of the customer complaints that will inevitably arise. If you just talk and don't act, word will get around very fast.
- Provide plenty of quality networking time. Users want to learn from you, but they also learn a lot from each other, and appreciate the chance to commune with their peers.

CLIENT CONFERENCES

User groups target the engineer or middle manager who actually uses the product in day-to-day business, with primarily an educational and troubleshooting objective. A client conference, on the other hand, is designed to engage a more senior managerial level, addresses more strategic issues and is often, in some respects, more sales oriented. The typical client conference pursues the following objectives:

- Deepen the customer relationship.
- Communicate company vision, culture, and strategies.
- Cross-sell and upsell.
- Encourage networking among peers.

A client conference may have any of the following components:

- Keynotes and breakout sessions.
- Exhibit hall.
- Meetings with sales reps and senior executives.
- Sports event, such as a golf outing.
- A client appreciation dinner.
- Entertainment.

Siebel Systems provides a case in point. Siebel runs the well-respected User Week Conference, twice a year, in the U.S. in October and in Europe in April. In the U.S., the event typically attracts 2,000 to 3,000 attendees. The three to four day program follows a standard format, kicking off with a general session keynoted by Tom Siebel, founder and CEO of the company. Siebel, who comes from a sales background, can be relied on to give a dynamic, rousing pep talk to the crowd. Then 180 breakout sessions follow, intended to educate customers on the current and upcoming products in a variety of industry vertical and horizontal categories. The evenings are reserved for entertainment and relaxation.

The conference includes a busy exhibit hall, where Siebel business partners set up booths in an area known as the Partner Pavilion, over 1½ days of the week. Hardware, software, and services partners like Microsoft, IBM, HP, Sun, and Accenture serve as premier sponsors. Partner participation in the pavilion helps defray the expense of the user group conference as a whole.

Siebel's primary objectives for the User Week Conference are:

1. Educate customers on products and applications, concentrating on the latest product theme, such as "On-Demand Computing."
2. Gather information about customer needs and concerns.

According to Susanna Hyatt, Senior Director of Events at Siebel, the conference's success is measured in three ways. First, Siebel conducts a survey of customers and business partners. "I am proud to say that 96% of attendees say they would recommend the conference to a colleague," says Hyatt.

Second, Siebel tracks—using its own CRM product, of course—leads generated at the client conference and reports on the resulting revenue. Leads are gathered using lead retrieval systems at the partner booths, and the Siebel sales reps are also instructed to gather business cards and turn them over to the marketing team for processing. The leads are coded to the conference and tracked to resolution.

The third metric is partner renewal rates. Hyatt notes with satisfaction that the business partners come back to the Partner Pavilion at a healthy 90% rate. "Our main sponsors have been with us consistently since the conference started in 1997, when we only had 100 attendees. It's with our smaller, newer partners, who might take just a 10 × 10 booth, where we experience any turnover," says Hyatt.

Concurrent with User Week, Siebel runs a special program for 30 to 50 senior executives from Fortune 500 clients. This event focuses on networking, and offers a different schedule—although the attendees are welcome to attend the rest of the User Week Conference if they like. The event gives top customers special access to the president and to the product division chief and gives Siebel senior management insights into problems and opportunities at key accounts.

Another excellent use of client conferences is suggested by Alan Cordial, of Calan Communications: the chance to influence an entire buying team from a client company. "At a trade show, where there are lots of distractions, it's hard to get everyone together and have an effective discussion. But at a proprietary event, you can bring in plenty of subject matter experts to engage with the engineers about productivity, the sales people can take the general manager out for golf, and your CFO can chat with their finance people about terms. It's a neat way to allow multiple, but integrated, conversations."

Cordial managed scores of client conferences for ATT in the 1980s, when they would bring as many as 4,000 customers into large venues like the Orlando World Center. ATT developed a standard template for the conference format, beginning with general sessions in the morning where senior corporate officers would communicate the direction of the company. Then, a well-known technology guru would come up and talk about the future—addressing such topics as wireless and global positioning. After the plenary meeting, attendees moved to break-out sessions on specific tracks, with presentations by subject matter experts from within the corporation. Finally, attendees migrated over to the exhibit hall, known as the TechnoZone, where customers could learn more about new products from the technical staff. "The beauty of these conferences," says Cordial, "is that we could get customers immersed in our sales presentations, in our culture, our thinking, and our strategy. We influenced their entire experience."

PARTNER CONFERENCES

Hosting a conference that involves your business partners can be a powerful way to sell. In most business marketing contexts, the term *partner* refers to any independent third parties who help you take your products to market; parties such as distributors, wholesalers, resellers, agents, retailers, OEMs, or value-added resellers. But the term can also mean companies with whom you cooperate in sales and marketing, such as non-competitors who are targeting the same market segments as you are. Occasionally, businesses even form partnerships with their competitors, when there is opportunity for servicing a large piece of business.

Partner conferences can be divided into two types:

1. A meeting where you gather your distribution partners together for purposes of education, strategy, and relationship building.

2. An event where you include your partners in a dedicated meeting for your customers and theirs.

The first type of partner conference has many of the same characteristics as a client conference. In essence the partners are your direct customers, so the same rules apply.

The second type has many of the same characteristics as a trade show, although instead of being the exhibitor, you are the show organizer, responsible for attracting attendees, recruiting exhibitors, putting together an appealing set of sessions and keynotes, organizing recreational and entertainment activities, and handling logistics of food, lodging, and meeting space. It's a big job, so most companies hire professional event management companies to help them.

Tips for success with partner conferences:

- Involve your partners from the get-go. Listen to their objectives and their preferences. If you don't already have one, set up an advisory board of influential partners to help keep you focused.
- Select dates that encourage attendance. Co-location with an existing industry event can help attract higher attendance levels.
- It's possible to break even on conferences where sponsors, exhibitors, and attendees pay a fee. But consider your objectives very carefully. If the goal is to educate customers and enhance partner relationships, then you won't want to go overboard on spreading out the expenses.
- Strategically, everyone involved in the event is your customer—from the partners, to the end-buyers, to the suppliers who will exhibit. So get very clear about your priorities so you can manage the decision-making process smoothly.
- Of all marketing events, partner events are perhaps those of deepest interest to senior management and to sales management. So be sure they are deeply involved from the outset. The goals for the conference should be their goals.
- The main value of the event to the partners is access to a sizable customer base as well as the other partners, who may be their prospective customers as well. So design the event so that everyone has plenty of access to everyone else.

- Some partners may want to be more involved than others, so offer tiered levels of participation, breaking out various sponsorship options to suit.

SINGLE-CUSTOMER EVENTS

Events focusing on a single customer can be a useful element of the corporate event marketing mix. Limited to top customers, these events can be as simple as an expanded client meeting, where the business carries on into ancillary activities like dinners or outings. Or they can be workshops, or facilitated sessions—whatever meets the sales and marketing objective.

One common type of single-customer event is also known as a "vendor day," when a large company arranges for suppliers to come in and show their wares. Essentially, these events behave like multivendor trade shows, but they take place at a single client site. Typically organized by the company's purchasing function, key suppliers are invited to set up a tabletop in a conference room or hallway, and company employees are encouraged to stop by during the day.

Some vendor days are organized by a third-party event manager or marketing agency. A prime example is the T&G Ingredient Tops Plus events, which bring food ingredients, food packaging, and lab instrumentation companies together with very large food manufacturers, like Kraft, Tyson, and Sara Lee. The events take place on site at the manufacturer's facility, and are limited to 15 vendors per event. Vendors must submit applications, which are screened by the event organizer and then approved—or rejected—by the host company. The event is attended by the technical, marketing, and purchasing staff—as many as 100 people—from the R&D division of the food manufacturer. The vendors gather at the company site for about five hours, including a lunch, and use a tabletop exhibit to show their samples, prototypes, and collateral material.

The prime benefit of these single-customer events is focus. Compared to a trade show, where you can meet a few representatives from many companies, these events provide richer access to buyers and influencers in a single—very large—account. The company attendees are highly qualified, and they attend specifically to learn about new products and solutions.

EDUCATIONAL SEMINARS

An educational seminar can be an appealing way to deliver product information within a larger business context—which adds credibility and also increases access to hard-to-reach customers. Most common are daylong or half-day seminar programs taught by a credible third party on a subject of strong business interest to your customers. If you include speakers from your own company, it's important to keep the tone of the presentation more about solving problems or sharing ideas, and less a blatant sales pitch.

One of the secrets to success in seminar marketing is balancing good content with amenities. Consider this wisdom from Mark Amtower, a specialist in marketing to government buyers. Amtower conducts seminars all over the country for clients and prospects as part of his sales outreach. "The seminar content is important," says Amtower. "But the food is how they'll judge the seminar overall. I have learned to provide great food, and plenty of it, and I get rave reviews—and new business—from my seminars."

Structural Graphics, a paper promotions company based in Essex, Connecticut, has made good use of educational seminars as part of its strategic account sales and marketing strategy. The idea is to use seminars for account penetration situations, where the company is looking to get larger jobs, or to cross-promote its services into other areas of the account. Their first seminar foray was with a large tobacco company, where Structural Graphics did quite a bit of magazine insert and direct mail work. Mike Maguire, the company president, felt that there was opportunity to grow the account. "Our primary contact for the magazine and mail work was the ad agencies, and we wanted to figure out ways to develop more direct contact with the client. We also wanted to make the company aware of the other areas where we could help them, especially with our expertise in point-of-purchase promotions."

So, while accompanying his sales rep on a call to the head of the tobacco company's production department, Maguire inquired about her needs and ways his company could add value. The department head said she was looking for new ideas for ways to lower costs and to do things better. Maguire offered to come in and do a seminar for her team on project management, an area where his company excels. He put together the content, and on the appointed day, delivered a 1½ hour seminar to 12 people in the department. The session got rave reviews. "While you usually expect to pick up a couple of ideas at a session like this, the attendees told their boss they had picked up five or six. The department head was very pleased, and we now have several pieces of point-of-purchase business with them," says Maguire.

Maguire believes that the cardinal rule of seminar marketing is credibility. "The fact that I was president helps. If I were too overtly involved in the selling process, they would never have reacted as they did."

The other key to success is relevant content. Maguire recommends that you probe carefully about the client needs, and shape the content very specifically to help them. "This is not about what you want to talk about," he says. "It's what is of real value to them."

EXECUTIVE SEMINARS

Executive seminars are intended to bring senior-level customers together for education, peer interaction, and face time with senior company representatives. Usually kept fairly small, repeated at regular intervals, and held in desirable locations, these events combine customer appreciation with sales opportunity. The primary hook to attract attendees is content, topics of strategic interest to senior managers. The events thus serve to position the hosting company as a partner as opposed to a vendor, a trusted resource who can be relied upon to help solve pressing business problems. Attendees appreciate the chance to learn about solutions and to network with their peers from other companies.

Siebel Systems runs an ongoing series of successful events for VIP customers. In 2004, the event is scheduled to take place once a quarter. The attendees are selected by the sales team about six months in advance. The event brings in 25 to 50 C-level executives, with a two-day program. In most cases, Siebel pays all of the guests' expenses, including their travel.

Like the Siebel User Week Conference, this proprietary event follows a standard format each time. The program is launched with a hospitality event, like a golf or tennis tournament, followed by an elegant dinner. Day two brings an executive session, with most of the content provided by the customers themselves, sharing business cases and experiences. The event is conducted like a United Nations roundtable, with a relaxed exchange of views. Also in attendance are five to seven top Siebel executives, including Tom Siebel himself, who gives a welcome speech.

This VIP event is measured the same way as the User Week Conference, with a post-event survey and leads tracked to closure. "This program provides a huge ROI for Siebel," says Hyatt.

CASE STUDY

The New York Stock Exchange Provides a Big Wow

Symbol Technologies, a manufacturer of wireless handheld computers, wanted to entertain C-level executives from its current customer base who were attending the NRF (National Retail Federation) show at New York's Javits Center in 2000. But this is a jaded group, who receive plenty of fabulous invitations for evening events from such behemoths as IBM and Microsoft. How could Symbol attract them? Assisted by their event marketing agency, Carat, Symbol's Director of Corporate Meetings and Events, Joe Spaccarelli, learned that any company listed on the New York Stock Exchange can use the exchange floor as a venue for events. Bingo.

Working with the sales team, Symbol selected 450 key executives attending the show for the invitation list. The invitation clearly stated that the offer was non-transferable, and the executives were discouraged from bringing along their mid-level IT colleagues. Symbol received 250 positive replies, and arranged for limo service to ferry the guests from the Javits downtown to the NYSE, where cocktails were waiting.

What executive wouldn't want to prowl around the stock exchange floor, chatting with the very trading specialists who make market for their stocks? Combine that with a classical music trio and a lavish spread of lobster and shrimp—the event was the talk of the NRF show. Symbol was pleased with the amount of business closed at the show, and the company's executive briefing center back at headquarters received 65 new visits as a result of the event. Total cost for the NYSE event: $30,000, or $130 per person.

Symbol's success in attracting C-level execs has become a tradition at NRF. In the ensuing years, Spaccarelli continued with the creative New York venue strategy, holding events at the United Nations, the Guggenheim Museum and the Good Morning America studios.

WEBINARS

In-depth sessions conducted via the Internet have emerged in the last several years as a valuable tool in the business marketing toolkit. Instead of running road shows around the country—hiring hotel meeting rooms, ordering doughnuts and coffee—you can instead invite your customers and prospects to log on from their desks and hear about your products. You get global reach, low costs, and enviable time savings.

The technology has by now evolved to be very flexible, with plenty of useful features. You can present slides or draw live on whiteboards. You can invite attendees to vote in real-time surveys. You can take questions from the audience, either publicly or privately. Attendees can correspond with each other using text chat while the speaker is presenting. You can even give an attendee control of the demo, to annotate a document, or move around a website individually, while the others watch.

Business marketers are using webinars for all kinds of purposes:

- Product demonstrations.
- Analyst briefings.
- Sales training.
- Channel partner communications.
- A substitute for, or supplement to, a face-to-face sales call.

Like regular seminars and road shows, the webinar's best use comes relatively late in the selling process, where you already are in contact with prospective buyers, and you want to communicate more detailed product information to move them along the buying cycle. However, some companies are finding them useful earlier in the process, even for cold prospecting.

As useful as a webinar can be, there are still myriad ways to blow it. So have a look at the following guidelines for creating a successful webinar.

- Keep the customer experience top of mind. No one likes to listen to a presenter drone on and on, whether it's live or online. Prevent your presenters from reading their speeches. Try putting a person in the room with the presenter, so the talk can be directed at an individual instead of a computer or a microphone. It will sound much more natural and engrossing to listeners.
- Use concurrent conference calling for the audio. Voice-over IP technology, or voice delivered live online, is getting better, but it's still a risk. There's nothing worse than slides that are out of synch with the presenter's voice.
- Be sure your content is compelling and relevant. Recast your message into benefits for the listener. Talk more about "you" than about "we." Boring offline is simply excruciating online.
- Listen to your audience. As they give their feedback via live chat,

make sure the presenter is responsive to comments like "slow down," or "speak up."

- Add variety. Use multiple presenters, and break their sessions into small bits, to keep a fast pace and maintain listener attention.
- Experiment with the speakers' phone equipment in advance. Headsets are preferred, but make sure the sound is clear and the fit is comfortable. Avoid using speaker phones, where possible. You don't need a more disembodied experience.
- Stay away from audio or video streaming. The technology is still too fickle.
- Build in a lot of interactivity, to keep listeners interested. Use the polling questions. Encourage listeners to type their ideas into a text chat box. Give prizes for the best answers.
- Record the event for later viewing. This will broaden your audience size and cut your cost per contact.
- Follow the rules of direct marketing to drive attendance. Offer an incentive, like a white paper or a book. Follow up with confirmation emails before the session, and a thank-you note at the end.
- Conduct a poll at the end of the webinar to further qualify attendees. Ask them their reactions to the product discussed. Ask them questions about their intent to buy, their authority to buy, and their likely time frame. And don't forget to ask them if they'd like to see a sales rep.

ENTERTAINMENT EVENTS

Events designed around social outings, or around food and drink, are most successful when linked to a specific sales objective. The attendees need to be carefully selected and qualified, since you don't want to be investing in entertaining the universe. Most companies find that entertainment events only work when they are driven by the sales team, and marketing assists in logistics and strategy. Some tips for successful entertainment events include:

- Co-locate them with other events where your customers and inquirers are already assembled, such as industry shows.
- Get creative on the venue and the activity. Entertainment events

can be built around bowling and billiards, on cruise ships and yachts, or around such worthy activities as a fun run for charity. Go crazy.

- But don't go completely crazy. In some industries, entertainment must be approached very carefully. Consider pharmaceuticals and medical devices industries, where recent guidelines practically ban all entertainment of customers and prospects.

Problems in Corporate Event Marketing

Compared with trade shows, corporate events sound like a dream. You can control the message, there's no competition, and you set the agenda and impress your customers to buy more and more often. But like any marketing opportunity, events can be problematic. Here are some pitfalls to watch out for:

- Can you attract the audience? As events have gained in popularity, the competition for customer and prospect time and attention has intensified. Much of the event cost structure is fixed, so if attendance falls, the cost advantages can disappear.
- Beware the dissatisfied customer. If customer gripes get out of control, the atmosphere at your event may be ruined. You need a plan for speedy, discreet resolution of complaints before they escalate.
- Customers may compare terms and conditions, another source of potential dissatisfaction. One way to counteract this is by assigning handlers, dedicated reps who will shepherd particular clients throughout the event.
- Comply carefully with industry regulations. The pharmaceutical industry, for example, has recently come under fire for questionable marketing practices, and new regulations place constraints on almost any kind of customer event.

Exhibit 7.3: Best Event Applications by Event Type

Event Type	Best Audience	Best Application	Comments
Road shows	Users, specifiers, prospects	Demo new products Deliver rich product information Create preference	Not to be confused with mobile marketing
User groups	Users, specifiers, current customers	Introduce new product information Solve problems Identify customer needs Install/use	Charging a fee helps qualify attendees and defray costs
Partner conferences	Qualified prospects (inquirers) Users, specifiers, influencers, decision-makers Current customer and prospects	Suited to various buying process stages Deliver product information/ demo Create preference Repurchase Multi-product cross-purchase	Can be structured to break even or make money
Single-customer events	All involved in the buying process Individual purchasing agents	New product information Repurchase/cross-purchase Identify customer needs	Often held at the customer's location
Educational seminars/ workshops	Prospects or customers All involved in the buying process	Consideration Preference Repurchase/ cross-purchase	Stress the educational benefit, and de-emphasize the sales pitch
Executive briefings	C-level, senior management Customers Decision-makers (possibly prospects)	Repurchase/cross-purchase Relationship building	Strongest benefit: networking with peers

Exhibit 7.3: *continued*

Webinars	Users, specifiers Purchase agents	Product information Problem resolution Install/use Repurchase/ cross-purchase	Break up the presentation with plenty of involvement devices
Entertainment events	C-level, segment decision-makers, users, specifiers, influencers	Preference Relationship building	Clearly articulated goals are essential
Trade shows	Prospects, customers Specifiers, users, influencers	Competitive positioning, sales lead generation, customer relationship management Press relations	Must be viewed as a strategic element of the go-to-market process

8

Lead Generation and Qualification

Since leads represent one of the most quantifiable success measures, and one of the most likely objectives on a business marketer's business event marketing list, this chapter focuses on lead capture and qualification at the business event. If lead generation is not one of your show objectives, feel free to skip over this chapter. If it is, be sure you consult not only this chapter, but also Chapter Nine, which discusses lead management and nurturing after the show, as well as Chapter Eleven, where lead tracking and metrics are covered.

The Semantic Problem: What is a "Lead," Anyway?

One of the most annoying practices in business marketing is the misuse of the term "lead." A lead, short for a "sales lead," can be defined as the name, contact information, and background information on a prospective buyer—preferably someone who has expressed some interest in your product or service, or your company. A qualified lead can be defined as a prospect who possesses the necessary attributes—by predetermined criteria—to become a customer.

Unfortunately, throughout the business marketing world, and especially at trade shows, the term "lead" is generally applied to contacts of all sorts, including:

- People who have simply passed by a booth and were tempted by an exciting prize drawing to drop a card in a fish bowl.
- Trade show attendees whose names appear on the pre-show mailing list.
- Compiled lists of contacts at various companies sourced through phone books or directories.

A better term for names of this sort is "suspects" or, if the prospect has actually expressed some interest in the company, "contacts" or "inquiries." Not that contacts have no value. In fact, they can eventually be converted into valuable leads through a series of ongoing communications. But calling contacts leads demeans the value of a true lead, and at the same time artificially elevates the presumed value of a mere contact.

In truth, a lead—especially a qualified lead—represents enormous value to a company. Consider this example. If your average order size is $12,000, and your lead-to-sales conversion rate is 30%, then each lead in theory represents a $3,600 value to the firm ($12,000 × .3). Approaching it from the other direction, nearly 1 in 3 leads will turn into a $12,000 sale to the company. So, each lead needs to be treated like gold. This is a key source of company growth and profitability over time.

Another way to appreciate the value of a lead is to calculate the cost it represents. If you spend $15,000 exhibiting at a trade show, and generate 300 qualified leads, your cost per lead is $50 ($15,000/300), assuming no post-show qualification expense is required. If your qualified leads behave as in the previous paragraph, meaning a 30% lead-to-sales conversion rate, then the lead-related cost of a closed sale will be $166 ($50/.3). On a $12,000 sale, this represents a very respectable 1.4% expense-to-revenue ratio. If a qualified lead is mishandled, that represents a cash loss of $50 and an opportunity cost of $3,600, in this example.

A contact, on the other hand, represents a lesser value. Additional effort must be invested to convert the contact into a qualified lead. If a contact is treated like a lead, and handed over to sales, then two things will happen. The sales force will waste its valuable time. And worse, the sales people will quickly determine that the "leads" they get from marketing are worthless, and they will not be inclined to work them.

So responsible business marketers will call a lead a lead and a contact a contact. They will develop a program designed to convert a contact to a lead. They will treat leads with respect. And they will endeavor at their events to generate the largest possible number of quality leads for hand-off to sales.

Contact Capture at the Show

Given the importance of lead generation at trade shows, it's remarkable how little attention is given to the capture of contact information from visitors. In fact, you might argue that data capture is the single most important activity at a trade show. Without it, there can be no follow-up, and the potential for relationship building—not to mention revenue—would rely entirely on the visitor's later taking the initiative or on the memory of the booth staff. Not likely.

The characteristics of an optimal contact capture system are as follows:

- Convenience. Any system that gets in the way of a conversation will reduce quantity and quality of the contact.
- Clarity. Your form or screen needs to be easy to read and easy to fill out. In paper-based systems, this means liberal use of check boxes, wide line spacing for filling in addresses, and plenty of room for comments. With computer-based systems, this means fast loading, clear type fonts and software designed so it can be filled out by either the booth worker or the prospect.
- Speed. In the frenetic atmosphere of a trade show, neither staff worker nor visitor wants to hang around while a form is laboriously filled out.
- Accuracy. Nothing annoys a prospect more than a misspelled name. One method for improving accurate data capture is requesting a business card, and attaching it to the paper-based form. Another is using a "lead retrieval system" provided by

show management, whereby the visitor's badge is swiped and the contact data is captured automatically.

What Information to Capture at the Trade Show

The first question you must consider is the exact set of data points that need to be captured. Each additional point carries a cost, in terms of time and accuracy. Attempt to capture too much, and your collection rate will suffer. Record too little, and you reduce your ability to sort, qualify, and assign value to the contacts.

Don't confuse the contact capture form with a marketing survey or questionnaire. Its intent is entirely different. The ideal level of information for contact capture is that which will tell you exactly how to handle the follow up with the prospect, for example, send information about certain products, call for a sales appointment, or hold for later contact. Your objective is to eliminate—as much as possible—the need for additional outbound communication before following up after the business event.

The interaction—conversation with the visitor—should result in one of three outcomes:

1. Identify non-prospects and eliminate them. These are visitors who will never buy, or refer, or influence a purchase decision. You do not want to capture their data at all.
2. Capture information about true prospects that will permit efficient and effective follow up after the business event. Essentially, you need their contact information, a few essentials about their characteristics, and an indication of how they want to hear from you. These are the show leads. Connecting with these people are why you are at the show.
3. Qualify the prospects who are ready to buy. Among the true prospects there will be a certain number whom you can convert to a qualified lead—ready to see a sales person—on the spot. For these, you need to have on hand the qualification

questions that you have developed in cooperation with the sales team.

Of course, it makes sense to try and identify the maximum number of qualified leads among the prospects, so these can be followed up immediately by sales and converted to revenue rapidly. Simply capturing name and address leaves you with the additional time and expense of qualification after the trade show. Not only do you then incur cost of the outbound contact—whether by phone, mail, email, or fax—but you also reduce the volume of the usable contacts, since you won't be able to get in touch with all of them after they have left the trade show.

But not all prospects will be ready for that step. As Mac McIntosh, President of Sales Lead Experts, points out, "Don't ask them to convert before they're ready. This is like asking someone to marry you on your first date." The bulk of contacts at the trade show will be prospects who will be ripe for follow-up communications. Many of these will later convert to qualified leads, and then convert to sales revenue. You need to capture enough information at the trade show to follow up, but have on hand the questions needed to qualify the lead fully, if appropriate.

Essentially, the form needs to capture the following categories of information:

- Contact information.
- Needs assessment or qualification assessment.
- Follow-up plan.
- Notes on the discussion with the rep.
- Name of the rep.
- Show name, location, date.

Discourage your staff from capturing data on visitors who have no potential of ever buying, influencing a purchase, or referring others. Why waste everyone's time? It's better to wrap up the conversation and move on.

DATA POINTS

Within the essential data categories lie numerous possible data elements to consider. Remember, you are seeking the perfect balance between too much and too little data, so choose carefully. When creating the forms, list the most important questions first, to improve the likelihood that their answers will be captured. Sales management input will help, not only in form design, but also in ensuring sales force cooperation in data capture and later lead management. Here are the categories of data to consider for inclusion on your form.

- Trade show name, location, and date.
- Name of staffer.
- Visitor (contact) name, title, company, address, phone, fax, email.
- Preferred contact method (e.g., phone, mail, email).
- Functional responsibility (because titles can be obscure, you may want to clarify what the prospect actually does, such as the department or the level of authority).
- Objective at the trade show.
- Buying responsibility (specifier, influencer, decision-maker, etc.).
- Industry.
- Company size (revenue or employees).
- Relationship category (dealer, supplier, end-user).
- Current customer (yes, no).
- Member of a buying team.
- Timeframe of intended purchase.
- Budget (size, availability).
- Product or service interest.
- Current supplier.
- Follow-up plan (send collateral, call for appointment, call with a quotation, resolve customer service problem).
- Contact quality (e.g., A, B, C).
- Referral to other contacts.
- Comments.

You may also want to provide the booth staff with a list of questions intended to elicit the information points you select. The discussion between rep and prospect at the booth is a conversation. You don't want it to become an interview. But booth staff members sometimes find it handy to have canned questions as reminders for them of gentle, but effective, ways to gather the data they need. Here are the kinds of questions you might provide:

- Why did you stop by our booth?
- What are you looking to accomplish at this trade show?
- How soon are you looking to make a purchase?
- How are you solving this problem today?
- Who else do you know who could use a product like ours?
- What's the best way for us to follow up with you?
- Is this the best phone number to reach you?

Capture Methods

A wide variety of inquiry capture methods are available, each with its own strengths, weaknesses, costs, and best applications. As you evaluate the options, just keep in mind that you have about 30 seconds to engage a visitor and begin the contact capture process. Make sure that whatever method you choose does not become a roadblock to prospect engagement or to data capture. Involve sales management in discussions about the options—you'll improve your chance of successful information capture at the event.

Using Teamwork to Motivate Data Capture

Doug MacLean, of MacLean Marketing, believes that teamwork can improve data capture at the booth. Pairing people stimulates cooperation and quality control. MacLean suggests you pair opposites, like a seasoned booth staffer with a newbie, or a sales person with a technical person. At the daily staff meeting, you can then report on the number and completeness of each team's contact forms, and offer recognition to the most productive team of the day.

The Out of Control Lead Sheet

Matt Hill, of The Hill Group, warns against a lengthy data capture form. Some marketers— if you let them— will see the form as an opportune venue for market research. "Don't let it happen," says Hill. "I've seen forms that include ridiculous questions like what magazines they read, what other shows they attend, and what competitors they know. Apple was once saddled with an 8-page lead sheet! These questions belong in market research, but not in lead generation." Get the information that you need to follow up, and no more.

PAPER-BASED PROCESSES

The simplest approach is to develop a "contact sheet" or form for each trade show. Many exhibit managers prefer a tall and narrow format, such as one-third of an 8½ × 11 inch sheet of paper, or a 5 × 8 or 4 × 7 inch pad. Other managers prefer a smaller form, like a 3 × 5 card, which is fairly easy to fill out when standing up. Just be sure you have enough room for all the questions you want to ask, and don't assume that all staffers will have neat, small handwriting—leave plenty of room for them to write. For a small show, you can create a form on a PC and photocopy it.

Exhibit 8.1: Sample Lead Cards

SIEBEL®

Name: ____________________

Title: ____________________

Company: ____________________

Parent Company: ____________________

Address: ____________________

City, State, Zip: ____________________

Phone: ____________ **Fax:** ____________

Email: ____________________

Product(s): ☐ Analytics ☐ Contact Center & Service
☐ CRM OnDemand ☐ ERM ☐ Field Service
☐ Marketing & Sales ☐ UAN
☐ Theater Presentation ____________________
☐ Other-Please Specify ____________________

Are you currently evaluating solutions from Siebel Systems?
☐ Yes ☐ No

Is there a formal initiative to evaluate in the next: ☐ 0-6 months
☐ 6-9 months ☐ 9-12 months ☐ 12+ months ☐ No formal initiative

Is this initiative budgeted? ☐ Yes ☐ No

Who is the executive sponsor for this initiative?
☐ CEO
☐ COO or VP of Operations
☐ CIO or VP of IT
☐ CFO or VP of Finance
☐ VP of Sales, Marketing or Service
☐ No sponsor

Are you interested in receiving future emails from Siebel Systems on new eBusiness initiatives and upcoming events?
☐ Yes ☐ No

Notes:

(continued)

Source: Siebel Systems, Inc. Reproduced with permission.

Exhibit 8.1: *continued*

<table>
<tr><td colspan="2">

Staple Imprint or Business Card Here

Make sure you have:
Shipping Address for Samples
ie: No PO Boxes
And Phone Numbers

</td><td colspan="2">

2002 ICE Lead Form

GENERAL INFORMATION - Please Circle

DAY: Wed.   Thurs.   Fri.

TIME: 9-10   10-11   11-12   12-1
          1-2   2-3   3-4   4-5

TAKEN BY: FAK   PMB   RB   WJB   ROB   LJC
RDC   CRF   CHF   JJF   SJK   SLK   MAM   DJM
RR   RJS
*Name (Reps etc.)*_____

CUSTOMER INFO: A   B   C

</td><td></td></tr>
</table>

Product	Product #'s	Sample	Literature	Other
NACURE & K-CURE				
K-FLEX				
K-SPERSE				
K-KAT				
NACORR				
DISPARLON				
K-STAY				
CURENOX/SAMCURE				
NEW GEN. BROCH.				
OTHER_____				

Remarks:

_____
_____
_____
_____
_____

Source: Bob Burk, CTSM—King Industries, Inc.

Some experts recommend that you create a unique contact form for each trade show. This allows you to adjust the questions to fit the audience, the products you are promoting, and so forth. However, keep in mind that the data needs to be key-entered for later use, so it is beneficial to use as many standard questions as possible. Similarly, if you organize the questions on the form in the same order that is used in your database program, you will save time and improve accuracy at the point of key-entry.

The other advantage of customized contact forms is that some items can be pre-printed on your form, saving the staff time. Some of the candidates for pre-printing include:

- Trade show name, location, and date.
- Check-off boxes.

Where possible, organize points into check-off boxes. Some points particularly lend themselves to this approach, among them:

- Current customer.
- Preferred contact method.
- Buying responsibility.
- Industry (when the show is narrowly targeted).
- Relationship category.
- Current customer.
- Timeframe of intended purchase.
- Budget.
- Product or service interest.
- Follow-up plan.

Some exhibit managers have found success using color-coded forms, allowing more specificity and differentiated handling. For example, light blue for prospects and white for current customers. Or a special color for customer service problems, which will be shipped back to home base nightly for speedy resolution. Or a different color form for contacts interested in different product lines—a method that works great when you only offer a handful of lines. Just don't select a paper color so dark that the writing is hard to read.

A clever variation on the paper form is converting it to an envelope. If you print the questions on the face of the envelope, then you can insert the prospect's business card inside. This eliminates the need for staplers, and reduces the likelihood that the business card will get lost.

Paper-based systems have been supplanted, or supplemented, by wide use of electronic systems today. However, it is not only Luddites who believe that paper is superior. Consider its flexibility, low cost, and immediacy. For very small conferences, and tabletop exhibits, paper is likely to be your only option.

ELECTRONIC "LEAD RETRIEVAL SYSTEMS"

Show organizers—actually a vendor designated by show management— will rent you a so-called lead retrieval system, which swipes, shoots, or scans the prospect's badge, allowing you to print out a contact form with much of the basic data pre-populated. These systems can improve the accuracy of data capture, and save time and aggravation versus filling out a form by hand. Typically, the systems can be rented for a few hundred dollars, and when you return it at the end of the show, you can pick up a diskette with your complete data, ready to transmit to a spreadsheet or your marketing database.

However, the technology is not perfect yet. These systems have a number of drawbacks:

- The attendee data pre-gathered by the show organizer may itself be inaccurate or incomplete.
- The systems are typically incompatible among trade shows, so you may have to fiddle with data transfer issues afresh for each trade show.
- If you have a large or busy booth, you may need to rent a number of boxes. No matter how many you have, they can still become a bottleneck.
- Most systems offer very limited opportunity to customize the form.
- Glitches and snafus are common, whether it's badges that resist scanning, or running out of paper tape at the busiest time of the trade show.

If you do decide to use such a system, here are some tips for increasing its effectiveness:

- Add a note-taking capability to the swiped data. One method is to scan the badge onto a label, and affix it to a larger paper form. The objective in data capture is to record the elements of the opening conversation with a prospect. If you simply swipe the badge without taking additional notes, you've wasted an opportunity, and squandered one of the most important advantages that a trade show offers.

- Experiment with the new alternative swipe hardware, if available. Many vendors now offer handheld devices that allow portable information capture anywhere in the booth.
- Don't let the system simply serve as an electronic fish bowl. If you only collect the contact information pre-populated from the data provided to the show organizer, all you have done is replicate—at a much higher cost—the value of the attendee list. Make sure your system is connected to your qualification questions whether they are programmed into the system itself or whether the answers can be attached to the printout by the staff member who is interacting with the visitor.
- Provide plenty of time and resources for training on the system, and have a back-up plan in place.
- Make sure everyone in the booth has the capability to capture contact information. The technology needs to be a helpful tool, not an impediment. Each booth worker must have access to the system. Don't plan on referring the prospect to a centralized "swiper" at a main desk.

You can also consider buying your own lead retrieval system and carrying it to each trade show. This solution is economical for frequent exhibitors, but also introduces the risk of incompatibility and technical problems that can ruin your show experience.

PC-BASED SYSTEMS

Many PC-based systems are now available with software packages you can customize. These systems can be connected to scanners of the electronic show badge or business cards. Or they can be pre-loaded with a database of customers and prospects, who are then looked up and qualified while they visit. One of the benefits of these systems is the ability to correct any data errors on screen while the visitor is still with you. Another benefit is daily (or more frequent) reporting of activity, and the ability to export files easily to your marketing database. However, this kind of system does not work well with "one-to-many" situations, like large demos or theater-type presentations.

Consider using your own customer and prospect database on a PC, in combination with the lead retrieval system. When the badge is swiped, a booth assistant key-enters the name while the visitor is in conversation with a sales person. If the visitor pops up as a current customer, the helper gives a signal, and the rep says thanks for the business and talks about new products or other cross-sell opportunities. If the visitor is identified as a prospect, then the rep steers the conversation to a set of qualification questions. The result is a nicely customized conversation with booth visitors.

ONLINE SYSTEMS

The Internet is rapidly being applied to the contact capture business at trade shows and events. The advantages of a web-based system are speed, of course, as well as integration with post-event lead distribution and follow-up.

Increasingly, the official registration contractors selected by show management are making web-based systems available to exhibitors. Other options include solutions provided by third-party vendors, or developing your own customized, in-house system.

The online information capture system is typically a stand-alone, proprietary device that includes a PC, a badge reader, and a printer. Data is downloaded from each PC and transferred via email to your lead processing system.

Wireless technology with direct access to the Web is the next step in contact capture at events. Already, such technologies as Bluetooth are being used with PDAs, cell phones, and laptop computers to grab information from visitors and transmit it to databases. The technology is evolving rapidly. What marketers need to keep in mind is the customer experience. Don't let the whiz-bang features get in the way of a satisfying personal interaction with visitors.

CONTACT CAPTURE IN A "ONE-TO-MANY" SITUATION

When conducting a theater-type presentation, contact capture becomes a real challenge. The old-fashioned solution is to place on each chair a clipboard with a form to fill out, and hope visitors will comply. Some exhibitors add an incentive to encourage visitors to take the trouble.

A number of new handheld technologies are now available to make theater audience contact capture easier. According to Ken Mortara, President of ShowValue, Inc., a neat solution is the "audience response system," an interactive PDA-like tool that puts a keypad in the hand of each person in the theater. The sophisticated versions allow the presenter to receive input from the audience throughout the presentation, and make adjustments to the script based on the needs of the audience. The challenge remains for how to capture information from people standing in the back of the theater area. Mortara suggests you close off the theater and invite visitors to scan their badges on entry.

Lead Qualification

The ability to qualify prospects on the trade show floor is one of the least understood secrets to trade show success, and an excellent source of competitive advantage. A number of elements point to the importance of on-the-spot qualification:

- Not all visitors will ever be in a position to buy from you or refer you business. There is no point in spending time on unproductive conversations.

Questions to Ask Lead Capture Technology Vendors

The technological options for contact capture are evolving rapidly. Whether cutting edge or tried and true, all systems need to be evaluated carefully. Nothing is more frustrating than technical glitches on site. Word to the wise: Be sure you bring along some paper-based form templates, for quick reproduction at the trade show, as emergency back-up. Here are some questions to ask potential vendors that may reduce your risk.

- How customizable is the system? If you can't capture the pieces of qualifying information critical to your company, steer clear.
- What badges can the system read?
- Will it work with your current marketing database?
- How much flexibility is there for capture at various locations around the booth?
- Provide references from current customers.
- What kind of technical support does the vendor provide?
- Is the deal a software sale, a license, or a service?

- Mere contact names are no more valuable than a mailing list. Contacts and inquiries must be converted to qualified leads before they will convert to sales revenue.
- If you don't qualify the contact on the trade show floor, you will have to invest in follow-up qualification after the event. Later contact piles on the additional expense of outbound contact. Furthermore, you are unlikely to be able to get in touch with 100% of the contacts, reducing your qualification rate and increasing your cost per qualified lead. (Please see Chapter Nine for more details about post-show qualification.)
- Think about your customers and prospects. Without a workable information capture system, you are forced to ask for the same information more than once, which annoys prospects to no end.

Essentially, you are at a trade show to learn about customer needs—far more than you are there to tell prospects about yourself. For one thing, prospects won't remember but a fraction of what they hear at a show. It's the exhibitor's job to establish a connection, gather as much information as possible about the prospects, and then take the initiative on following it up.

SETTING QUALIFICATION CRITERIA

It is marketing's job to provide qualified leads to sales. Sales then work the leads until they convert to revenue—or are declared otherwise "closed." This division of labor increases the productivity of a highly skilled and expensive sales force by ensuring that sales people spend the bulk of their time in front of qualified prospects. But the system only works if:

- Sales and marketing agree on the definition of qualified.
- Marketing never, ever, hands an unqualified lead over to the sales force.

The qualification criteria must be developed in concert with sales. The best way to go about this is for marketing to sit with a few senior sales people and sales managers, and pose the following question:

"Who is your ideal prospect?" Or asked another way, "What kind of prospect would you like to stand in front of every day?" If you ask this question in enough different guises, and pose it to enough seasoned sales people, eventually you will get a clear sense of their definition of quality.

But you will also need to use some judgment. Keep in mind that sales people have a natural suspicion of marketing's role in the process. Some reps will demand, for example, that marketing keep them informed about all contacts into their territory. They may say, "Give me any contact you get. I'll figure out how to work it." The danger in this approach, however, is that the rep's patience will quickly expire in the face of working unqualified contacts. The sales force will conclude that they are getting nothing of value from marketing. And marketing will find that reputation very hard to shake.

The rule that marketing should never pass an unqualified lead to sales holds true for contacts and inquiries from all marketing channels. But trade show leads have developed a particularly bad reputation among sales teams. The reason for this is obvious: you need look no further than the notorious fish bowl. For years, exhibitor managers have been deluded into thinking that their objective was simply to grab business cards and names. Focusing on quantity over quality is, in fact, the kiss of death for a trade show program.

QUALIFICATION CATEGORIES

At a trade show, the meaning of "qualified" differs somewhat from its traditional context in campaign-oriented lead qualification. In the sales lead management world, the qualification strategy is to ensure that the prospect is ready to see a sales person. The objective is to increase sales force efficiency, and make sure the sales team is only in front of prospects who are likely to buy. So the qualification criteria are very well defined and tightly accommodated.

In the case of a business event, however, all you are trying to do is separate the wheat from the chaff. You want to eliminate visitors with whom you can never do business. So you might screen out students, spouses, or hangers-on. But you want to begin a relationship with any prospects who might eventually become a buyer, influencer, or specifier. Or prospects who might be a good source of referrals, in their own companies or elsewhere. So, your booth-level qualification criteria are likely to be fairly broad.

Here's an example. The pneumatic seals company, seeking to introduce a product line to the plastics industry for the first time, is exhibiting at a show where 15% of the 5,000 attendees are expected to be from the plastics industry. Their show goal is to demonstrate the seals to half of them, or 375 prospects. In this situation, the booth staff might have decided to capture any prospects who are in the plastics industry, in any capacity.

Most business marketers find that sales people are looking for qualification around the following categories. The degree of detail needed will be a function of the complexity of the buying process.

- Budget. Is the purchase budgeted, and what size of budget does the prospect have available? You will want to set up categories or ranges, for easier scoring. Some companies also request information about the company's credit history.
- Authority. Does the prospect have the authority to make the purchase decision? If not, you should try to find out who does, and capture the additional contact information. You may also ask about other roles in the buying process: who is the specifier, the influencer, the end-user, the purchasing agent, etc.
- Need. How important is the product or solution to the company? This criterion may be difficult to ask directly, but it can be approached by roundabout methods. "What is the problem to be solved?" "What alternative solutions are you considering?" "How many do you need?" "What product do you currently use?"
- Timeframe. What is their readiness to buy? When is the purchase likely to be? Depending on industry and sales cycle length, this can be broken into days, months, or even years.
- Potential sales volume. How many departments in the company might use this product? How much of, or how often, might they need the product?

- Account characteristics. Company size, whether number of employees or revenue volume, industry, parent company.
- Contact history. Is this a current or past customer?
- Would they like to meet with a sales person? A desire to continue the discussion may be such a powerful indicator that it trumps all other qualification questions. Don't forget to ask.

It's also important to find the right balance between lead quality and the booth staff's ability to run through the questions efficiently. The trade show floor can be a noisy, distracting environment. You can't expect visitors to answer a lengthy survey. During busy hours, you may want to have a fall-back strategy that focuses on capturing the basics, and postponing the other qualification questions for later outbound communications. In such a crunch situation, the essential elements to capture are:

- Contact information (name, title, company, address, email, phone).
- Preferred method of contact.
- Agreed-upon next steps (send product information, have a sales person call, etc.).

On the other hand, the trade show floor is a fertile environment for initiating sales conversations. Booth staff should be encouraged to record as much information about the prospect as possible. A detailed account of the conversation becomes, in itself, part of the qualification criteria. The nuances and the insights enhance follow-up, and make the next stage in the relationship easier to achieve. And don't forget that, if it the information is not recorded, the prospect will be annoyed at being asked the same questions by a representative of the same company in the future.

STANDARD VERSUS CUSTOMIZED QUALIFICATION CRITERIA

You must decide whether to develop a new set of qualification criteria for each business event, or whether to standardize your criteria across the entire business event marketing program—or even your entire marketing communications program. The advantages of the one approach comprise the disadvantages of the other. Consider this:

- Customized qualification criteria provide more relevance, especially at business events focused on specific customer segments or product categories.
- Standard qualification criteria allow consistency across marketing vehicles, making data capture easier and reducing confusion and error.

Whatever you decide, make sure that your database is set up to capture the criteria. Better yet, list the questions in the order they will be slotted into the database, for ease of later data transfer.

LEAD SCORING SYSTEMS

There are many ways leads can be sorted and scored. You will select the system that best suits your sales team and your industry. Remember to get input from the sales team about their preferences.

One of the most common strategies is a simple alphabetical ranking by A, B, and C. Here's an example of how this might work:

- The A category means the prospect is ready to see a sales rep. Either the prospect said so (e.g., "Have a sales specialist call me."), or the predefined qualification criteria for a sales call have been met.
- The B category means the prospect still needs nurturing, but the outbound communication should be shifted to the sales team. This might involve a telephone call to establish the relationship, in anticipation of an imminent readiness to buy.
- The C category means the inquiry is not ready to be handled by sales. It still needs nurturing, to be done by marketing.
- You may include a D category, to indicate an inquiry that is not worth nurturing. At that point, a decision needs to be made whether to put the inquiry into the marketing database for ongoing communications, or whether to mark it "cold" or "dead."

Lead ranking systems vary widely. Some companies classify leads as "hot," "warm," or "future" leads. Some call them "hard" or "soft" leads. However they are organized, the criteria must be set up in consultation with the sales team and applied consistently. No unqualified leads should ever be passed to sales.

IMMEDIATE FOLLOW UP

Occasionally, miracles happen, and a visitor at your booth proves on the spot to be qualified. In that situation, you want to deliver the lead to sales immediately. If the right sales resource is already at the trade show, you can arrange for a sales appointment or further conversation on site. If the right person is back at the office, then the lead needs to be transferred by email, phone, or fax for rapid follow up. The sales person will have to decide whether to contact the prospect via cell phone or email while he or she is still at the trade show.

THE DANGER OF FOCUSING ON QUALIFICATION

While qualification on the spot is an essential part of the lead generation process, don't let the qualification process blind you to the potential of apparently non-qualified prospects. Your booth staff needs to spend its time with the highest potential prospects. But keep in mind that:

- Not all potential buyers are immediately obvious. Business people shift their positions, their functions, even their companies, regularly. Be aware that today's dud may be tomorrow's hot lead.
- Someone who may never be in a buying—or even influencing—mode for his or her own company may very well be a profitable source of referrals. You may want to adjust your qualification form to include acknowledgement that the contact is still someone worth keeping in the communications stream.

So train your booth reps to be sensitive to contacts who have potential but are not—and many never be—qualified. Here are some signs to look for:

- Doesn't have a need. In many cases, the prospect may not even know he or she has a problem that can be solved by your product or service. This may be an opportunity to educate the prospect about the potential of improving his or her business. This prospect is more likely classified as a "suspect." But the potential is there if you have a process in place to keep in touch and explain the benefits of your product.
- Long lead time. Many sales people don't want to talk to a prospect whose plan includes a purchase far down the road. But these are exactly the prospects marketing should nurture along, keeping in touch with them until the budget becomes available—or whatever conditions need to be in place before they are ready to buy.
- No budget. What if the prospect is interested in your product, but has no money budgeted at the moment? This prospect may not be ready to absorb a sales person's time, but certainly marketing will want to keep the relationship warm until the budget becomes available.
- Is a consultant, or journalist. Your booth workers need to be aware of the power of influencers in the buying process. Consultants may be a rich source of referrals. Journalists can help establish positive word of mouth. If everyone in the booth is fixated on slavishly generating qualified leads, real opportunity can be lost.

Ultimately, a trade show is an environment where relationships are initiated and deepened. There can be a thin line between chit-chat and sales development.

ONLINE QUALIFICATION SYSTEMS

A variety of new software solutions are available to allow you to capture the results of your qualification discussion on a computer, for easy access, storage, and transfer. The data can be entered by booth staff, or by booth visitors themselves. Offering touch screens, color PDAs, or attractive kiosks for data entry will improve the likelihood that attendees will complete the process.

The systems are typically preloaded with attendee data, so the first step is asking the visitor to confirm the data that comes up. Then, you can move into the pre-determined qualification questions, like products currently used, communication preferences, and so forth. Just as with offline methods, the questions must be developed in concert with the sales team, and keep them limited to the most essential.

Data Transfer

What are you going to do with the contact forms or the data you have captured? Speedy follow-up is a virtue, so many exhibitors arrange to ship the information back to their home offices each night. Thus, leads that are already qualified can be worked immediately by a sales person.

In other cases, it makes sense to carry the data back with you at the end of the trade show. Whatever you do, don't leave the forms in the booth—there are too many stories circulating among trade show marketers about opening a closet when setting up a booth, and finding last year's "leads" pouring out onto the floor.

If you have captured the data electronically, then the next step is to transfer it, via email or upload, to your marketing database.

The contact data needs to be sorted, and distributed appropriately:

- All contacts are logged into a marketing database. Duplicates are identified and purged.
- Leads that are fully qualified go to the sales team.
- Contacts that have missing information must be further qualified.
- Contacts that are unqualified go to a nurturing process.
- Promises made must be kept, whether it's sending additional product information, scheduling an appointment or resolving a customer service problem.

Staff Training

Your staff training plans must include particular focus on contact data capture and qualification. Here are some tips for getting it right:

- Include hands-on practice with the contact capture systems and processes as part of your pre-show training.
- Train the staff to complete their discussion with each visitor with a question about the accuracy of the data they have recorded.
- At the end of the day, ask the booth staff to review the contact forms they have written during the day and be sure their handwriting is legible. Notes taken under the pressure of a busy trade show can sometimes make no sense to the poor person assigned to do the later key entry. As time passes, the rep is also less likely to be able to remember what the illegible notes were supposed to mean.
- The same quality review can apply to information captured electronically. Have the reps look over the list of contacts they were involved in to add any details that might have been overlooked in the heat of the moment.
- This quality review works especially well if conducted jointly in an end-of-business daily review meeting. Each contact can be discussed, and additional information from reps involved can be recorded.
- At the opening of the trade show, have a senior sales person conduct quality control on two or three contact forms for each sales rep in the booth, and coach the reps on ways to improve the forms' quality or completeness.

9

Lead Management and Nurturing

Most companies evaluate their trade show and corporate event results based, at least in part, on the quantity and quality of leads generated. So this chapter focuses on guaranteeing—not losing—your results.

Typically, as many as half of all business people who make product inquiries will at some point make a purchase in that product category, so it is imperative that inquiries be treated properly. No sense in letting that purchase intent migrate to the competition, especially if you already have some kind of contact in place with the prospect. Contacts developed at a trade show are valuable—and vulnerable.

The Value of Event Leads

Compared to sales leads that come from other sources, like demand generation campaigns, website visits, or even referrals, trade show and corporate event leads can be an extremely valuable asset to the company. Why are business event leads so valuable?

For one thing, they are the result of a concrete engagement. The sales process (or, from the prospect's point of view, the buying process) has already begun. The prospect has met with a representative of your company, or perhaps seen a demo or a presentation.

Certainly he or she has experienced some kind of interaction with your product, your company, and your brand.

Furthermore, the prospect voluntarily came to the business event, visited the exhibit hall, and stopped by your booth. The entire trade show atmosphere is about buying and selling, about solving business problems. People visit trade shows to learn about new products and services. The person visiting your booth is inherently more likely to be a prospect for your offering than a business person on the street. And the prospect is very likely to be a decision-maker, specifier, or influencer in the business buying process. If you don't follow up, you'll insult the prospect's interest and position yourself as an amateur.

According to the Center for Exhibition Industry Research (CEIR), trade show leads convert 230% better than leads generated in the field. A trade show lead takes only 1.6 sales calls to close, versus the 3.7 needed for a field lead.

In dollar terms, there are three ways to value leads.

1. Calculate the cost per lead generated at the business event. This calculation can be divided into two parts: the cost per contact and the cost per qualified lead. The former is calculated by dividing the entire trade show budget (including all variable costs, like travel and hotels) by the number of contacts generated at the show. The cost per qualified lead is a bit more complicated, since it involves a cost for post-show lead management. But in either case, you'll discover that your company has spent a lot in generating these contacts, so you don't want to squander that investment.

2. Another approach is to consider the value of a converted lead to your company. Essentially, this means the average order size of a product or service sold by your company, multiplied by the lead conversion rate. So, if your company typically sells $12,000 worth of product at a time, and each qualified lead is likely to convert to a sale at a 30% rate, then the value of a qualified lead is $3,600. This amount represents the opportunity cost of not working the lead.

3. The true cost combines the cost already invested to generate each qualified lead plus the opportunity cost of not working the lead.

With all this value at your fingertips, solid follow-up is essential to convert the opportunity to revenue.

Principles of Excellent Post-Event Follow Up

Nearly everyone has a trade show horror story relating to post-show follow up. The most common tale is about no follow-up at all. Consider to this story from Jane Lorimer, who at the time managed the Coors Brewing Company trade show program: "One year I was looking for transportation companies for Coors. We were doing about 300 events a year and needed a shipping resource to support our program. At the TS2 show that year, I stopped by the booths of seven transportation companies who were exhibiting, and left my contact info with them. I told them we were going to bid and asked them to contact me within two weeks to set up appointment. Of the seven, only three called at all. Of those only two called within the specified time frame. We solicited from an additional two others and actually selected one of the companies whom I met at the show. I was a hot prospect at the show, but experienced a number of cold sellers!"

One wonders why these companies were exhibiting at all. If you're not going to convert the business to revenue, why promote yourself in the first place? Lack of follow-up is particularly egregious in the world of trade shows, since the contact was relatively expensive to produce, and the follow-up was very likely promised by a real person. So, the waste in this situation is compounded by a breakdown of trust and the erosion of the value of the brand.

With a bit of effort, however, post-show follow up can be very effective. The secret lies in planning, process and accountability.

ROLES AND RESPONSIBILITIES

As discussed in Chapter Two, marketing is in a service role to sales, and one of marketing's key contributions to the productivity of the sales force is lead generation and management. In terms of a business event lead generation program, marketing is on the hook for the following:

- The contact capture and qualification process at the business event.
- Analysis of the contacts and distribution of qualified leads to the sales team.
- Post-event follow up with all contacts as appropriate.
- Post-event qualification of leads as needed.
- Nurturing of unqualified leads until they are ready for handover to sales.
- Distribution of leads, once qualified.
- Tracking and reporting of sales conversion results and business event ROI.

The point here is that marketing is in charge not only of the exhibit and the marketing planning that surrounds it. Marketing is also in charge of managing the entire lead process, and delivering the leads generated at the business event—the qualified leads—to sales. So, a marketing team that focuses only on the pre-show promotions and the marketing activities at the show has failed in its mission. The post-event follow up is also marketing's responsibility—and essential to its success.

One of the reasons trade show and corporate event marketing has developed a questionable reputation is that the focus has been on the business event itself. An exhibit manager must focus on the buiness event certainly. But marketing is responsible for making the business event a financial success. Marketing must accept accountability for ensuring that the business generated at the trade show or corporate event is converted to sales, and that those results are reported. You can't manage what you don't measure. So take a look at Chapter Ten for a discussion of metrics and measurements.

PLANNING AND BUDGETING FOR POST-EVENT FOLLOW UP

As they say in the Marines, "Prior planning prevents poor perform-ance." An ounce of planning is worth a pound of frenetic execution. Be sure that your plan includes a clear strategy for follow up, with detailed notification to all who will be involved. The plan should in-clude specifics on how to handle show contacts, with details on:

- Contact data delivery back to the office.
- How contacts and leads will be sorted.
- Fulfillment materials that will be sent.
- The qualification and nurturing process.
- How leads will be distributed, tracked to closure and analyzed.

A common failing in trade show and corporate event marketing is a budget that funds the wrong elements. A glitzy booth or a delightful party is only part of the process. The true leverage in trade show and corporate event marketing is in post-show follow up of all the rela-tionships that were kicked off at your fabulous booth or your dy-namic hospitality suite. So, be sure to budget at least as much for post-show follow up as you do for pre-show promotion.

SPEED IS OF THE ESSENCE

The most important element of post-show follow up is that it be done in the first place. But the second most important element is speed. Business buyers are looking for solutions. They want answers. If they don't hear from you, half of them will buy from someone else. So get them their follow up information fast.

Ideally, follow up should take place within 24 hours. A week is reasonable if the prospect is still at the trade show for a few days. After 30 days, you are probably too late to serve the prospect's needs—or appear in any way professional. Your fulfillment perform-ance, in effect, is seen by prospects as an indicator of what it's like to do business with you. Can they rely on you to deliver? Here's your first opportunity to establish your credibility.

Performark, Inc., a Minneapolis fulfillment and lead management company, conducted a revealing study that illustrates this point. In 1995, and again in 2001, Performark researchers conducted a test in the marketplace. They gathered a large sample of business-to-business advertisements in trade publications, and submitted responses to 1,000 of them. These were all paid advertisements, each with some kind of response device, whether an offer for more information, a website, an 800 number, or a reply card. Performark's objective was to see how well the companies managed these inquiries. How many of them would follow up? How quickly?

The answer was: It's pathetic out there. In the 1995 experiment, 43% of the responses received *no* follow up over a 60-day period. By 2001, when the arrival of the Internet was expected to increase the speed of business, the situation had actually worsened. A whopping 61% of the 2001 responses were ignored over a 60-day period. Obviously this is trending in the wrong direction.

But there are two positive signs buried in this experiment's results:

- Of the companies that did follow up on these inquiries, 75% of them managed to get the information to the prospect within one week. The companies that have a process in place understand the value of speedy follow up.
- Since 61% of the businesses out there are not following up, a major competitive opportunity is available to businesses that do get it right. Make sure you are one of them.

Here are some tips for how to improve your chances of successful follow up:

- Recognize that this is a process. It's not the exciting end of marketing. But it's not rocket science. Put in place a clearly defined, written process. Make it part of people's job descriptions and compensation plans. Report on results regularly.
- Mystery shop the process. Hire someone to visit your booth, go through the process, and report to you on how quickly and professionally he or she was contacted after the trade show.
- Own the responsibility. If the trade show revenue is coming entirely from the leads generated, then treat them like gold. Make them part of your performance objectives.

SORTING AND SEGMENTATION

The first stage in handling the trade show contacts is sorting them. Most companies will sort them by some combination of the following criteria:

- By value. Leads that are ready to see a sales rep should receive top priority. Others can be sorted and handed based on potential.
- By product interest. If your company is organized by product division, and there is little opportunity for cross-selling, then this sortation strategy makes sense.
- By sales territory or distribution channel. When lead handling varies by channel or territory, the first sort may well be along these lines.
- By preferred follow up method. If you collected communications preferences from the contacts, you should respect their wishes.

The point here is that not all contacts are created equal, and you want to treat the most productive ones first. You also want to respect your prospects' preferences.

FULFILLMENT OPTIONS

Often post-event follow up involves sending the prospect additional information, a process known as fulfillment. Information can be sent by mail or email, delivered as a web download, or hand-delivered by a sales person. Here are some tips for ensuring that your fulfillment is efficient and high quality:

- Differentiate your fulfillment material and delivery method based on the prospect's value. A typical fulfillment kit can cost $10 to deliver through the mail. Why send the same material to everyone? To the less valuable prospects, you might send a business letter, a postcard, or an email and refer them to your website for more detailed information. A highly qualified lead, especially one who has indicated an interest in seeing a sales rep, would merit a sales call or an overnight express package.

- In the interest of speed, use the Internet for fulfillment where possible. Web-based collateral material is not only fast, it is infinitely flexible for continuous updating and for customization to the individual prospect's need. It's also cheaper on a per-piece basis.
- Keep the contents relevant. You may be tempted to consider adding additional product or company brochures, or whatever spare collateral material you have lying around—but then the package will end up appearing disorganized and unprofessional.
- Remember that the purpose of the follow up is to move the prospect closer to a sale. Tailor the contact method to the prospect's level of urgency. Make sure the contents provide the information that the customer needs at that particular stage of his buying process.

The Fulfillment Kit Checklist. A number of best practices have emerged in the world of fulfillment. How does your fulfillment measure up against the best?

- ☐ It is flexible, so you can differentiate the contents.
- ☐ It uses personalization. After all, you have already had a face-to-face contact with the recipient. At least address the prospect by name in the cover letter. Better yet, customize the letter to refer to the meeting, address the prospect's specific needs, and sign the letter under the name of the person who handled the contact at the booth, or the sales rep who covers the account's territory.
- ☐ It reminds the recipient of its reason for arrival. In the subject line of the email, or on the outer envelope of the direct mail, it says something like, "Here is the information you requested at the event."
- ☐ It tells the person what to do next. Your objective is to move the prospect along the buying process. Don't miss the opportunity to request the next step, whether it's calling for an appointment, or visiting a website, or attending a webinar.
- ☐ It tells them where to buy. You never know—maybe the prospect is ready to buy. So include a list of dealers or the name of the sales person on the account or whatever information the prospect needs to take action.

Why Trade Show Leads Are Mishandled

Exhibitors suffer from a bad rep—probably deserved—for mishandling the contacts and leads they generate at trade shows. How have we arrived at this sorry state of affairs? The reasons are numerous:

- The people running the exhibit are not properly trained and motivated. Marketers must take responsibility for lead management. They can't expect it to be delegated successfully to a team that is focused on logistics.
- The organization is divided up into silos, and roles and responsibilities are unclear. Often, the decision to participate in a trade show is made jointly by several divisions in the firm. If no particular marketing function has responsibility for the P&L of the business event, the lead process can go untended.
- The marketers are caught up in the glamour of the "front end" of trade show planning and execution, and neglect the critically important, but less exciting, "back end" processes.
- A large volume of leads is dumped into the sales pipeline, without the proper capacity for follow up. Business events represent a one-shot opportunity to generate a lot of lead activity. You must have a plan to deliver the leads according to the ability of the sales force to absorb them.
- There is confusion about the meaning of a qualified lead. If the exhibitor staff is unclear about its mission, and focuses on quantity versus quality, the result will be a disillusioned sales force and a lot of wasted effort in pursuing what are essentially cold prospects.
- The business event budget is misallocated, and the lead management function is under-funded.
- The team is beat. Planning and working a trade show are exhausting. Plus, work is piling up on your desk back at the office. So when you return from the trade show, you're diverted to focus on your inbox and ignore the post-show follow up. Don't succumb to temptation.

The Lead Management Process

A marketing department experienced in lead generation and management is likely to have a process in place to handle leads from a variety of marketing activities—direct mail campaigns, advertising, Internet marketing, and trade shows. In this case, you should feed your show contacts and leads into your existing process.

Some exhibit departments feel the need to set up a dedicated process for show contacts. They try to make the case that trade show leads are a different animal, and need to be managed separately from leads generated through, say, direct marketing campaigns.

But this approach is wrong-headed, for two key reasons:

1. If there are problems with the lead management system internally, then those problems should be addressed and corrected. Building a redundant system is not the answer.
2. The company owns the relationship with the customer. If one department establishes a separate record of the relationship, everyone loses. The company loses a complete view of the relationship, its needs, its value, and its opportunity. Worse, the customer will quickly become confused.

Laura McGuire, founder and CEO of Qgenisys, Inc., a lead management firm, wisely observes, "These problems are usually about process or about politics. If the process is broken, fix it. On the political side, the company must agree, at all levels, that the prospect and customer relationships belong to the company as a whole, and not to any one department."

Post-Event Qualification

The best approach to qualification is to front-load it onto the trade show floor. If you can get the qualification questions answered at the time of initial contact, you will speed the process, reduce costs, and increase the conversion rate. However, not all contacts gathered at the trade show can be qualified on site, for various reasons. For example, during busy hours, booth workers may be unable to conduct complete conversations with each visitor. And most prospects will simply not be ready to have such a detailed conversation with you.

Contacts with incomplete information must be qualified through an outbound communications process. An excellent qualification process has the following characteristics:

- Speed. As with fulfillment, an outbound contact for qualification purposes is most effective if it is immediate. For one thing, the prospect is more likely to remember you and be responsive to your request. For another, the chances are better that the prospect will not have solved his or her business problem elsewhere. Experts recommend a follow up communication go out within five business days of the trade show's end.

- Persistence. It's hard to get anyone on the phone these days. But if you can't reach the prospect, the contact will be entirely wasted. A series of attempts is needed. However, define in advance your tolerance limit for touches, based on a reasonable number of contacts. For example, if the prospect is unreachable after five phone attempts and three emails, call it quits.
- Multiple channels. Traditionally, qualification has been the province of the call center, and the key medium for qualification was a series of outbound telephone calls. Recently, email has proved to be a potent medium for qualification. In some cases—when the prospect has provided no other contact information, for example—direct mail and fax are also effective.
- Dedicated resources. You may use full-time, dedicated staff for qualification, whether in house or outsourced, or you may assign the job to staffers who also have other duties. However you handle the function, make sure the qualification staff is motivated and compensated to encourage 100% handling of the contacts in short order. If making the outbound qualification contact is not on the top of the person's to-do list every day, it's unlikely to ever happen.
- Segmentation by value. Not all contacts are created equal. Sort them by pre-determined criteria—very likely the same criteria you used to sort them for fulfillment treatment—and differentiate your qualification strategy based on the expected value of the prospective lead.

ONLINE QUALIFICATION STRATEGIES

Like many business processes, qualification has benefited greatly from the Internet in terms of convenience, accuracy, speed, and cost. If your lead management system is Internet-enabled, it's a short hop to including a qualification module to the system.

Typically, online systems that allow contacts to be recorded on the trade show floor can be extended to permit automated lead follow up. The critical element in the process is collecting email addresses, since email is the most efficient means for post-show follow up communications. If the email is collected at the trade show, then the following elements of the process can be automated:

- A follow up thank you note containing whatever product information was promised at the show.
- An email qualification form requesting additional information.
- Attachments or hotlinks to product information.
- A post-show survey to capture information about the trade show experience.

One of the key benefits on online qualification is credibility. When the form is filled in by the prospect , then the lead will pull more weight with a sales person than a form filled out by a tele-qualifier.

The other advantage of an online process is the ability to automate the distribution of qualified leads to the sales force, and to manage lead disposition effectively. Ideally, an online lead distribution system will include the following:

- Complete qualification data on the lead, including the ranking.
- An acceptance indicator. If the sales person does not accept responsibility for the lead in a reasonable amount of time, it needs to be rerouted to another rep.
- A disposition indicator, with incentives for the sales team to fill in the information about the lead's status as it migrates through the sales pipeline.
- The ability to deliver the information to the sales force in a variety of formats, like the PDA and the sales force automation software platforms. This is especially true for leads that will be distributed to third-party distribution channels, which may use any number of systems.

CASE STUDY

How TruLogica Got 100% of Its Hot Trade Show Prospects to Respond to Follow-Up Communications

CHALLENGE: Many business marketers make a common mistake. They gather prospects' emails at trade shows from zapping attendee badges or gathering business cards in a fishbowl. Then they dump the names into their main email file and start sending them stuff on a regular basis. With ire rising against unwanted email, this could get your company blacklisted, or cause you to lose an RFP.

"We don't assume that getting an email address gives us permission to mail them indefinitely," says Margaret Herndon, TruLogica's Field Marketing Director. "We mail them one time and try to get permission to do even that. You can't ram this stuff down anyone's throat."

Coming back from her company booth at a Gartner show, Herndon had a pile of names with some good prospects buried in them. She allowed herself just one follow up email, so that message would have to work extra-hard.

Stakes were high. TruLogica's average sale is $500,000 to $1 million, so each good lead was gold. Her email campaign could either be the opening to a beautiful relationship . . . or ignored.

CAMPAIGN: Herndon began with the basics—organize your leads and segment them. Immediately after the trade show she huddled with the sales persons who manned the booth and put each visitor name they'd gathered into one of three categories:

Category #1: Hot Prospects
This was a small percentage of visitors. They had purchasing power or serious influence, plus (and this

was critical) they recognized that their organization had a problem that TruLogica's technology could solve. Some even pro-actively asked to be called by a sales rep when they got back to the office after the trade show.

Because these leads were already self-educated in the type of problem TruLogica solved, Herndon didn't want to send them the 101 white paper she usually used for direct response offers. She had to find content that would be compelling to more educated prospects.

There wasn't time to create a new white paper in-house, so for under $10,000, Herndon purchased the limited distribution rights for a META Group paper that accomplished the same objective. "Our company wasn't specifically noted in the white paper," she notes. "It focused on tangible metrics and numbers to measure value from this particular [technology]. It validated our approach. It was a great draw for someone who needed to be taken to the next level on how to measure ROI."

Herndon turned this third-party branding to her advantage in the copywriting in the emailed invitation she sent to hot leads for the paper. The brief letter notes META's brand name twice and states that "This is NOT a sales brochure" in order to entice more clicks.

Each note featured a personalized first-name salutation, and was sent "from" the personal email account of the sales rep that the prospect had spent the most time with at the show. If the prospect replied, the response would go directly to the rep, instead of a general mailbox.

Next, Herndon used three tactics to make sure her landing page converted the maximum number of clicks into white paper downloaders:

Tactic A: The landing page was visually similar to TruLogica's show booth. "Visitors stop by so many booths that it is easy to get them mixed up," explains Herndon. "We wanted them to know where the email was coming from."

Exhibit 9.1a:

Subject line: Gartner Conference Follow Up
From: Tony or Richard

Dear first name,

Thank you for visiting TruLogica's booth last week at the Gartner IT Security Summit. I enjoyed meeting you and describing TruLogica's new approach to Identity Management.

You had requested that I give you a call after the conference to continue our conversation. In the meantime, I thought you'd enjoy reading a recent presentation from the META Group on the ROI of Identity Management. This is NOT a sales brochure -- but a white paper from a respected third party analyst group. It makes a compelling case for adopting a business process-centric solution, like the one TruLogica offers.

Please simply **click here to get your copy of "Identity Management in a Virtual Work Environment" by the META Group.**

Thanks again for stopping by our booth this week. I will get in touch with you in the next week once you've had a chance to **read the report.**

Best regards,

Tony Carpinelli
VP, Sales
TruLogica, Inc.

Souece: MarketingSherpa, Inc. www.marketingsherpa.com. Reproduced with permission.

Exhibit 9.1b:

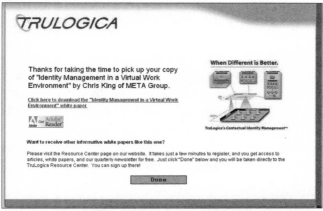

Source: MarketingSherpa, Inc. www.marketingsherpa.com. Reproduced with permission.

Tactic B: The cleanly designed page had very little copy, lots of white space, and only three links (one to get the white paper PDF, one to get the download for Adobe's free PDF reader, and one to go to TruLogica's site Resource Center to sign up for additional emails). It's worth noting TruLogica's regular site navigation was not on this landing page—Herndon didn't want to risk losing the attention of these hot prospects to other links not specifically suited for this stage in the relationship. She focused their eyes on the META paper, and only after that, allowed them to go to the main site.

Tactic C: Visitors were not required to enter any information whatsoever to access the white paper. After all, Herndon already had their contact information in her database, which tied to email campaign results, so she didn't need to put this artificial barrier in front of people to get names. Plus, her sales reps were already calling these hot leads. The campaign goal was to shorten and sweeten the sales cycle, not re-gather leads.

Category #2: Tepid Prospects
These names were classic semi-qualified leads. They might not understand the problem that technology like TruLogica's solves enough to be ready to shop for solutions; or, they might work for the right target company but in the wrong position.

In this case, Herndon's goal was to educate them a bit more, and perhaps get permission to continue to email the most interested of the group so that someday they might turn into hot leads. So, her standard 101 white paper was the perfect offer. The email and landing page they saw were very similar to that of the hot leads, except the paper offered was different.

Category #3: Cold Prospects
Thanks to all of the "win a Palm" offers marketers have been running to generate trade show traffic for years now, businesspeople have been trained to stop by every single booth at a trade show and get their badge zapped to increase their chances of winning something.

Herndon realized most of the names on her list were these auto-zappers—people who stopped at the booth out of habit rather than a genuine interest in or qualification to purchase TruLogica technology. She put these names into the "cold leads" pile. They too got a personalized email that also thanked them for stopping by the TruLogica booth.

However, she realized they probably wouldn't care about a specific white paper, so instead she sent them her most generalized offer—a link to the site library, which included a wide variety of information such as articles and information on relevant upcoming conferences.

RESULTS: It's certainly rare that a landing page could convert 100% of click-throughs into white paper downloaders, but TruLogica's landing page for the hottest leads broke records to get a 100% download rate from visitors. Plus, some of the visitors forwarded the link to colleagues, so the final download rate was around 125%.

"We kept seeing this individual continually download this paper and we were really concerned the guy was not able to download it," says Herndon. She was so concerned, that the link wasn't working, that she had the appropriate sales rep send the prospect a polite email asking if everything was ok. Turns out the prospect was perfectly happy with the download, so much so that he'd forwarded it to about two dozen other people.

Since the campaign went out in June 2003, several of the analyst paper downloaders have become serious sales prospects and at least one has already entered the buying cycle.

More data:

- More than 30% of hot prospects visited the download site. 8% of these clickers took two actions, 1. they got the white paper, and 2. they also registered to receive more information from TruLogica's library.
- 27% of the tepid prospects visited the download page and, of these, 27% downloaded the 101 paper. This huge difference in conversion rate from click to

download shows that lead quality counts, and also that a third party branded white paper offer can be more powerful than an in-house paper. Also, none of the tepid leads took the next step and registered for the library.

- None of the cold leads clicked on their emailed offer.

These results prove that differences in lead quality, even for attendees of the same niche show, can be profound.

These results also prove that it's worth it to split your campaigns by lead-type for measurement purposes at least, even if you don't do different creative. If Herndon had jumbled all the leads together in one lump campaign, she would have never learned that the landing page conversions were so different depending on lead type. It might, in fact, have changed her perception of the landing page's overall ROI.

Nurturing

When a prospect is not ready to buy—that is, the contact remains unqualified—the lead needs to move to a nurturing process designed to keep the relationship going until the prospect is ready to see a sales person. Also known as "incubation" or lead "development," nurturing is a marketing function that can dramatically improve the sales results of trade show leads. Consider a typical example of the qualification status of 100 contacts generated at a trade show (see Exhibit 9.2).

Notice how relatively few contacts (five) were ready for sales follow up immediately after the trade show. But twice that amount (11) were converted to qualified leads through additional outbound qualification. The balance was put into a nurturing process, which generated another 25 qualified leads over time. Thus, thanks to post-show outbound qualification, this trade show generated 300% more qualified leads than it would have at the trade show alone. And thanks to post-show nurturing, the trade show's productivity increased 500% over the lead generation at the trade show site.

**Exhibit 9.2: Qualification Status of One Hundred
Contacts Generated at a Trade Show**

At Show		Qualified Leads
Contacts generated	100	
Immediately qualified	5	5
Unqualified at show	95	
Post-show		
Lead pool	95	
Contacts reached (60%)	57	
Qualified via outbound communication (20%)	11	11
Nurturing pool	84	
Qualified via nurturing (30%)	25	25

Nurturing involves a series of communications intended to build trust and awareness, and keep a relationship going until the prospect is ready to buy. The series of communications can vary widely, using all communications media, and all kinds of sequencing and timing strategies. To keep things simple, however, you should devise a standard process and then continue to refine it as experience shows you what works best.

CHECKLIST OF NURTURING TACTICAL OPTIONS

Some of the communications tactics that business marketers have found effective in nurturing include:

- ☐ Additional qualification questions, via phone, or email.
- ☐ Seminar or webinar invitation.
- ☐ Event invitation.
- ☐ Request for appointment at the next trade show.
- ☐ New product announcement.
- ☐ Catalog mailing.
- ☐ Newsletter (email or print).
- ☐ Press release.

☐ Survey or needs analysis.

☐ Videotape, audiotape, DVD, or CD mailing.

☐ White paper, downloaded or mailed.

☐ Article or chapter reprints.

☐ Case study, executive briefing, or checklist.

☐ Tip sheet or guide.

☐ Personal communication, like a birthday card or holiday card.

☐ Letter from various sides of the company, such as the CFO, customer service department, engineering, or senior executives.

☐ Letter from a third party endorsing your product or service.

You may reach a point in the process where it's no longer economical to continue nurturing a contact in the hopes that it will convert to a qualified lead. That point arrives in different places for different companies, depending on many factors, such as the complexity and length of the sales cycle, and the conditions inside the prospective account. But when the point is reached, you should remove the contact from the nurturing process and return the name to the marketing database for fresh promotion.

There may be some controversy internally about whether nurturing is a function for sales or for marketing. Some companies split the difference, and create nurturing teams that report into the sales organization. Other companies put nurturing in marketing and loosen the qualification criteria so that more leads will flow to sales earlier in the process. However you decide to manage nurturing, be sure you recognize that it is a separate function, and one that can be staffed by lower-cost resources than your sales people. That said, however, those resources will be in regular contact with prospects, so make sure they are professional and well trained. You want them to be able to act as an appropriate representative of your company to the outside world.

The objective of the nurturing program is to stay in touch with the prospect until he or she is ready to buy. Things change rapidly in businesses. The only way you can know when the prospect is ready is through regular communication.

Inside Versus Outsourced Lead Management

Professional lead management companies can provide welcome services in the area of lead capture, fulfillment, database management, qualification, nurturing, distribution, tracking and reporting. The advantages of outsourcing are many:

- Easily manages the natural peaks and valleys of lead flow. Trade shows are notorious for dumping unwieldy volumes of contacts into the system. You may not want to build the capacity in house.
- Shifts technology risk. The professional lead management company will invest in the latest technology to manage the process.
- Reduces your management headaches. Let someone else worry about the day-to-day management of the function. You have your own job to do.
- Their core competency, not yours. The lead management company does this for a living. For you, it's a minor staff function.
- Manages the closed-loop process by maintaining contact with the sales force on your behalf. It can help to have someone else taking the heat.

Before outsourcing, give serious consideration to the following:

- Is lead management a function of strategic importance for your company? You may decide to invest in managing the function yourself.
- On a variable basis, the cost of outsourcing may be higher in the long run.

Other Post-Show Follow-Up Steps

An often neglected, but productive activity is post-show thank you messages to the parties involved. As an exhibitor, you are of course a client of the show management. But you will be well served by politely acknowledging the contribution that the various parties made to your success. Here is a checklist of possible candidates for thank-you notes:

- ☐ Booth staff.
- ☐ Neighboring exhibitors.
- ☐ Show sponsor.
- ☐ Show organizer (account rep, PR contact).
- ☐ Booth visitors.
- ☐ Exhibit manager.
- ☐ Exhibit designers, builders, agency.
- ☐ Hospitality or event planners.

Press and Publicity

Trade journalists cover trade events. It's so obviously a public relations (PR) opportunity, it's a wonder why more companies do not take advantage.

Well, maybe it's not a wonder. Very likely, it's due to the organizational gulf in many companies between business event or exhibit management and the PR function. Another problem may be a lack of familiarity with PR on the part of marketers involved in trade shows and corporate events. But a public relations focus can add such lift to business event marketing results, a press and publicity strategy is a must.

Much of trade show publicity is simply an extension of your ongoing public relations effort. You can use the same tools, and integrate your trade show and corporate event activity into the larger PR plan. So, in a sense, trade show PR is business as usual.

However, there are two angles that need to be considered. First, publicity is one of the great under-leveraged opportunities in trade show marketing. Most exhibitors neglect even the basics of PR. Of course, this means a greater likelihood of success for the company that gets it right.

Second, there are a handful of differences in organizing a public relations program around a trade show, compared to traditional PR. A review of the differences will illustrate the rich opportunity.

The key point is this: after sales and sales leads, the second most powerful marketing benefit of a trade show is press coverage. Trade reporters cover trade shows. They are looking for things to write about. So, whatever your trade show objectives, it makes sense to add PR to the list, and put in the relatively modest effort required to support the publicity function. The ROI on media relations can be huge.

Business Event PR Strategy

Journalists are looking for news. So, if you have an opportunity to save up a newsworthy item—a product launch, for example, or a new business partnership agreement, or some thought leadership delivered in a new white paper or study—the trade show can provide an efficient place to disclose the news. With real news available, your PR strategy at the trade show can be fairly straightforward. You might reveal the content on embargo to one media outlet before the trade show, and release the news to the rest of the media at the trade show.

What can be positioned as news? Here are some suggestions from Barbara Axelson of Axelson Communications:

- A new product.
- An acquisition.
- A major personnel change.
- A new initiative.
- A new service.
- An award.
- A new distribution channel or partnership.

Without actual news, there is still plenty of PR opportunity to be tapped at a trade show. A baseline strategy might be "get acquainted" sessions with the journalists on site. The trade show is probably the most concentrated availability of trade journalists you'll ever see. Take advantage of the chance to build good will and awareness among the press in your industry.

Connie LaMotta, President of LaMotta Strategic Communications, notes that trade show PR is most effective when it is part of your larger public relations strategy. If, for example, a certain trade show represents a concentrated communications opportunity for a product launch, then it's wise to schedule that launch to coincide with the trade show.

The critical step, she cautions, is to bring the PR people and the corporate event marketing people together, early and often, to plot strategy as a marketing team. The company's marketing plan itself should contain a PR component. And the business event marketing plan must include a PR plan.

For example, when considering the PR strategy for a certain show, you ask the same questions that are asked for marketing planning:

- Who is the target audience at the show?
- How are our products and services differentiated?
- What key messages do we want to deliver?

While news is the most effective attractor of press attention, what happens when there's no news to announce? Create some, says Connie LaMotta. For a major trade show, LaMotta recommends that you invest in a small piece of research on a subject of interest to your target audience's business needs. The minute you have some actual numbers to share, your story gains traction with journalists. "Reporters can only do two or three stories a day, and you are competing with hundreds of other exhibitors for your share. If you have numbers, your pitch is ten times more likely to be picked up," she observes.

The secret of the quick survey, according to LaMotta, is selecting a topic that is of business interest to your customers—the very targets of trade journalist attention. "It's not about what interests you, but information that helps your customer do his or her job better."

Creating research-based news is not a last-minute strategy, but you only need a few months' lead time and a small investment. "With 50 to 100 respondents, you'll have some reasonable validity," says LaMotta. "And a survey administered from your own website costs next to nothing."

The other critical step in developing PR strategy is to set clear, measurable objectives. Are there particular publications where you want to appear? Is it a certain gross number of mentions? Are you seeking a particular number of meetings with journalists? With objectives in place, your results analysis will be straightforward.

Trade Show PR Execution

WORKING WITH SHOW MANAGEMENT

Show management recognizes the value of publicity, and will have a PR staff on hand that is responsible for both publicizing the trade show itself and assisting exhibitors in getting coverage. Building a relationship with the trade show's PR team will pay off. Consult with them early, explaining your objectives and probing for opportunities to get press attention. Be sure you keep track of their deadlines, which will be published in the exhibitor manual. Lead times can be as much as three months.

Show management may be running contests or new product showcases. While they sound tacky and might seem not worth the trouble, in fact contests tend to be easy to enter, and easy to win. "You don't need to submit only new products," says Wayne Dunham of Dunham Communications, a company specializing in trade show publicity. "In a field of 3,000 exhibitors, I've seen situations where there were only 11 submissions for 12 awards. Why not get the extra exposure?"

The trade show's website will also contain a section devoted to exhibitor press releases. According to Dunham, this is an easy way to get in front of qualified prospects as well as journalists. "The press release area is typically the most widely read page on the trade show site, because people actually want to learn what's new."

Show management's publicity department has as its primary duty to gain press attention for the trade show itself. But exhibitor news plays a large role in attracting that attention, and can mean in a win for both sides. Advanstar's Industry (212) show, for example, solicited input from exhibitors for use in its pre-show press release, which persuaded journalists to attend the trade show in the first place. According to Victoria Pace, with Goldstein Communications, Ltd., the new products scheduled for introduction at the trade show became the major news hook that attracted the editors. "We asked all the exhibitors to provide input about their product launch plans, and what recent press mentions their companies had received. With that information, I could go to fashion and trade magazines and let them know that news related to the companies they were already covering would be announced at the show."

Reed Exhibitions sends out a questionnaire to exhibitors to solicit fodder that can be used to attract press to the trade show. According to Beth Blake, Director of Public Relations, the Reed PR department is looking for such items as:

- Do you have new product announcements to deliver at the trade show?
- Are you scheduling a celebrity, VIP, or industry guru at your booth?
- Are your company officials speaking at the trade show?
- How telegenic are your product demos, for possible use in broadcast coverage?
- If you are a public company, do you have an important corporate announcement scheduled for the trade show?

The Reed PR team will then work in tandem with the PR agency of the exhibitor, to take advantage of mutually beneficial opportunities to stimulate coverage.

For exhibitors who have no PR resources available, the show organizer's PR department can serve as a temporary but valuable resource. "I make myself available to consult with our exhibitors on public relations," says Blake. "I will review their press releases and make suggestions. I will help them format their releases. I am happy to advise on their press conference strategies. It's a free service, and I wish more exhibitors would take advantage of it."

For one apparel show, Goldstein Communications developed a pre-show press goody bag, and invited exhibitors to contribute product items for distribution. "We advised the exhibitors who wanted to participate that they should include their booth number with the product," explains Victoria Pace. "A number of exhibitors wrote to thank us for the extra exposure, saying that journalists had thanked them for the gift."

Exhibit 10.1: Public Relations Services Form

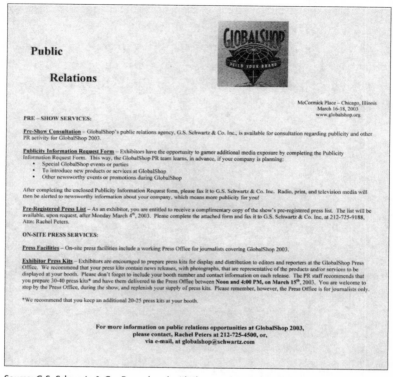

Source: G.S. Schwartz & Co. Reproduced with the permission of Rachel Honig Peters.

The National Association of Store Fixture Manufacturers arranged for its public relations agency to provide exhibitors with a variety of support services at the Global-Shop show.

PRESS APPOINTMENTS

The best results accrue from setting up appointments for press representatives with your key executives, especially when you have real news to share. Get a list of registered press people from the show management's PR services group. Ask for the previous year's press list, which will include journalists who did not pre-register but came to the trade show anyway. Also inquire among your own contacts in the industry whether they will be attending the trade show.

Your pitch can relate to product announcements or other news items you are saving for the trade show. Or it can be simply an opportunity for the journalist to get acquainted with you. The press representatives are moving around the trade show looking for ideas, buzz, news, and trends. A conversation with your senior management can help them meet their objectives, if the executive has something to say.

Before contacting journalists, it makes sense to research their backgrounds and story history, so you better understand their interests and you can personalize your pitch. Says Peter Shankman, President of The Geek Factory, "There's nothing more appealing than a pitch that begins with how much you enjoyed my recent article."

Chet Dalzell, Director of Public Relations for Harte-Hanks, recommends that press appointments with senior company executives be limited to occasions when there is some breaking news or particular story to discuss. He saves "getting to know you" meetings for himself to handle.

Connie LaMotta agrees. "Working journalists are under pressure to fill their daily story quota. Save the get-acquainted meetings for before or after the trade show, when there's no agenda. That's the way to set your executives up as a resource for the journalists, and you can conduct the interviews via phone. Diverting them from their objectives during the trade show is just wasting their time."

When meetings are scheduled with press representatives at a trade show, Dalzell recommends that you find a quiet place off site. He also suggests that media training in advance can work wonders for senior executives' ability to stay on point and deliver the key messages effectively.

Trade publications may send several journalists to a single show. In that case, focus your attention on a single reporter. "Don't call every reporter in the news room," cautions Ken Magill of *The New York Sun*. "The staff will divvy things up. Better to make one contact and stick with it."

Breakfast meetings are particularly welcomed by journalists. They like to eat, and early in the day tend to be open to a more leisurely discussion. A classy dinner at a first-rate restaurant for a key journalist and some of your top executives is another excellent strategy. This is not intended for breaking news, but for quiet conversation and relationship-building.

Some industries have fostered entrepreneurial new opportunities for trade show press contact. ShowStoppers is an example of a new service that makes life easier for marketers—while challenging the hegemony of show organizers. At major trade shows like Comdex, PC Expo, and CES, ShowStoppers offers an evening reception where companies enjoy three hours of quality face time with key journalists, such as Walter Mossberg of *The Wall Street Journal,* for a reasonable sponsorship fee. Compaq successfully introduced its iPAQ pocket PC at the Comdex ShowStoppers event without even taking a booth at the trade show. Sponsoring companies set up tabletop demos, and reporters welcome the chance to look at new products in an efficient venue—plus, cocktails.

WORKING THE TRADE SHOW FLOOR

At larger trade shows, a common PR tactic is to roam the exhibit hall looking for people with press badges, and approaching them cold. Rachel Honig Peters, Senior Vice President of G.S. Schwartz & Co., has this down to a science. "Journalists are less likely than ever to register in advance for shows. They just show up. So it's impossible to know exactly who will be there—not to mention book an appointment in advance. So I move about the show floor, introduce myself to anyone wearing a press badge, and try to persuade the journalist to visit my client's booth."

Peters also recommends that outside PR agency personnel have business cards made up that give not only the PR person's contact information but also names the client, so the journalist will remember the connection. Her company affixes transparent stickers to the back of her regular business card to serve this purpose.

PRESS RELEASES

If you have any kind of news to tell, a press release is the basic tool for communication. Essential distribution points for the release include:

- Mail it to the press list in advance, if appropriate. This provides the hook for setting up at-show appointments with reporters.
- Place a pile of releases in the press room.
- Send it to the trade show daily. Or prepare separate releases for the trade show daily for each day of publication.
- Hold a stash at the booth for distribution to journalists who stop by the booth.
- Send to customers, partners, and employees, if appropriate.

PRESS KIT

A simple press kit—namely, a folder with a press release, product spec sheets and photos, and perhaps a company brochure—is an inexpensive method to get your point across and provide journalists with basic background about your company and products.

The basic elements of the press kit include:

- Press release (the most important element).
- Fact sheet about the company spokesperson.
- Fact sheet about the company.
- Backgrounder on the new item.

The kit should be neither too heavy nor too light. Barbara Axelson, President of Axelson Communications, observes "Don't put any junk in the press kit. But don't let it be simply a press release in a folder, either. And be sure you include clear information about your company's press contacts at the show and back at the office as well."

The kit should be placed in the press room, with additional kits held at the booth in case journalists stop by the booth. According to Wayne Dunham, only ten percent of exhibitors ever submit kits to the show press room. "It's amazing to me that exhibitors miss this obvious chance to get low-cost publicity," notes Dunham. "But those that do submit are ahead of the competition."

Consider mailing the kit in advance to show management's PR team, and to the press list for the trade show. Then, when you follow up with a phone or email request for an appointment at the trade show, the way has been paved.

An alternative press kit strategy is recommended by Chet Dalzell. "We've gotten away from using kits in press rooms. Instead, we just put out a release, and have a few kits available on request. Reporters are really looking for the news. Our experience is that kits just get dumped."

Some PR professionals advise that the press kit be mailed to key reporter contacts' offices during the trade show, to serve as a reminder of your news on the reporter's return, and provide contact information for easy follow-up.

Place an electronic version of your press kit on your website, for journalists who prefer to download it after the trade show, or for additional journalists who are not attending the business event.

THE PRESS ROOM

The press room is dedicated by show management as a resource for journalists covering the trade show. It tends to be open long hours, and offers coffee, snacks, and computer terminals.

Some press rooms are off limits to anyone but registered press. Whatever the policy, the press room provides your best chance to meet journalists and get to know them better. But you have to behave appropriately. If a journalist is busy filing a story, it's probably not a good idea to interrupt with pitches or invitations to the booth.

Hanging around the press room entrance can be an effective way to establish face-to-face contact with journalists, even if the press room itself is off limits. As Barbara Axelson observes, "The show is often your best chance to meet some journalists who may inaccessible to you back home. Go to the press room and get to know them. Take them to breakfast—they're always hungry."

Some trade shows make the press room available for sponsorship, and at a relatively low price compared to the other sponsorship slots on offer. This is a fairly new concept among association-run trade shows, so you can cut an attractive deal. With for-profit conference organizers, the deals may be leaner, but still good value.

Chet Dalzell has sponsored the press room at his industry's annual convention for several years, and feels that as a result, Harte-Hanks has earned a special place in the minds of the journalists. For about $5,000, he can place signage in the room, and distribute small gifts like notebooks, pens, mousepads, and screen savers. The sponsorship also earns him free access to the room, and the chance to build relationships with the press attendees.

Connie LaMotta offers an important reminder: "Reporters come to the press room several times a day to find out if there's anything new. They are hungry for your material. When you have news, you should make it known to everyone—the people running the press room, the show organizer's PR people, anyone who can let reporters know what's going on, when they ask."

PRESS CONFERENCE

Unless you are a major company with hot news to announce, a press conference is not likely to be a productive at a trade show. The problem is competing attractions. The journalists have a lot of other things to do during any given time slot, so it may be hard to get enough attendance to justify the expense of a room and catering. If you do decide on a press conference, work with show management's PR team to get it scheduled. And be sure to invite other interested parties, like association officials, customers, prospects, business partners, and sales people.

Some show organizers offer press conferences as a routine part of their services to exhibitors. Reed Exhibitions, for example, sets aside a room at each trade show it manages, and creates a master schedule for exhibitors who wish to conduct press conferences there. Still, the Director of Public Relations at Reed, Beth Blake, recommends that exhibitors only sign up for the room if they have a newsworthy item that needs to be delivered to many journalists at the same time. "To announce a strategic alliance that will have wide industry impact, a press conference is ideal," advises Blake. "But for a new upgrade to a software product, it's better to schedule one-on-one demos with journalists."

THE TRADE SHOW DAILY

Show management often publishes a daily newspaper during the trade show. They need content, so be sure you pitch the trade show daily every day, following the guidelines in the PR section of the exhibitor kit. "In 25 years of trade show public relations," notes Wayne Dunham, "I have never had a story rejected by the show daily."

TRADE SHOW ISSUES OF TRADE PUBLICATIONS

Pitch the special trade show issues of your industry trade publications. Show management will have a list of who is doing special trade show coverage. You are likely to find both pre-show and at-show special editions available.

Some trade publications cover the latest trade show news through their websites, so be in early touch with those reporters in order to participate. You can give them an early look at your press release, your new products, or your booth.

STAFF PREPARATION

Some companies insist that only trained media relations people talk to the press. Whatever you company policy, all employees should be trained on how to handle a press inquiry. Make sure all booth staff know the badge color that indicates a press representative.

Pamela Parker, Managing Editor at *ClickZ*, a web-based journal on interactive marketing, notes her frustration when booth staff are untrained in this area. "When I am walking the show floor and drop by a booth at random, there is nothing worse than being told 'Sorry, I am not authorized to talk to the press.' Don't they realize journalists will be there?"

The lesson here: at least one person at the booth should be trained to speak to visiting journalists. That person must have the ability to offer journalists meaningful content, and not just direct them elsewhere. The other booth staffers should be trained to refer journalists to that designated person. And the person must be available on the floor at all times.

POST-SHOW FOLLOW-UP

Here are some tips for gaining additional leverage after the trade show:

- Thank all reporters who either had meetings or gave you coverage.
- Keep in touch with the reporters, over time. Have lunch with them when you are on their turf. Drop them a note when you see an interesting article they have written. Send them case studies when you have them.
- Send additional product information as requested.
- Always deliver on your promises.
- Keep track of which reporters were unable to make their appointments with you. Follow up with them to offer an interview or a demo of your new product.
- Send a thank-you note to the unsung heroes in the show management PR department.

Other Trade Show Publicity Opportunities

No surprise, trade shows offer plenty of ways beyond the traditional press release for gaining the attention of journalists and other influential parties in your industry.

Your past PR initiatives can pay off for your trade show marketing, as well. Post framed copies of feature articles and other notable press mentions on the walls of your booth. Or offer article reprints as collateral material for visitors to take away.

SPEAKING ENGAGEMENTS

If your company will be exhibiting at a trade show, it makes perfect sense to gain additional exposure by placing your executives in speaking opportunities on the content side. Most trade show programs include such slots as:

- Breakout sessions with a single speaker.
- Panel sessions that need multiple panelists and a moderator.
- Roundtable sessions with a moderator.
- Keynote speeches.
- Conference chairmanships.

Ask your account executive for an introduction to the head of programming at the trade show. Most trade shows disavow any quid pro quo connection between exhibiting and speaking engagements, but there is certainly an obvious overlap in interests: you are exhibiting because you have products or services of interest to attendees. Your company's expertise in the field will, if properly positioned, provide value to trade show programmers.

When reviewing session proposals featuring your company executives, trade show programmers will react favorably to a positioning of objectivity. Some tips for improving your chance of being selected include:

- Avoid any whiff of a sales pitch.
- Stress your speaker's ability to deliver detailed case studies and success stories.
- Include a customer in the session, for instant credibility.

If you think your company executive has a chance at a speaking level higher than a mere session, by all means pursue it. Keynotes and conference chair slots require some effort, but the payoff can be substantial.

According to Ellen Shannon, an experienced business conference programmer, the easiest way to become a keynote speaker is to have been a keynote speaker. "Most keynoters work their way up from small conferences or company events to larger venues," she says. Here are some tips for making the grade:

- Keynote speech topics must be broad. Prepare speeches on themes like emerging trends, the future, or the state of the industry. Also prepare topics around the themes of conferences you are targeting.
- Videotape your speeches and make the tapes available for review by programmers. You might stream the tape from your website. Also list your past speaking engagements at the site.
- Prepare a speaker profile sheet, or kit that includes a tape or DVD, a list of potential topics, and a list of past engagements.

Becoming a conference chair is usually a function of a high profile and plenty of connections. Shannon observes that programmers are looking for conference chairs who are:

- Well known, whether themselves or their companies.
- Well networked, so that they can be relied upon to recruit other speakers.
- Organized, responsive and helpful.

Program development for the trade show's session content usually has a longer lead time than even required for reserving booth space. Count on at least six to nine months—often 12 months—in advance for session proposal deadlines.

If your executives are placed in speaking engagements at the business event—whether keynotes or regular sessions—take advantage of the publicity opportunity as well. Prepare a press release for distribution to trade journalists before the trade show and in the trade show press room. Trade editors are likely to cover sessions, especially if they contain new ideas or information that readers can use to apply to their businesses. Journalists are more likely to cover your executive's session if they've been pitched it in advance.

If the session has general interest beyond the confines of the trade show, distribute your press release to the news radio and television outlets, including local media. They may be inclined to cover your event as well.

Speaking Engagements: How Exhibitors Can Improve Their Chances

There are certain steps you can take to improve the odds of placing your executives in speaking opportunities at trade shows where you are exhibiting. Ellen Shannon, President of Publication and Conference Development Partners, and a 25-year veteran of business conference development, provides her recommendations here.

1. Find out who makes the program decisions. Ask how the programmer wants to receive your information, whether by email, hard copy in the mail, or fax. If there is an advisory committee involved, the programmer will probably want everything by email, for easy forwarding.

2. The exhibit sales person will give you the contact information for the programmer. But then be sure you get in touch with the programmer directly—don't go through your account person. Like journalists and editors, programmers prefer to maintain a church-and-state separation of exhibit sales and program content.

3. Call the programmer before submitting proposals, and do it early in the programming schedule. Make sure you understand the size and scope of the program, its contents, and its attendees. The program is likely to have a slightly different focus from that of the exhibit hall.

4. Here are the topics you should cover in your discussion with the programmer:

   - Is the program separated into tracks? If so, your session will need to fit into one of them.
   - What are the evergreen topics, meaning the ones that get covered every year? A proposal for one of these will have the best chance of selection.
   - What are the hottest topics in your area of expertise?
   - What are the top "pain points" for the audience?
   - What is the programmer's focus this year? Is there a theme, a new track, or some new area of programming that is getting special attention?
   - Is there a specific need or hole in the program that is waiting to be filled?

5. Once you identify one or more program areas of interest, develop several topic ideas. Strive for a balance between breadth and specificity—you want to interest a sizable audience, but still address a particular business problem that the attendees need to solve. Choose topics that are benefit and solutions oriented. Then, check back with the programmer and share your ideas. If you get a positive reaction, go to the next step. If not, go back to the drawing board.

6. Submit several proposals, using the programmer's designated form or format. Write strong benefit-laden headlines for your session, and suggest two or three possible headlines for each. A good example of a strong ses-

sion topic headline: "21 Proven B-to-B Lead Generation, Management, and Fulfillment Techniques." A bad headline for the same session: "How to Improve Your Lead Generation Program." In your session copy, state guarantees or promises of what the attendee will learn. A tip: check with your own customers for ideas on what they would want to learn in these sessions. Attach any articles that you've written, speaking references or experience, or session scores you have received from other conferences. Your objective is to establish that you are an expert in the area, and that you are a good public speaker.

7. You will significantly increase the chances of your session's being chosen if you create a panel with your customers, or present a case study with client participation. This way, your ideas will be validated by someone in the same boat as the attendees, and you will gain enormous credibility. Confirm the panelists and submit their names, titles, and company affiliations on the session proposal—don't simply promise to deliver this information later.

8. Make it very clear in your proposals that you do not view participation as a sales opportunity. Communicate that you view yourself a knowledge leader at a connected company. Attendees will approach you if they think that they can learn from you. They will run if they think that you are trying to sell them something.

9. Get back in touch with the programmer late in the program process to find out if they are having trouble putting a specific session together that they need. Offer to help.

10. See if there are any panels that you can join. Also offer up your customers as people who can help fill panels. Placing your happy customers on panels can pay off—invariably someone will ask them about their vendors.

11. If you aren't chosen, find out why. This knowledge will help improve your submission at the next conference. If you are chosen, exceed the expectations promised for your session. A good score will get you included again and again.

12. Carry a presentation with you whenever you travel. Make yourself known to conference programmers as a possible emergency stand-in, in case any speakers cancel at the last minute.

PARTIES AND COLLATERAL EVENTS

While your parties and collateral events may be designed with customers and prospects in mind, do not neglect the trade journalists. Reporters like a good party as much as anyone. Not only will they appreciate your thoughtfulness, they may also come up with a juicy story idea at your event that can gain you extra exposure.

This is another point where the business event marketers and PR people need to cooperate closely. At both planning and execution stages, ensure that representatives from these two functions are in the same room as plans are made for parties, hospitality, and collateral event activity.

Publicity for Corporate Events

Compared to trade show PR, publicity strategy for corporate events is much closer in nature to corporate PR in general. Trade press cover trade shows as a matter of course. But when it comes to a customer event you are organizing, such as a user group or a distributor conference, getting coverage is a long shot.

The exception to this rule, of course, is a company that is essentially newsworthy in itself, a market leader, or a hot stock, for example, especially one with a colorful, media-savvy senior management team.

But lesser luminaries in the corporate world can also find leverage in a corporate event for "ink" if they concentrate on news. Here are some tips for improving your chances:

- Match the topics to be covered at your corporate events with those that are being followed in the media you are targeting.
- Invite a star speaker.
- Present real news at the corporate event. The media may find your corporate event particularly appealing because it will offer a variety of perspectives—your news, plus the reactions of your customers or your business partners.
- Create an old fashioned publicity stunt.
- Use a professional media relations firm to help you craft the messages and attract the press representatives to attend.
- If media do show up, then make it as easy as possible for them to do their jobs. Provide them with access. Make sure they have the technology and the comfort that keeps them happy.

Ed Niehaus, co-founder and former CEO of the technology PR firm Niehaus Ryan Wong, advises that you hire the best media professionals you can afford. "Ongoing professional counsel can manage the company's and the executive's relationships with the press, focus upcoming news, provide creative ideas, and give the press a high level of service before, during, and after the event. As with anything else, you get what you pay for. The PR pro is an intermediary, influencing but not controlling the media, so you are paying to improve the odds of good results. There is no guarantee, because successful event PR depends not just on the professionals, but on everyone involved—including the media—to make the conversation more interesting, entertaining, and newsworthy."

Post-Event Results Analysis

W hy measure? The answer is obvious: how else will you understand the results of your marketing effort, and be able to make rational decisions among competing options for marketing investments?

In the world of trade show and corporate event marketing however, there are additional reasons for a focus on measurement. Unfortunately, the business event world has a history of fuzzy metrics. Companies have in the past been satisfied to participate in trade shows because they feel they "have to be there." And companies have been willing to evaluate the results based on such subjective measures as management's impression of whether it was a good show or not. At the same time, the cost of exhibiting has risen, and some companies have begun to question the value of trade shows at all.

Large budgets combined with fuzzy results reporting are a recipe for disaster. When companies have no clear visibility into the effectiveness of their trade show investment, they naturally look to reduce their participation and channel the budgets into more measurable programs. This means throwing out the business event baby with the unmeasurable bath water. What a waste of an important element of the business marketing toolkit.

In fact, trade shows and corporate events are highly measurable for marketing purposes. All it requires is planning and discipline.

Measurement will both provide you with the knowledge of whether you've been successful, and also provide the benchmarks you need for continuous improvement over time.

Measurement Strategy: Objectives Drive Metrics

If you did the right thing up front, in the planning stages, and you set clear, measurable objectives for your participation in the business event, then your measurement strategy is fairly straightforward: you need to collect data on the defined metrics, analyze the data, and report on your results. Sounds easy.

But a few challenges remain. Among them:

- Selecting the best method to collect the data you need. You must decide—in advance—the optimal tools that will help you collect the data, and make sure the resources are available. That means you need to plan for measurement, *and* you need to budget for it. Marc Goldberg of Marketech recommends allocating 1–3% of the total trade show budget to measurements.
- Doing it. In the throes of business event activity, not to mention planning for the next season's set of business events, results analysis can represent an unwelcome chore that you'd rather put aside. Don't succumb to this temptation. In short order, your ability to manage your marketing mix will go up in smoke.

From Exhibit 3.1 in Chapter Three, here are a variety of possible business event objectives and associated metrics, along with suggested tools that will help you capture the data needed for the metric selected. This is just an illustrative sampling. You will want to put together your own set of metrics and measurement tools against the primary and secondary objectives selected for your event.

Exhibit 11.1: Business Event Objectives and Associated Metrics

Primary Objective	Associated Metric	Measurement Tools
Introduce new product	Number of demos given Number of leads gener- ated by product	Daily self-reporting by booth staff Lead volume by product
Gather new prospects	Number of prospects gathered Number of new accounts added to the database	Visitor badges swiped at booth
Sales	Revenue	Sales lead management system
Awareness	Pre-post show awareness levels Number of press mentions	Pre-post show survey of attendees Press coverage analysis
Competitive research	Number of competitors at the trade show	Count competitors among attendees, sponsors, speakers, and exhibitors
Competitive research	Competitive analyses completed	Qualitative audit of com- petitors' presence at trade show
ROI	Return on investment ratio	Did-you-buy survey
Retain current customers	Number of customer appointments	Reporting by booth staff and salespeople attending the trade show
Retain current customers	Revenue closed from current customers	Financial system reporting on customer appointments Trade show contact data

Philosophically, the best strategic approach to selecting metrics is by assessing actions. What is it that you want customers or prospects to *do* as a result of your participation in the business event? Measure those actions, and you'll be set.

CASE STUDY

How HP Classifies Its Trade Show Metrics

Rob Aston, Director of Global Brand and Communications at HP, organizes his trade show objectives and related metrics into four categories, or "buckets." As reported in *Exhibitor* magazine in 2001, Aston uses the data to report to senior management on results and to refine the elements of his show program. The buckets are as follows:

1. Sales. Number of qualified leads, purchase intent, and cost per lead.
2. Audience. Visitor demographics, budgets, and purchase authority gathered by pre-show and at-show surveys.
3. Brand image. Message effectiveness and audience brand awareness, as measured by at-show and post-show surveys.
4. Media. Press coverage for HP and its competitors, researched by an outside service.

STANDARDIZED METRICS

The more you can standardize your metrics across marketing channels and over time, the more valuable they will be. For example, the cost to generate a qualified lead is a metric that allows you to compare investments in a variety of marketing communications arenas, such as direct mail campaigns, search engine marketing, and trade show marketing.

Similarly, if data is collected the same way over time, it can reveal important trends. For example, if you notice that your cost per contact at trade shows is increasing year on year, you will want to investigate ways to lower costs in that channel.

In the world of trade show marketing, a number of industry

standard metrics have emerged, pioneered by research companies such as Exhibit Surveys, Inc., who are dedicated to helping exhibitors assess their programs. Some of these include:

- Potential audience. Primarily used in trade show selection, space requirements and staffing, this metric estimates the portion of the audience who represent your true prospects. The criteria for judging prospect potential are specific to your objectives, such as industry, title, or product interest.
- Exhibit attraction. The percentage of the potential audience attracted to your booth, and a useful metric for companies that are focused on awareness and image objectives. Exhibit Surveys has tracked this factor for years, and reports a national average of 79% for all trade shows in 2003.
- Exhibit efficiency. Measures the degree of face-to-face contact your booth achieves with its potential audience. Most useful for companies measuring their results based on lead generation and sales results. This metric is the percentage of net attendees who stopped by your booth, took a demo, or had some other face-to-face interaction with your booth staff. If it is lower than expected, you may need better staff training or more staff assigned to the booth. Exhibit Surveys reports a national all-show average rate of 47% in 2003.
- Personnel performance. The helpfulness of your staff, on a qualitative scale (e.g., "excellent," "good," "fair," and "poor") as reported by your visitors. Other criteria to assess your staff could be knowledge or credibility. The most common failing found by Exhibit Surveys is insufficient product knowledge or inability to answer questions. Exhibit Surveys's 2003 national average of "poor" ratings is 2%.
- Sales person's rate. The average number of visitors handled per sales person

Seven Ways to Measure Events

The George P. Johnson Company, a business event agency founded in 1914, produces over 4,000 business events through its 16 offices around the world. The company has developed a set of seven business event measurement categories for their clients to consider:

1. Lead quantity and quality.
2. Audience quality and delivery.
3. Message effectiveness.
4. Competitive presence, or "share of voice."
5. Audience behavior.
6. Sales opportunities.
7. Press impact.

per hour. Complex, technical products usually experience a lower rate than average. Exhibit Surveys finds an all-show national average of 10 visitors per sales person per hour.

Exhibit 11.2: Benchmarks and Industry Averages

2003 Specific Industry Averages

	HITECH	RETAIL	MED*	MFG/IND	2003 ALL-SHOW
AUDIENCE QUALITY INDICATORS					
Total Buying Plans	51%	63%	57%	46%	**54%**
Net Buying Influences	85%	89%	78%	83%	**83%**
Final Say	35%	53%	30%	36%	**39%**
Specify	29%	26%	25%	33%	**28%**
Recommend	58%	48%	60%	53%	**55%**
AUDIENCE ACTIVITY INDICATORS					
Avg. Hrs. Spent Visiting Exhibits	9.1	10.3	7.5	9.5	**8.9**
Avg. Days Spent Visiting Exhibits	2.2	2.2	2.63	2.1	**2.3**
% from Surrounding State	52%	41%	17%	44%	**38%**
Within 200 Miles	26%	39%	11%	29%	**23%**
Over 400 Miles	62%	56%	77%	55%	**64%**
First Time Attendees	35%	30%	21%	32%	**30%**
Previous Show Attendance	37%	45%	44%	35%	**40%**
Attend No Other Shows	39%	36%	31%	33%	**36%**c
Regular Attendee	29%	32%	32%	28%	**30%**
AIF*	--	--	--	--	**54%***
Traffic Density	2.4	1.4	1.7	2.1	**2.0**
EXHIBIT PERFORMANCE CHARACTERISTICS					
Exhibit Attraction	82%	78%	78%	78%	**79%**
Exhibit Efficiency	48%	43%	55%	44%	**47%**
SIR (Staff Interaction Rating)	55%	50%	65%	51%	**60%**
CVR - Exhibit Attraction CVR*	$118	$124	$129	$132	**$117**
CVR - Exhibit Efficiency CVR*	$218	$242	$201	$225	**$200**
Personnel Performance					
Excellent	23%	37%	35%	23%	**30%**
Very Good	34%	32%	36%	35%	**36%**
Good	33%	20%	29%	31%	**25%**
Fair	8%	9%	6%	8%	**7%**
Poor	3%	2%	3%	3%	**2%**
Too Crowded	14%	7%	7%	9%	**8%**
No One To Talk To	4%	2%	4%	3%	**4%**
Previous Personal Contact	26%	10%	12%	24%	**16%**
Visitor Quality					
Product Interest	82%	63%	85%	72%	**78%**
Buying Plans	39%	35%	50%	28%	**43%**
Buying Influences	79%	76%	77%	74%	**77%**
Memorability	90%	96%	83%	94%	**83%**

* - 3 year Avg
c - 51% with no answer

Source: Exhibit Surveys, Inc.

Post Mortem Meeting

Immediately on returning from the business event, it's a good idea to assemble the booth staff and key representatives from marketing functions for a post-mortem discussion. This can be done face-to-face, by teleconference, or by web conference. The key is that it takes place soon after your return, while the details are still fresh in people's minds. Topics to be covered in the meeting might include:

• Look at the results against stated goals.
• Review actual costs versus budget.
• Feedback from staff, customers, other exhibitors, and show management.
• Gather recommendations from the staff for future events.

Measurement Tools: Quantitative

The term "quantitative measurement tools" is used here to mean, essentially, surveys. In the world of trade shows and corporate events, surveys are in wide use for evaluating results. Even if you use lead production or sales revenue to measure ROI on a busines event, a survey will help you understand the reasons why the business event performed the way it did.

In quantitative measurements, a sample of the target audience is surveyed, and the results are projected to the whole. Where possible, the sample size is large enough to support a statistically reliable projection, but the acceptable confidence levels may vary with the importance of the subject being investigated. Purchase intent, for example, may demand a higher level of confidence—and thus a larger sample size and more expense—than questions about image or awareness.

Generally, exhibitors take advantage of three major types of surveys.

1. Pre-post show surveys.
2. Exit interviews or at-show surveys.
3. Post-show surveys.

PRE-POST SHOW SURVEYS

Often used to measure fairly fuzzy variables like brand awareness or perceived competitive positioning, pre-post surveys sample a group of attendees on their way into the exhibit hall at the beginning of the trade show, and then sample another batch as they are leaving the exhibit hall toward the end of the trade show. According to Ken Mortara, President of ShowValue, Inc., the objective with this kind of survey is to evaluate any changes in the perception of the attendees. "If we talk to them before and after, then we can reasonably conclude that the changes in perception came as a result of the investment the company made in exhibiting," says Mortara.

Pre-post surveys are effective in measuring such variables as:

- Brand awareness.
- Memorability or recall.
- Attitude or image.
- Message.
- New product awareness.
- Audience profile.

The trick in pre-post surveying is ensuring that the populations sampled in each segment are statistically similar. You have a number of options to consider for survey media—mail, phone, Internet, or personal interview at the trade show. Getting the help of a professional research organization is highly recommended.

EXIT INTERVIEWS AND AT-SHOW SURVEYS

To measure the immediate effectiveness of the booth and attendee experience there, an exit interview can be helpful, especially for exhibitors using a sizable booth footprint. An interviewer intercepts visitors on their way out of the booth, and requests that they answer some questions. Exit interviews can explore such questions as:

- What prompted you to visit the booth?
- Were you treated well by the staff?
- Did someone approach you right away?

- How useful was the product demo?
- Did you see more than one product during your visit?
- Were you able to find the information you needed?
- What message did you take away from the signage?
- As a result of your visit to the booth, how likely are you to add the company to your short list?
- Did the booth design evoke any particular emotion?
- Was the booth staff knowledgeable?

Exhibit 11.3: Example of Booth Exit Survey

Source: ShowValue, Inc. Reproduced with permission.

Check with your show organizer, since some trade shows require special permission to conduct exit interviews on the trade show floor. The surveys should be administered throughout the trade show, with the possible exception of the last day. The number of completed surveys required is a function of the size of the attendee population and the degree of confidence required.

One of the big advantages of the exit interview, when done early in the business event, is that it allows mid-course correction. For example, you can adjust your signage, or retrain your staff, in the midst of the trade show, in response to visitor feedback.

Surveys can also be given to visitors at the booth, using paper forms or PC-based survey tools. You can set up kiosks around the exhibit and invite visitors to swipe their badges, confirm the data that pops up, pose some qualifying questions, and ask a few survey questions about their experiences at the booth. When companies offer an incentive to complete the survey, some report a compliance rate as high as 50%.

POST-EVENT SURVEYS

Contacting a sample of attendees to ask questions about their experience is a standard method of evaluating trade show and corporate event results. Depending on your objectives, you may want to survey the entire attendee population, the people that visited your booth, or the group that participated in a certain activity at the business event. At a trade show, if you want to evaluate the quality of the attendance and the relevance of your exhibit to the trade show population, you will want to survey a random sample of all attendees, excluding exhibitors, students, staff, and press.

Surveys typically support the following objectives:

- Detailed reporting and benchmarking of the attendee profile.
- Feedback on your exhibit's ability to attract and communicate with high-potential prospects.
- Benchmark your performance against the competition.
- Document the value of your business event investment compared to competing options in the marketing mix.

Traditionally, the survey instrument was administered by phone, fax, or mail, and sometimes by personal interview. More recently, web-based surveys have become very popular due to their flexibility and relatively low cost. No matter what the medium, however, the challenge facing post-show surveys remains the response rate: it is increasingly difficult—and expensive—to recruit a large enough sample to complete the survey. Some researchers are also concerned about the bias that is introduced by low response rates: Trade show attendees who are willing to complete the survey may not be representative of the total population.

Ian Sequeira, Vice President of Exhibit Surveys, Inc., suggests that a mail sample of 1,000 to 1,500 attendees is likely to be sufficient to produce reliable result projections. In his experience, if you include a $1 incentive, a personal cover letter, and a postage-paid reply envelope, you can expect a 20–25% response rate to a mail survey of trade show attendees.

Internet samples can be larger, since they are cheaper to administer, but will likely result in survey response rates of around 10–15% of attendees.

Post-show surveys can be used to explore such issues as:

- Audience quality.
- Audience motivation for attending the trade show.
- Attendee activity at the trade show.
- Strengths and weaknesses of your exhibit, staff, design, signage.
- Competitive comparisons.
- Which products are most effective to exhibit or demonstrate.
- Effectiveness of promotions and premiums.
- Other trade shows attended.

Skip Cox, President of Exhibit Surveys, suggests that you will probably have to limit post-show surveys to the major trade shows in your calendar because of the investment required. He also suggests that you check with show management to find out what information they plan to provide relating to the details about the attendee population. No point in paying to collect data that someone else is already collecting.

Ken Mortara offers these tips for improving the effectiveness of your post-show surveys:

- The best time to administer the survey is within one week after the business event. Thereafter, you may want to conduct follow-up surveys at three months, six months, nine months, or 12 months, depending on the metric you seek to measure. For example, if you want to understand the memorability of your brand, you might survey at one week and then again at three months.
- Limit the questions to those relevant to your trade show objectives. The problem with research is that it tempts curiosity. Stick to the most important questions only.
- Design the questions so they are easy to answer. Use ranges for quantitative categories. Use multiple choice boxes, but don't offer too many options, or you will depress response.
- Provide an option in case none of the choices applies. For example, add "other" or "none" or invite write-in answers.
- Integrate your survey results with your other metrics, like contact and lead quality and quantity. Surveys can project purchase intent, for example, while lead management can measure actual revenue generation.

Skip Cox points out that the post-event survey can provide marketing with important additional insights into the "why" of event results. "If sales from events fall short of expectations, you have to decide whether the show should be dropped, the expenses reduced or the exhibit improved," he observes. "But to understand the root causes, you need more information. Was it a low attendance? The wrong audience? Was it your exhibit, or your staff, or lack of sales follow up?" A survey can help you understand these intermediary effects.

POST-EVENT LEAD SURVEY

Most companies focus on lead quality and quantity as measured by results, meaning the sales conversion factor. But in some cases, it makes sense to evaluate lead output using surveying methods, for

Exhibit 11.4: Sample Trade Show Report

Incremental Revenue Opportunity

54,000 Registered Visitors to SuperComm 2001

28,000 Non-Exhibiting Visitors

10,829 Aware of the XYZ Exhibit

6,336 Visited XYZ Theater or Demo

1,267 Qualified Prospects

177 (14%) intend to purchase from XYZ

Average Lead Amount = $118K

177 x $118,000 = $21 million
incremental revenue opportunity

The following points will further explain the inverted pyramid (or funnel) depicted above.

- The top level reflects the total number of registered visitors to Super-Comm 2001.
- Level two shows the numbers of potential business prospects who are non-exhibiting trade visitors.
- Level three was estimated and gathered from another independent survey and reflects the number of attendees who visited the XYZ exhibit.
- Level four is also estimated from that same independent survey and depicts the number of people who stopped at the XYZ Exhibit and were exposed to theater or solution stations.
- The fifth level shows the position of the 6,336 visitors who are classified as actual prospects in terms of being qualified by lead capture on site.
- The sixth level represents people in XYZ's post event survey who intend to purchase additional products, services, or solutions from XYZ as a result of their visit to XYZ's exhibit at SuperComm2001.
- The final amount is the incremental revenue opportunity for XYZ as a result of exhibiting at SuperComm2001. It is derived by multiplying the number of people determined in level six by $118,000, which is the average additional amount that the visitors said they intend to purchase.

In addition to the incremental revenue opportunity, described above, other incremental benefits stemming from XYZ's exhibit at SuperComm2001 were measured, but are more difficult to measure in terms of financial return. For example,

- 19% of the visitors to XYZ's exhibit reported, that as a result of their experience, they may purchase new XYZ technology that they currently do not have.
- 31% said that, as a result of their visit to XYZ's exhibit, they may include XYZ on their approved vendor list.

example, when the leads will be handed to a third-party distribution channel with little chance of reporting back, or when the sales cycle is so long that marketing cannot wait for true conversion results before planning for future business events. In such situations, you may want to evaluate the lead quality soon after the trade show. Note: this approach fulfills a purpose different from the did-you-buy survey described later in this chapter, which is a method for calculating sales lead revenue closed.

The Six Components of an Effective Business Event Measurement Strategy

Exhibit Surveys, Inc., advises its clients to design a business event measurement system that:

1. Measures the potential audience. Combine audience data from show management with exhibitor surveys to assess audience quality and quantity. This metric allows you to select the right trade show in the first place.
2. Profiles the potential audience. Analyze their demographics, needs, and motivations, so your marketing can be optimally effective.
3. Identifies the exhibit's performance. Evaluate all the tactical elements of the booth, including traffic flow, graphics, live theater, and staff, against the needs and expectations of visitors. This metric will ensure continuous improvement.
4. Assesses trade show performance against pre-defined objectives. The objectives must be specific and measurable.
5. Benchmarks the business event results. Compare results against previous trade shows or against competitors.
6. Keeps metrics consistent from trade show to trade show and over time, so you can monitor trends.

For a post-show lead survey, you may use mail or phone, but the Internet is likely to be most efficient as the survey medium. Your survey can explore such issues as:

- Perception of the company as a result of visiting your exhibit.
- Effectiveness of the exhibit experience (products, signage, staff, etc.).
- Impact of the exhibit on the purchase decision.
- Total lead potential at the show (how you did versus your competitors).
- Intention to buy.
- Standard qualification questions.

- Demographics.
- Quality of lead follow-up

Be sure you coordinate the survey sample with your lead qualification and nurturing plans. You don't want to annoy prospective customers by asking them the same questions twice. Neither do you want research to get in the way of sales strategies.

Measurement Tools: Qualitative

Qualitative metrics, while not projectible to the entire population, can be very valuable in assessing your performance. One word of caution: do what you can to manage the informal feedback loop. Too often, exhibitors rely on the impressionistic input of booth staff and senior management when assessing the value of the trade show. Such comments as "Booth was crowded," "Mostly junior people," and "Felt light to me" can do more harm than good.

Far stronger is analysis based on your trade show objectives. If qualitative tools are right for assessing one or more of your targeted objectives, then conduct the research accordingly. The best way to be sure you are approaching this objectively—and to gain additional credibility with the reporting—is to involve an independent third party in your qualitative research.

MYSTERY SHOPPING

One stratagem for analyzing your booth's effectiveness is to hire a professional evaluator to "mystery shop" your booth and assess the experience from the point of view of a customer or prospect. Many trade show consultants offer this service. John Guthrie, President of Guthrie & Company, provides a mystery shopping service he calls the "visual audit." Guthrie attends the trade show in the guise of a C-level executive or physician (he wryly notes that his graying temples lend credibility to the pose). He then rates the exhibitor with a ten-point scale on 14 specific criteria, such as the booth design, the signage, the integration of messages on and off the trade show floor, and the performance of the staff and the business partners. He takes discreet photos or videotapes to support his conclusions.

Guthrie argues that the best assessment of an exhibitor's effectiveness is based on the customer's point of view. "I am not there to critique the booth design per se," he notes. "I am looking at the brand experience. Where I see shortcomings, I also offer a set of recommendations. My objective is to help the exhibitor improve areas of weakness next time. It is a constant learning process."

One of Guthrie's recent cases involved a pharmaceutical company that was celebrating its 150th anniversary. Their intended key message for the trade show was about how innovative and technologically advanced a company they are. But as Guthrie visited the booth, he was struck by the focus the exhibit put on the company's history, and the past. It was a dignified, even clinical experience. Guthrie concluded that the company had a serious disconnect between its intended message and its execution.

According to Guthrie, there are two main benefits to the mystery shop approach to assessing trade show performance:

1. The trade show is a place where many marketing techniques come together. Sales, marketing, marketing communications, public relations are all involved. A holistic view of the customer experience is the best way to assess how the entire mix is working together.
2. With narrow target audiences like C-level executives or specific job functions, it can be expensive to find a large enough sample size to support a booth exit interview strategy. Furthermore, senior executives may be loath to take the time to answer questions.

STAFF FEEDBACK

The booth staff is your first line of customer contact, and a rich source of data about the quality of just about every conceivable variable. You should poll them for insights daily, and then again at the end of the trade show. Here are some of the questions that may be relevant:

- Rate the traffic quality and quantity.
- What products drew the most interest from visitors?
- What questions did you hear most often from visitors?
- Which key accounts came to the booth?
- What did you hear about the competition?
- What question was the hardest to answer?
- Which tools at the booth did you use the most?
- What was most and least helpful in the staff training and pre-show meeting?
- Did you see any notable "best practices" at other booths on the trade show floor?
- Should we exhibit at this trade show in the future?
- What should we do differently?

Results from staff feedback forms can be used for continuous improvement in the training, for data about the exhibit's effectiveness, and for making mid-course corrections in your marketing tactics during the trade show.

Mim Goldberg of Marketech suggests that you also conduct a post-show review with your vendors and contractors. "If you don't ask, they won't tell you anything, so ask them. They tend to see more than you do about what's working and what isn't."

KEY ACCOUNT OR KEY PROSPECT ANALYSIS

Doug MacLean of MacLean Marketing suggests that keeping track of key account attendance can be an important success metric, especially at trade shows where you expect a relatively high level of current customer attendance. MacLean recommends the following process:

- Make a list of key accounts, noting which were invited in advance by the sales team to visit the booth or attend a business event.
- Distribute the list to all company representatives at the trade show, both booth staff and others. Ask them to check off any who were engaged in conversation. Also, ask them to make

notes on the details, such as the customer status, impending activity, competitive influences, business conditions, upcoming changes in people or products, and interest in new products or upgrades.

- Review the results at daily staff meetings. You might want to keep a list that shows daily progress as customers are contacted at the trade show or corporate event. Review and distribute the ever-shorter list as the trade show progresses, so all staff members will know which key customers remain to be contacted, and will keep an eye out with increasing vigilance.
- Report on the results as part of the post-show reporting. For example, "We saw 16 of our 40 top accounts on the first day of the trade show," and "We learned they were interested in these products and those potential upgrades."

This process can also be applied to a list of key prospects targeted by the company. In both cases, you will improve results reporting by making more concrete what are otherwise fairly intangible customer conversations.

COMPETITIVE ANALYSIS

Assessing the presence of the competition is best approached qualitatively. Check the trade show guide to see who among your competitors is exhibiting, speaking, or sponsoring events. Assign competitive sleuthing duty to several of your booth staff and other company attendees, if possible. Provide them with a form to fill out that covers such items as:

- Booth size, location, features (e.g., live theater).
- Products and services featured, new products introduced.
- Key messaging.
- Number of demo stations.
- Booth staff: number, functional specialty (e.g., sales people versus technical people).
- Traffic levels.

- Visitor experience (booth staff attitude, attentiveness, knowledge level).
- Promotions, premiums, literature.
- Lead capture, qualification questions.
- Speaking engagements (take notes on what competitors say in their sessions).
- Sponsorships or other events (e.g., hospitality suite, party).
- Press mentions.
- Competitors who exhibited last year but not this year.

At the end of the trade show, include a competitive analysis as part of your results reporting.

Metrics

There are a number of approaches you can use to evaluate the best choices among results metrics. You should base your selection on the following criteria:

- What numbers are available, or can be generated economically.
- Whether the metrics are accepted as reasonable by senior management, especially financial management.
- Are the metrics similar to, or consistent with, those used to evaluate other marketing investments.

WHAT ITEMS TO INCLUDE IN PROGRAM COSTS

As a marketer, you are part of the chain that drives value for the firm. So, when you assess the value of the investment in an event, you must take the point of view of the shareholder. Not all relevant costs will necessarily live within your budgetary control. And some issues around accounting procedures will need to be addressed. One of the big questions that will arise is: what items should be included in evaluating program cost?

The optimal approach is to think about the expense to the firm on an incremental basis. If you had not done this event, would the company have incurred this cost? Here are some examples on how this might work in real life:

- You build a booth for $15,000 and expect it to last for five trade shows, with repairs and refurbishment costs of $5,000. So, each show would be assigned 1/5 of $20,000, or $4000 in booth costs. If the booth manages to limp along beyond the five trade shows, the additional trade shows would get a free ride, in terms of incremental booth expense assigned to their program costs.
- Five employees sign up to work the trade show, and they all pay their travel, hotel, and meal expenses out of their own T&E budgets. Those costs were incurred incrementally by the company, and must be added to the program cost. But what about their salaries? Some companies would argue that salaries are a fixed cost, and would have to be paid whether the employees worked the trade show or not. But, on an incremental basis, the time devoted to the business event took them away from other tasks, and should be included, if only on the basis of a rough estimate. By adding in a portion of such fixed costs, you get a more accurate comparison among business events that are more or less time intensive, as well. If, on the other hand, all your business events incur roughly the same time and overhead, then that item can be eliminated from consideration.
- What about an executive who attends the trade show as a speaker? From the incremental point of view, this item should be included in your program cost. The executive is representing your company, and composes part of the business event PR program—whether you arranged the speaking engagement or not. With luck, the engagement will also result in some sales leads passed back to marketing for qualification and follow-up.
- Allocating the expense of a creative department that develops event graphics and promotions can also be problematic, when the department handles a variety of marketing communications activities. But some allocation of that department's overhead, along with the direct fixed costs they incur, should be applied to your program.

COST PER LEAD

Cost per lead (CPL) is perhaps the most fundamental unit of trade show measurement. It is generated by dividing total program cost by the number of qualified leads generated. A few caveats are in order, however:

- Use the fully loaded program investment number as the numerator.
- Eliminate unqualified contacts from the denominator.
- Add in to the denominator the contacts that are still in the qualification and nurturing process but are expected to convert to qualified leads—in effect, the pipeline revenue generated from the event.

The main benefit of tracking cost per lead is the ability to analyze costs on a consistent basis over time, and to compare the value of competing marketing investments. For example, ranking the annual trade show calendar by cost-per-lead results can serve as a benchmark for making future event-selection decisions.

COST PER CONTACT

Another useful number is the cost per contact, which is generated by dividing the entire program investment by the gross number of contacts generated. Only a percentage of these contacts will convert to sales revenue, of course, but the others can be qualified, nurtured, and otherwise managed in the marketing database.

Cost per contact becomes an important benchmark for evaluating competing marketing investments, especially within the business event category. However, cost per contact can be dangerous if used on its own to evaluate the relative value of a business event. Better to combine it with an additional metric that emerges later in the selling process, like cost per qualified lead or ROI. If left to stand on its own, the cost-per-contact metric can encourage such questionable trade show marketing practices as fish bowls and contests, where marketers slavishly attempt to gather gross quantities of names, instead of focusing on quality .

Some exhibitors use cost per visitor reached, meaning the program cost divided by the number of potential prospects who visited your booth. According Exhibit Surveys, the national industry average for cost per visitor attracted is $116 and the cost per visitor reached, based on having had a meaningful face-to-face interaction at the exhibit, is $208.

CASE STUDY

Custom Metrics

Consider the value of developing metrics specific to your company's particular market and sales cycles. Bob Burk is Marketing Communications Manager for King Industries, Inc., a specialty chemical manufacturer in Norwalk, Connecticut. Bob is a certified trade show marketer (CTSM), with over 15 years of experience. King's sales cycle can be as long as five years, from the initial contact through laboratory and field testing to developing the product approved for a customer's specific formulation. As a result, Burk has developed a set of trade show metrics that are specific to King's marketing objectives and Burk's constant struggle for program efficiency. Over time, and across shows, Burk tracks the following:

- Leads per product line. King Industries typically features one or two product lines at any given trade show, and they find that a featured product line will result in five to ten times the interest of a non-promoted line. This metric allows Burk to analyze the relative value of the additional promotional investment.
- Leads per hour. Breaking out lead flow by hour helps Burk figure out his most efficient staffing schedule.
- Leads by prospect type. A somewhat subjective metric, this allows Burk to sort leads by quality and analyze his lead results in more depth.
- Sample requests. As a custom chemical supplier, King knows its prospects are serious about buying when they request a product sample for testing in their labs

and in the field. A sample request initiates, in effect, the first stage of King's sales cycle.

EXPENSE TO REVENUE RATIO (E:R)

Dividing the total revenue associated with the business event by the total expense incurred is a standard marketing communications metric in business marketing. The benefit of using E:R is that it makes the relative cost of the marketing communications tactic easy to compare with other tactics of its sort. The company might impose a maximum E:R threshold—2.5%, or 6%—for example, to establish control of marketing communications expense.

The reason E:R has come into wide use in business marketing situations is that business-to-business revenues tend to be very high compared to a single marketing tactic, thus making ROI calculations faintly ridiculous. Furthermore, most business-to-business revenues result from multiple sales and marketing investments, so claiming an ROI on any one "touch" is risky and inaccurate. E:R makes no such claim.

ACTIVITY-BASED METRICS

When sales results are too difficult to get, some marketers retreat to a set of metrics that are fully under their control, most of which can be characterized as based on marketing activity, rather than sales results. These include such indicators as:

- Number of visitors to the booth, year on year.
- Booth visitors by target (penetration of certain accounts, industry breakdown, etc.).
- Number of qualified leads.
- Number of sales appointments confirmed.
- Number of credit applications or RFPs received.
- Lead quality mix (percent of A, B, C, etc.).
- Lead mix by geography, or by product interest.
- Lead mix by day or hour of the show.

- Cost per qualified lead.
- Cost per contact added to the database.
- Cost per demo given, or live presentation viewed.
- Cost per visitor reached (people who passed the booth).
- Cost per current customer met.
- Qualification rate.
- Actual costs versus budget.
- Whether the exhibit arrived and was set up on time.

Activity-based metrics can be helpful in keeping marketing communications programs on track, year after year. Keep a record of the categories that interest you, and review the trends annually, trade show by trade show, or corporate event by corporate event. Select the categories that are the most powerful indicators of a prospective sale for your company. But don't track too many items—keep it to a maximum of three that you will benchmark. Some of these, like cost per lead, can also be helpful in comparing trade show activity to other marketing communications options. What is the cost of a demo at a trade show, versus the cost of giving a demo in the field, for example?

As to the pros and cons of activity-based metrics, some trade show experts believe that it is unreasonable for a business event marketer to be responsible for sales results. Marketing activity, they say, should be evaluated based on elements within the marketers' control. Allen Reichard, a thought leader in trade show marketing strategy, and now a vice president at The Freeman Companies, endorses this approach. "Financial measures like ROI are impossible for trade show marketers to deliver," says Reichard. "When they

Using a Key Code to Measure the Effectiveness of Pre-Show Promotions

Pre-show promotions are most easily measured if they are set up as direct response communications. All you need is a key code, a response device, and a reason the prospect should act. Once the prospect takes the action, the key code is collected from the response device and the results can then be analyzed.

A common pre-show direct response strategy involves:

- An outbound direct mail piece as the communication.
- A puzzle piece, treasure chest key, or the letter itself as the reply device and key code.
- An offer of a free premium waiting for you at the booth as a reason to act.
- Respondents who come to the booth with the response device are then analyzed for response rate and quality.

Without a key code, the best method for analyzing the results is data matchback. Compare the contacts collected at the booth to the original pre-show mailing, either on an individual contact level or on a company or site level, and infer that the pre-show mailing was a factor in the attendee's decision to visit your booth.

have no control over how their activities eventually result in sales dollars, marketers simply cannot be judged on sales results of the event. Instead, marketers should set measurable objectives that are under their purview—number of leads, quality of leads—and report based on those objectives."

This is a compelling argument, and makes sense when it comes to the performance measures by which, say, an exhibit manager will be evaluated. However, a marketing manager who is clearly in a sales support role cannot survive for long without a clear connection to sales results. Marketing management must have the ability to report on a program ROI in order to select among competing investment options and serve the shareholders wisely.

One final note: when the exhibit situation allows business to be transacted on the trade show floor, sales metrics are easier to assess. But be sure you add to the revenue from orders written at the trade show an estimate of future pipeline revenue expected from the sales leads that were not closed on the spot. This will give you a more accurate picture of your results.

CASE STUDY

King Industries Case: Analyzing the Results of Trade Show Promotions

Since promotions represent a discrete set of investments within your trade show budget, you may want to analyze them on their own merits. Bob Burk, of the chemical additives manufacturer King Industries, shares the results of his promotional expenses for the 1997 International Coating Exposition, where King was featuring a product line for urethanes called K-KAT Catalysts. From the pre-show attendee list, Burk selected those who would likely be interested in this product, and added to them names from King's house database of past visitors, for a total of 1,500 mailers. The offer invited visitors to the King booth to enter a contest with a $1,000 grand prize. Burk received a 42% response to the mailing, including responses received both before the trade show and at the booth. He also tracked sample requests for the K-KAT product at the same trade show over three years, with satisfying results. Finally, Burk analyzed the cost per show contact versus inquiries generated through trade publication advertising. Note: Burk analyzes the pre-show campaign on a variable basis, including only the cost of the direct mail promotion and prizes, not the total cost to exhibit.

Exhibit 11.5 Analysis of a Pre-Show Campaign

Promotion	Costs
Printing 1,500 pieces	$725
Postage	$480
List rental	$300
Grand prize	$1,000
100 consolation prizes	$987
Total	$3,492
Promotion Responses	**Results**
Responses prior to show	99
Responses at show	533
Total promotion response	632
Total response rate	42%
Promotional cost per lead	$5.53
Product Sample Requests	**Number of Requests**
1997 ICE show	109
1996 ICE show	14
1995 ICE show	3
Comparison to Trade Ad	**Trade Ad Results**
Average cost for ad	$2,735
Average inquiries	37
Average cost per inquiry	$73.92

BUSINESS EVENT ROI

Ultimately, business event marketers must demonstrate a return on their marketing investments. This means a financial return, either in sales revenue or cost savings. The return on the investment is calculated by subtracting the incremental expense from the incremental variable revenue that was driven by the marketing program, then that number is divided by the expense itself. The result is expressed as a percent. A zero indicates a program that broke even, and a negative number means a loss on the investment. If you spend $1 million to generate $1.2 million in new margin, you've achieved a 20% ROI.

$$ROI = \frac{\text{Gross margin} - \text{Expense}}{\text{Expense}}$$

Why use margin versus revenue: because margin represents the true contribution to overhead that was generated by the incremental marketing activity. Using gross sales overstates the benefit that the marketing activity generated, and also disguises any unprofitable sales transactions that may have resulted. Marketers should use the gross margins on the sales, that is, subtracting out the variable cost of goods sold and the direct cost of sales.

Is the gross margin the number that results from the initial transaction? No, it should reflect all the incremental margins generated from that investment. So, if as a result of your trade show marketing activity, you acquire a new account, then all margins accruing from that new account need to be added in. Margins that will accrue in the future must be discounted back to today's dollars, to recognize the time value of money. In other words, the term "gross margin" here represents the lifetime value of the new account to your firm.

Jim Lenskold, author of *Marketing ROI*, encourages marketers to look beyond the initial sale, and capture the full increase in customer value that is generated from the customer relationship. The incremental customer value consists of the present value of the future profit stream—the monthly profits less expenses, discounted to reflect the time-value of the cash flow—that result from acquiring, cross-selling, or retaining customers. This number will be a projection, and thus introduces some uncertainty. But it will be a more accurate portrayal of the pay-off to the company than the margins from the first transaction from the customer. As Lenskold observes, "To truly assess event marketing, it is critical that the marketing impact be tracked all the way through the sales cycle and include an estimated profit value for new business generated. Where business event marketing is a key component of a larger campaign, ROI should be measured across the entire campaign with some analysis in place to determine the degree to which each channel contributes."

Exhibit 11.6: Costs and Results Metrics from a Hypothetical Manufacturer's Trade Show Program

Metrics	Costs & Results
Event costs, fully loaded	$500,000
Qualified leads generated	200
Cost per lead ($500k / 200)	$2,500
Lead-to-sales conversion rate	40%
Leads converting to sales (200 x .40)	80
Average order size (or average incremental revenue)	$100,000
Cost per sale ($2,500 / .40, or $500,000 / 80)	$6,250
Sales revenue (80 x $100k)	$8 million
Gross margin rate	45%
Gross margin on the event revenue ($8 million x .45)	$3.6 million
E:R ($500k / $8 million)	6.25%
ROI ([$3.6 million–$500k] / $500k)	620%

A simpler approach to ROI metrics is often used in the world of trade shows. In this approach, the numerator is sales revenue resulting from the trade show, and the denominator is the total trade show expense, meaning all variable costs, including staff T&E, but not staff salaries. The resulting number is expressed in dollars, and represents the number of gross dollars returned for every incremental dollar invested. Essentially, this metric expresses E:R upside down. Marc Goldberg of Marketech advises his clients to look for a 10:1 objective, meaning that you seek to generate 10 revenue dollars for each dollar invested in trade show marketing. He also points out that the objective will vary from company to company. Consult with your colleagues in finance to arrive at the right target number for your marketing activities.

This approach to ROI is relatively simple to calculate, which is a benefit. However, it overstates the value of the revenue to the company, and fails to express profitability.

Exhibit 11.7: Post-Event Expertise to Revenue Analysis

2001 NSSEA Ed Expo Show Summary
March 15 - 17, 200
New Orleans, LA

Booth Staff: jane quinn

Booth Size: 10 x 10

Costs:

Booth Space	$1,075.00	
Booth Furnishings	$613.82	
Electricity	$62.94	
Cleaning	$0.00	(included in furnishings)
Drayage	$89.76	
Carpet	$0.00	(included in furnishings)
Travel	$1,016.74	
Travel	$0.00	
TOTAL	**$2,858.26**	

Orders:

New Customers	$2,410.70	9	orders
Current Customers	$10,253.92	23	orders
TOTAL	**$12,664.62**	32	orders

ROI: **$4.43**

Recommend for 2003

Exhibit?	yes
Booth Space	10 x 10
Personnel	1 Sales Manager

Additional Comments:
Very busy, makes day go quickly
Must have a separate promo for show

This company generated $4.43 in revenues for every dollar invested in its activity at an educational products show.

Source: Exhibit Surveys, Inc. Reproduced with permission.

Tracking Leads to Closure

If you buy the argument that marketing must take responsibility for tracking, analysis, and reporting of sales results from the leads they generate, then you must select among the options available to marketers for tracking leads to closure. There are several methods available. Each has its strengths and weaknesses. None is perfect, but each has its best applications, and some can be successfully applied in combination.

CLOSED LOOP SYSTEMS

A closed loop system strives to track each lead to closure, either by hand, or using software that aids in the tracking. Such systems require that the sales person working the lead periodically report on the lead status, such as rejected, lost to competition, or closed. Marketers may need to hound the reps, or build in management systems that motivate them, to take the time out of their sales activities to update the records.

Closed loop systems are best applied in high-ticket, relatively low volume environments, where the expense of tracking each lead from generation to closure can be justified. They are most successful when actively supported by senior management, which can influence all parties to make the system work. A closed loop system is extremely difficult to put in place when a third-party distribution channel is involved.

Such systems tend to under-report sales conversion, however, since inevitably reporting on some leads will fall through the cracks. And they need to be supplemented if you want to track external factors, such as sales lost to the competition, or the relative contribution of the business event to the sales process. The closed loop system benefits both sales and marketing, offering a fairly reliable pipeline

---

What to Do with Contacts Generated Elsewhere than the Trade Show Booth?

An integrated trade show strategy is likely to result in contacts and leads generated elsewhere than the booth. Your company representatives may be collecting contact data at speaking engagements, entertainment, off-site meetings, hotel bars, parties, outings—wherever there is interaction with attendees. The best way to handle these contacts is to pull them into the same data capture process you are using at the booth. If you are using a paper-based lead form, you might ask all your company representatives to carry the forms around during the day and evening, so they can both gather the data and include answers to the qualifying questions. If they balk, at least ask them to pass along the business cards they collect, so you can include these prospects in the show follow-up and the metrics.

analytic tool for sales forecasting, and detailed insight into marketing campaign effectiveness.

DID-YOU-BUY SURVEYS

Regular surveys of a sampling of qualified leads from your business event is often the most reliable, and least expensive, method for assessing the revenue results of the program. You can conduct the survey via any number of media, whether mail, phone, email, or face-to-face contact. A statistically reliable sample size can then be projected to the whole, allowing you to claim, legitimately, the resulting revenue as having been generated from your business event.

You may want to conduct separate surveys by product segment. If you mix high-end and low-cost products together, the results may be skewed. You may further decide to separate surveys by lead quality, with separate samples for A, B, and C leads. Include a sample of nurturing and abandoned contacts.

One tricky issue is how long to wait before conducting the did-you-buy survey. Ideally, you should wait until the sales cycle is likely to be complete. But, with a very long sales cycle, you may not want to wait before planning your future events. So, if you need information earlier, you can conduct multiple surveys at intervals and get an interim sense of lead quality.

Your response rate and quality will improve if you keep the survey "blind," by not identifying your company. Keep the survey short—avoid the temptation to throw in market research questions. Also, tabulate the results, especially from a small sample, using a median instead of an average. In either case, throw out "outliers" that will skew your results.

Here are some of the questions to include in the survey.

The Marketing Database

A critically important tool in event metrics is the marketing database, where customer and prospect records are maintained and analyzed. Clean, accessible data is the lynchpin that holds together everything from pre-show promotions to lead tracking and results reporting. Ideally, the marketing database is supported by the IT department, but managed within marketing or marketing operations. Business data tends to degrade quickly, at a rate of 3–4% per month, so be sure you have regular hygiene processes in place to maintain its quality. Some companies prefer to maintain a prospecting database separate from their customer database, for easier management of inquiries and leads as they move through the qualification, nurturing, and sales conversion process.

- Did you buy the product since attending the business event?
- From whom?
- Why did you buy (price, features, relationship, etc.)?
- What marketing and sales contacts factored in your decision (sales calls before the trade show, visiting the booth, other companies' booths, sales calls after the event, etc.)?
- Did you receive a follow-up communication from an exhibiting company after the business event?
- If you didn't buy, are you still in the market?

The key advantage of did-you-buy surveys, beyond their low cost, is that they provide a sense of competitive purchases, and they can give you insight into the impact of various marketing and sales touch points. But there are two potential problems with the method. First, surveys offer the potential to overstate the role of a single marketing event. Most business purchases are made after a number of interactions. And you don't want to imply to the sales team that your marketing event was the sole driver of the revenue. One way to avoid this problem is to adopt a term from basketball, and report the event's contribution as an "assist."

The other problem with surveys is that they can annoy customers, if overdone. It can be risky to conduct a did-you-buy survey after every business event. One solution is to schedule surveys at regular intervals, semi-annually or quarterly, and include samples from several marketing events at the same time.

TRADE SHOW SPECIALS

When you make an exclusive offer at a business event, all sales closed on those terms can reasonably be credited to the business event. So, trade show specials can become a convenient way to track revenue without expensive closed loop processes.

DATA MATCHBACK

Data matchback is a low-cost and low-effort method that can be used as often as you like to assess the sales associated with a business event. Wait for the period of a typical sales cycle to elapse, and then analyze sales into all the accounts for which leads were generated at the business event. The one caveat with data matchback is that it may overstate the impact of the business event itself. Certainly, any sales person will resent the claim that all sales into the account in the period after the business event be credited to the business event. But if you report the results with care, data matchback can serve you well.

Outsource Versus Do-It-Yourself Metrics

Some metrics are best collected and analyzed internally, among them closed loop systems, special offers, and data matchback. Methods involving surveys can also be handled in-house, at low cost, especially if you use one of the Internet-based tools available. Consider including a small incentive to increase response and keep the number of questions small.

However, when metrics involve surveys of customers and prospects, a good argument can be made for outsourcing the collection process. Among the reasons for outsourcing are:

- Objectivity. You don't want to be open to accusations of bias or self-interest.
- Professional skill. No sense in collecting faulty data. Worse yet is making decisions based on faulty metrics.
- Getting it done. You have plenty to do with your day job.

Some elements of the measurement toolkit are particularly well suited to outsourcing, among them:

- Booth exit interviews.
- Mystery shopping.
- Pre and post surveys.
- Did-you-buy surveys.

Mike Hamilton, President of Synchronicity, a business event marketing firm, makes a powerful case for outsourcing your survey work. "People are more likely to be truthful if they are asked for their opinions by a third party. When you ask on your own, they are probably going to pull their punches. If you decide to conduct the survey yourself, I recommend that you disguise its origin. Use a dummy post office box, or URL, and pose as a third party. You'll get better answers, and a higher response."

Measuring PR Effectiveness

While the benefit of publicity is that it's relatively inexpensive and delivers a nice dose of credibility, the problem with publicity is that it's hard to control and harder to measure. If you have invested in media relations—created press materials, set up press appointments, arranged for speaking engagements—your results will come primarily in the form of editorial coverage. There may be some fringe benefits in terms of good will and potential future press mentions, but these are nearly impossible to tie back to the trade show-related PR activity.

But all is not lost. First, compare your results to your objectives. Did you get the number of mentions you sought? Were the stories in the publications you targeted?

To answer these questions, you will count and evaluate the press mentions that result from your releases, kits, and meetings. You can tackle this informally, keeping an eye on the articles written by the journalists attending the trade show, or you can hire a clipping service or a PR agency to keep track for you.

In order to put a concrete value on the press mentions your activities garnered, you may calculate their dollar value. There are two general approaches to deriving a dollar value of editorial coverage:

1. Advertising equivalence: the value of the total column inches of the mention if it were paid ad space. This approach can apply to print advertising or to banner advertising for web-based articles. Barbara Axelson of Axelson Communications argues that editorial is in fact more valuable than paid advertising, so she recommends that you calculate the value of column inches at three times the ad rate.

2. Cost per reader: divide by the total cost of the show by a multiple of the number of press mentions times the publication's readership.

Like other business event-related marketing efforts, PR results metrics can be approached by a combination of activity-based and results-based strategies:

Activity based:

- Number of press meetings.
- Number of press kits distributed.

Results based:

- Number of articles generated.
- Number of company mentions in the articles.
- Quality of mentions—did they communicate your key messages or discuss your featured products?
- Favorable, unfavorable, and neutral mentions.
- Ad equivalent value.
- Cost per reader.

Another strategy in assessing the value of your PR investment is to analyze the quality as well as the quantity of the press mentions. This approach involves ranking the mentions by their influence on business buyers. For example, a cover story would be more valuable than a feature, a feature would be more valuable than an industry round-up, and so forth. A national business magazine would rank higher than a regional magazine. A cover blurb on a trade publication increases the power of the article inside. A targeted readership trumps a general circulation.

You can also take the approach that your PR is a competitive weapon, and analyze your press mentions in the context of how well you did in the press compared to your competition. This approach is time consuming and expensive if you hire a clipping service to assist. See Exhibit 11.8 for an example.

Chet Dalzell of Harte-Hanks offers another perspective on measuring the value of your PR program. Perhaps more important

Exhibit 11.8: Press Analysis

MEASUREMENT REPORT   INDUSTRY TRADE SHOW

PRINT AND MEDIA COVERAGE	XYZ	Cisco	Lucent	Nortel	Alcatel
High Circulation	2	8	8	5	7
Med Circulation	2	19	18	14	2
Low Circulation	1	20	13	16	7
Business Articles	1	2	4	1	2
General Articles	2	16	16	11	7
Specialist Articles	2	18	13	16	6
Technical Articles	0	11	6	7	1
Positive Tone	2	3	4	2	1
Neutral Tone	3	40	25	26	15
Negative Tone	0	4	11	7	0
High Mention	1	5	17	4	5
Med Mention	0	11	10	9	6
Low Mention	4	31	12	22	5
Front Position	0	4	3	4	2
Middle Position	5	36	34	29	13
Back Position	0	7	2	2	0
Headlines	3	5	13	7	3
Records	3	47	39	35	15

Print and broadcast media were monitored worldwide, two weeks prior to the event, during the week of the event and two weeks after the event. Included were all media that had mention of SuperComm 2001 and XYZ as well as its competitors. The resulting numbers were classified by circulation, type of article, positive/neutral/negative tone, extent of mention, position of mention within the article and whether the vendors' name was mentioned in the headline. The table to the right provides the details:

XYZ's participation at SuperComm 2001 was covered in five print articles. Of these five articles, three included mention of XYZ in the headline, two were in high circulation publications and two provided positive coverage of XYZ (one was neutral). New products covered in the articles included Product #1 and Product #2, Product #3, Product #4, and Product #5. Favorable coverage included an interview with XYZ's CEO that addressed the company's future financial outlook. Relative to competitors, XYZ was covered in fewer articles, but with comparatively better placement, higher circulation and more favorable treatment.

Source: ShowValue, Inc. Reproduced with permission.

than the tangible results like quantity and quality of press mentions are the intangibles, like the relationships fostered with the press. "Face-to-face time with reporters has a longer-term payout," says Dalzell. "I gain a lot when I can pick up the phone and talk to a reporter who knows who I am. It's hard to quantify, but the number of conversations and interactions with journalists at the event has value in itself."

Measuring the Results of Corporate Events

Most of the strategies and methods described in this chapter apply to measuring the effectiveness of corporate events as well as trade shows. The metrics should emerge from the objectives set for the corporate event. Companies are likely to select from the following metrics:

- Attendance growth. Not only registrations but also verified attendance. This metric applies only to corporate events that are repeated regularly, versus one-off corporate events. If customers are clamoring to get into your user group meetings, that's a good sign. This can also be measured by the length of time customers are willing to spend at your corporate event.
- Growth of sponsors and partners, as measured by dollars invested, or number of participants.
- Retention rates, or repeat attendance, on the part of customers and partners.
- Leads generated, and resulting revenue.
- Attitudinal shift among attendees.
- Press coverage.

Perhaps the most widely used tool in corporate events is the post-event survey, administered to attendees on site at the end of the corporate event, or by follow-up communication. Surveys typically ask for feedback on the following:

- The content and delivery of information at sessions.
- The food, hotel facilities, and amenities.
- The keynote speakers.
- Would you recommend the corporate event to a colleague?

In a complex sales environment, you may need to set up a series of surveys that measure the prospect's movement through the buying process. Mike Hamilton of Synchronicity describes a program he put in place for a medical supplies company whose surgical instrument sales are strongly influenced by doctors and nurses. Hamilton operates a series of trade shows, seminars, and road shows intended to demonstrate the superiority of his client's products. After the business event, he administers a survey to visitors asking about their intent to test the instruments. After the test, he conducts a mail survey asking whether the clinician will recommend the product to the hospital administrator who makes the final purchase decision. Finally, he conducts a did-you-buy survey among administrators. "It sounds obvious," says Hamilton, "But the best strategy for evaluating event results is to know your audience and know what you want to get out of the event."

Results Reporting

Business event results should be reported the same way that any marketing tactic is evaluated. Reporting can be specific to the business event itself, or as part of the period (quarterly, semi-annually, annually). A report will accomplish two objectives: 1) it will assess the ROI of the business event itself, and 2) it will serve as a record for future marketers in your company to consult for benchmarks and trends.

A thorough report will include the following elements:

- Statement of business event objectives and metrics.
- Business event budget.
- Review of tactical programs, such as pre-show promotions, booth size, key messages, ancillary events, post-show follow-up, etc.
- Review of measurement tactics, such as lead analysis and surveys.
- Feedback from booth staff.
- Competitive activity analysis.
- Sessions attended or educational activity.
- Results against objectives, including event ROI.
- Recommendations for future programs.

In terms of lead reporting, it's a good idea to expand the detail beyond number of qualified leads and cost per qualified lead, to include a breakout of such details as:

- Titles and job functions.
- Percentage who plan to buy immediately, in three months, six months, nine months, or a year.
- Percentage who have budget, and how large is the budget.

This kind of detail will provide insight into the quality of the business event and your ability to attract the right people.

Case Studies

Case Study Index

- ☐ AIRxpert Systems
- ☐ Apple Rubber Products
- ☐ The Broadmoor Hotel
- ☐ CAS
- ☐ Hubert Company
- ☐ Lake Group Media
- ☐ MTS Systems Corp.
- ☐ Saab Aircraft
- ☐ Woolpert
- ☐ XMPie

AIRXPERT SYSTEMS:
LEVERAGING PR FOR A LARGER SPLASH

Summary: *A ventilation monitoring systems company worked in partnership with the convention center and sponsoring organization at its largest industry conference to measure the air quality in the exhibit hall. The results were picked up by the industry trades, making the company one of the central stories in the coverage of the trade show.*

As part of the launch plan for its main product, a system that monitors ventilation system performance in large buildings, AIRxpert Systems, Inc. (www.airxpert.com), started exhibiting at the annual Greenbuild Conference sponsored by the U.S. Green Building Council (USGBC). In the world of building design and operations these days, the trends of "green" and "sustainable design" are hot, so a solution that helps measure building air quality can generate considerable buzz. Steve Wallis, president and founder of AIRxpert, recognized that with a cleverly crafted PR plan he could extend the power of his 10 × 10 exhibit.

AIRxpert's first year of participation was in November 2002, when the show took place in Austin, Texas. The prior June, Wallis approached senior management at the new Austin convention center and offered to provide a free assessment of the air quality during the trade show.

Convention center management declined, possibly out of fear that the results might be unflattering. At the show, Wallis went ahead informally and set up a ventilation monitoring demonstration in the aisles surrounding his booth. The results were dramatic. At first, the data showed relatively poor ventilation in the exhibit hall. So Wallis called the building engineers and suggested that they adjust the ventilation system controls to bring in more outside air. Within minutes, he and his technical staff could feel the difference—better circulation, and fresher air for attendees to breathe.

"I can't say that fresher air necessarily improves productivity," observes Wallis. "But it certainly provides a better customer experience in the exhibit hall. We tracked the air quality for the rest of the week of the show, and it stayed nice and high."

Wallis wrote up the data about the Austin experience, and it was published in an environmental trade publication, "Environmental Business News," two months later. The article had an immediate impact. As planning began for the next year's show, Wallis learned that the show sponsors had decided to make their convention city selection based on the "green" factor in the convention center and the surrounding hotels. Not surprisingly, the USGBC responded favorably to AIRxpert's offer to provide monitoring services at the trade show. When Pittsburgh won the contract for the November 2003 event, their trade show services company, Stetson Convention Services, was instructed to support the temporary installation of the AIRxpert system in the hall.

AIRxpert recorded three fundamental air quality indicators—carbon dioxide, carbon monoxide, and humidity levels—throughout the Pittsburgh trade show. Fortunately for the conference center, the results came out positive. Except for temporary elevations of carbon monoxide concentrations associated with forklift trucks that were moving display crates around the hall on the day before the trade show, the air quality inside the hall was similar to outside—the objective of a good ventilation system.

AIRxpert produced a white paper recording the Pittsburgh results, and submitted it to publications in the environmental and building trades. The fact that a trade show focusing on environmentally friendly buildings is dedicated to providing a "green" atmosphere at its own business events is a story that is likely to appeal to journalists. By harnessing the overlap between his product and the trade show's theme, and cooperating with the show sponsor and trade show services provider, Wallis was able to expand his presence at a key industry show, at minor additional cost. In 2004, he plans to provide the same services—and get even more publicity—at the trade show in Portland, Oregon.

APPLE RUBBER PRODUCTS: HOW A HOSPITALITY SPONSORSHIP CAN POSITION A SMALL COMPANY AS A BIG ONE

Summary: *A small manufacturer created a huge presence at a trade show attended by its key target audience by sponsoring a refreshments area, and using the personal contact to begin a business relationship with a large number of qualified prospects.*

Apple Rubber Products, Inc. (www.applerubber.com) makes O-rings and seals for OEM companies large and small. A $25 million privately held outfit near Buffalo, New York, Apple Rubber distributes directly using inbound and outbound telephone sales. It's a fairly technical sales process, since their customers—design and mechanical engineers in all kinds of industries—need parts designed to their particular specifications.

In 1989, Apple Rubber began exhibiting at trade shows, and, in short order, this channel became the company's primary source of new business. Over the years, the company has tried all kinds of venues, from national engineering events to regional conferences, typically exhibiting with a 10 × 10 booth. But it wasn't until they hit on the idea of sponsoring a hospitality space at the leading national engineering show that Apple Rubber's event strategy really paid off big.

Lynne Parry, Show Manager, runs the trade show function for Apple Rubber single-handedly. She sets the show calendar (14 a year), sends out the pre-show promotions, handles all the booth logistics, and mans the booth herself. Parry quickly became a trade show maven, grew active in the trade show industry affairs, and eventually served as board chair of the Trade Show Exhibitors Association (TSEA). Parry also earned two exhibition management certifications, the CME (Certified Manager of Exhibits), which is conferred by the TSEA, and the CTSM (Certified Trade Show Marketer), conferred by the Exhibitor Show.

Parry's major event for Apple Rubber was the National Design Engineering Show (NDES), a Reed Expo event at Chicago's McCormick Place every February. This trade show attracted a qualified audience for Apple Rubber—24,000 engineers in Chicago as part of Manufacturing Week. But Parry was concerned that she'd have a tough time doing all the business she wanted with a 300-square foot presence on the trade show floor. So in 1991, Parry decided to sponsor a 40 × 60 foot hospitality area that Reed managed, where coffee and doughnuts were available to attendees.

"The first year was a bit of a disaster," reminisces Parry. "They were always running out of food, the signage was pathetic, and no one was effectively monitoring the entrance to the hospitality area. There were as many exhibitors as attendees in there drinking the coffee—at $25.00 a gallon. So, the following year, we stepped up, and not only sponsored the area, but managed it as well."

Parry christened the space the "Engineers' Club," and organized the refreshments to arrive in batches throughout the day. She also managed the entrance to the space, ensuring that visitors were qualified, and that exhibitor entry was limited to those exhibitors who were Apple Rubber customers and prospects. The new hospitality space was an immediate hit. And in the ensuing years, Apple Rubber became associated in the attendees' minds with this friendly, warm environment. "We always run across engineers at other shows, or over the phone, who thank us for the free coffee. The sponsorship made us look like a big company—although we knew we were relatively small."

In consideration of the $37,000 sponsorship, Reed included Apple's eye-catching logo (a bright red apple) on all trade show promotions, including the VIP tickets, the show preview notices, the attendee recruitment mailings, the badge mailing, and, of course, the conference program and directory, for a total of 1.4 million impressions.

Sales results were impressive. From the 1992 experience, Apple generated $258,000 is sales from leads generated, and by 1994, seven of the top trade show prospects had become Apple buyers.

The Engineers' Club sponsorship was a hit with Apple Rubber customers as well as prospects. "We don't have any sales force actually calling on our current customers," notes Parry. "That's why shows are so important to us—they give us a chance to see our regular buyers face to face. I would invite 1,500 customers to visit us at the National Design Engineering Show, and was happy to be able to offer them a cup of coffee and a doughnut in such a nice space."

Over the years, Parry's sponsorship took on a life of its own. "We kept asking Reed for more. One year we'd add big signs. Then the next, we'd get both signs and big banners. Once I distributed 70,000 bags. One year I pinned a button on all Club visitors and asked them to wear it around all day. Most of them did! It was great exposure for us."

Some of the lessons Parry learned through the experience at NDES:

- Don't just sit back and assume the fact of sponsorship will be all the work you have to do. Parry did all the right marketing moves to make her hospitality spot a success. She created an appealing name for the space. She promoted it to customers and prospects.

Exhibit 12.1: The Engineer's Club

Source: Apple Rubber Products. Reproduced with the permission of Lynne Parry, CTSM, CME.

She managed the logistics carefully. And she worked the space the same way she would a booth: collecting names, qualifying prospects, and beginning an ongoing business relationship.

- Reduce your presence when the trade show stops working for you. After about 12 years, the trade show had declined in productivity for Apple Rubber. Parry now focuses on niche shows, like those catering to the medical industry. "Don't dwell in the past. Every show has a life cycle. Keep moving forward."

THE BROADMOOR HOTEL: TECHNOLOGY FOR DATA CAPTURE AND FOLLOW-UP

Summary: *The Broadmoor Hotel marketing team applied online contact capture and email communications technology to add leverage to its modest booth at a highly targeted trade show for meeting planners, resulting in sales and sales leads that far exceed its objectives.*

The Broadmoor Hotel (*www.broadmoor.com*) is a five-star, five-diamond, year-round golf resort in Colorado Springs seeking to attract meeting business to fill its guest rooms and conference space.

Trade shows in the meeting and corporate event planning industry represent an important source of new business for the Broadmoor. For its exhibit at the MPI (Meeting Planners International) show in September 2002, the Broadmoor Hotel's marketing department set a clear objective: 25 qualified leads resulting in five sales calls after the trade show. For this trade show, they decided to use proprietary on-line technology called Get Feedback, to capture leads, conduct follow-up communications, and track sales results.

The Get Feedback software was installed in two laptops at the 10 × 10 booth. Visitors had their badges swiped, which populated a profile page on the laptop with the visitor's name, company, and contact information. Visitors were asked to edit the information, and add their email addresses, if missing. The profile also pulled up a customized set of seven survey questions that the prospects could answer by themselves. The questions had been developed in collaboration between marketing and sales, and included things like "What does the Broadmoor mean to you?" "Have you been to the Broadmoor?" and "How many of your meetings would be suitable for the Broadmoor?" After the prospects finished, the booth staff could make additional notes on the system.

The system then generated an instant follow-up HTML email, thanking the visitor for stopping by the booth, reselling the Broadmoor's benefits to meeting planners, and reminding the prospect of the upcoming prize drawing for a digital camera. Laurie Meacham, Director of National Sales at the Broadmoor, notes that their decision to give away a digital camera proved to be a powerful incentive. "In the meeting industry, everyone gives away hotel rooms. Our offer was unique at that show."

The email featured a photo of the Broadmoor's splendid façade—truly one of the more dramatic hotel images in the business. It also invited recipients to click through and take a streaming-video tour of the hotel—the spa, the meeting rooms, and the golf courses. This option later proved useful to the sales force, who were then able to tailor their follow-up contact by referring to the area of the facility the prospect had visited.

A week later, a second email was generated, this one signed by the

Exhibit 12.2

Dear [[name]],

The Broadmoor is giving away a three night, four day vacation of your dreams at the legendary Broadmoor Hotel.

If you'd like to be included in this drawing, all you need to do is simply click on this link.

You'll be entered into the drawing and can take a 'virtual' tour of the property right from your computer.

We hope you'll enjoy our world class amenities and five star, five diamond service in our magnificent foot hill setting. We've recently completed a major multi-million dollar rennovation project, and welcome the opportunity to host your next event.

Sincerely,

Michal

Michael Dimond
Senior Vice President of Sales & Marketing
(800) 633-7711
mdimond@broadmoor.com

P.S. The winner will be announced on September 18th. Don't miss your chance to be pampered at The Broadmoor, click here to be entered into the drawing.

Package Includes:
- Round trip limousine service to and from the Colorado Springs Airport
- A fabulous Colorado welcome basket, a luxurious suite overlooking Cheyenne Lake with breathtaking mountain views.
- A "Rocky Mountain Revitalizer" spa experience for two.
- A round of golf for two at one of our championship golf courses.

General Information | Accommodations | Golf | Tennis | The Spa
Recreational Activities | Dining & Wine | Meetings & Conventions

The Broadmoor
1 Lake Avenue
Colorado Springs, Colorado 80906

This message was sent to the [[email]] email address. If you no longer wish to receive this sort of message from The Broadmoor, please click here.

Source: Laurie Meacham, Director of National Sales, The Broadmoor.

sales rep assigned to the account, and inviting the prospect to click through to see who won the digital camera. For the non-winning prospects, the landing page contained a pre-populated "contact me now" form, with a submit button to press. Meacham comments, "As the soccer coach always says, 'The ball will not come to you. You must go to the ball.' We need to provide the easiest possible method for our prospects to stay in touch with us. A pre-populated submit form is vastly easier than expecting them to pick up the phone or send an email."

Three weeks after the show came a third email, this one sent to the trade show contacts as well as the larger Broadmoor prospect database (see Exhibit 12.2). It offered a drawing for a four-day "dream vacation" at the Broadmoor, including round-trip limousine service to the airport and a lavish array of amenities, such as a spa visit and round of golf for two. Recipients wanting to enter the drawing clicked through to find a registration form and a "contact me now" form. Of the 3,100 emails sent in the third round, Meacham received 350 contact requests. "We sort of overwhelmed the sales force," she notes ruefully. "This campaign educated us at the Broadmoor to the value of email marketing. We now do everything we can to capture email addresses from customers and prospects."

The Get Feedback system allows the contact-me leads to be forwarded automatically via email to the appropriate sales rep for follow-up. Meacham and her team could keep track of the lead status through the online system, analyzing the lead flow by customer type, industry, and whatever other variables had been captured. She could also look at the email response results, checking delivery, open rates, links clicked and pass-along rates.

Over the three-month period after the trade show, the MPI event had generated 58 new leads and five closed sales, with a total revenue result of $245,000. The $15,000 campaign cost meant a cost per lead of $259, a cost per sale of $3,000 and an ROI of $30 returned for each $1 spent. Not bad, especially when the original MPI show objective set was for 25 leads and five sales calls. The specificity of Meacham's reporting allowed her to gain additional funding from senior management for business event investments.

CAS: CREATING A BIG BUZZ ON A SMALL BUDGET

Summary: *A company with a small booth in a large trade show used a Martini Hour event on the second day of the trade show as a way of standing out from the crowd. The business event was so successful that they have repeated it at every trade show where they exhibit, establishing a memorable brand image for themselves, as well as a regular stream of names that can be added to their marketing database.*

Jim Grace, Director of Marketing at CAS, knew he had a challenge. The Omaha, Nebraska, list and database company (www.cas-online.com) was considerably smaller than its competitors, and couldn't afford to buy its way into notoriety at the trade shows in its industry, direct marketing. "We can't compete with booths the size of two city blocks that dominate these shows," he commented. "We needed a way to increase the attention to our company, but we couldn't spend a lot."

So in early 2000, Grace and his marketing coordinator Marilyn Monohon cast around for a gimmick, and hit upon the martini hour.

"We looked around at what other people were doing, and noticed that food and beverage seemed to be most popular. We saw booths baking free cookies, or having an open bar for a half hour. But we needed something more dramatic."

Grace and Monohon decided to jump on the then-nascent martini craze. Beginning with the DMDays of New York trade show in May 2000 at the New York Hilton, they designated a cocktail-hour time slot, and invited everyone to a martini party at their booth. The event was an immediate success, and became the talk of the show.

Since then, CAS has repeated the business event 12 times, at direct marketing trade shows all over the country. They have experimented with various twists and new ideas, made some mistakes, and refined the process to the point where it runs like clockwork. The business event contains the following elements:

- Monohon begins planning three months before the trade show, talking to show management, making sure they allow a cocktail event at the booth, and getting an introduction to the hotel or caterer involved.

- She schedules the business event for the second night of the trade show, usually around 4:30 to 5:30 p.m.
- Two weeks before the trade show, she sends out a 6 × 9 postcard to the attendee list rented from show management [see Exhibit 12.3]. The front of the postcard is a color illustration of an elegant martini glass and an invitation to a "Martini Hour." The back of the postcard is one color, including the company name, logo, and address, the booth number, a blurb about the company's services, and information about any new products or deals being introduced at the trade show.
- A poster board, with take-ones, stands at the booth to announce the event to passers-by. Grace and Monohon walk the floor handing out invitations, typically distributing 300–500.
- At the event, the hotel bartenders pour freshly made vodka or gin martinis in stem glasses, charging CAS by the drink.
- Guests line up, allow their badges to be swiped, and enjoy a welcome libation at the end of a long day.
- The names are entered into the CAS marketing database, and a telemarketing follow-up call is scheduled for the week after the trade show. CAS also sends a thank-you letter to all visitors to the booth.

Grace estimates that he averages about 200–250 prospects from the event. After follow-up, the prospects might convert to seven to eight sales and additional referrals.

The CAS sales people love the event. Grace stands at the head of the line, pressing flyers on the thirsty guests. Monohon swipes the badges, keeping an eagle eye out for early birds who try to come back for seconds. (They politely decline to serve the same guest twice.) The sales people work the crowd, which inevitably is snaking in a line around the floor, or, with drink in hand, spilling out into the aisles, and in a very receptive mood.

The costs? The hotels charge by the drink, on average $8.95 to $10.95, depending on the city. The highest Grace has had to pay was

Exhibit 12.3: Business Event Invitation Postcard

Source: CAS. Reproduced with the permission of Michael Garrean.

$12.95, in Orlando. There is often an extra fee for the bartenders. Grace expects to pour 250 drinks during the hour, and will keep the business event going for an hour and a half at the larger shows.

Grace and Monohon point out some lessons they have learned:

- Don't take it for granted that the hotel people will show up. "By noon on the martini day, I am over at the catering office, double checking on everything," says Grace.

- Get them to set up earlier than the appointed time, if possible. "The presence of the bartender and the lines of bottles attract additional attention and create more buzz."
- Remember Murphy's Law. "In Chicago we were told at the last minute we'd have to supply our own table for the bartenders. I ran over to the lunch area and quietly borrowed a folding table from them," Grace observes.
- Keep it simple. "We tried distributing stickers, or hiring models to hand out flyers on the days before the event. But there are so many variations in the rules in different cities. We have now boiled it down to the simple—and inexpensive—methods to promote the event."
- Be polite. "At first we were concerned that other vendors would come over for the free drinks. And they do. But now we realize that they are going to be a source of referrals for us. Of course, we're seeking end-users, but we don't block anyone. If the line is still going at the end of the hour, I try to get everyone served," notes Grace.

How does Grace evaluate the results of his event? The leads are, of course, a tangible outcome. But he values even more the attention the business events have created for his company. "I don't measure this event on a strict ROI," Grace says. "I treat it like a magazine ad. I know we've landed business from it. But my main measure of success is how much brand-building impact we've had. We had limited dollars to spend. We have a 10 × 10 booth. But for an hour, we dominate the entire show."

After three years, the Martini Hour event has taken on a life of its own. CAS is known throughout the industry for the event, and, inevitably, Grace will be greeted at a trade show with "Hey, it's the martini guy! Are you guys doing the martini party again this year?"

HUBERT COMPANY: PARTNERING WITH NON-COMPETITORS TO ENHANCE YOUR SALES STRATEGY

Summary: *Business events can be all the more powerful if companies team up to go to market together. Hubert, a food merchandise supplier, was able to add power to its sales strategy by exhibiting in concert with a design firm at the Food Marketing Institute show. Also, by making its facilities available for corporate events, Hubert enhances its relationships with its business partners.*

The Hubert Company (www.hubert.com) of Harrison, Ohio, just outside of Cincinnati, is a $100 million supplier of merchandise targeted to supermarkets and the food industry. Hubert offers 23,000 SKUs, everything from a $9 rubber carrot used in food displays to an $8,000 reach-in freezer, through a multi-channel mix of catalog and e-commerce, outbound telephone, and a 30-person field sales force that calls on large food retail and food service accounts. A key sales prospect for Hubert is a supermarket that is being built or renovated, and will need stock at high volumes, versus standard replenishment.

In the 1990's Hubert decided to experiment with a new selling strategy. The company re-directed its sales force to focus on the store planning and development people at food retailers. These people were responsible for building new stores and re-models of existing locations. "Our problem had been price sensitivity," notes Andy Hallock, Vice President of Marketing. "When stores are working their way through the project, and they get to the point of buying the fixtures and displays, the discussion is all about price. We needed to move upstream in the process, where we could become more involved in the initial store design, and have our products specified as a result. So, we decided to partner with a Canadian firm that manufactures and designs supermarket fixtures and signage and go to market together."

In 1998, the partnership was launched at the Food Marketing Institute show at McCormick Place in Chicago. Hubert had exhibited at the show for 18 years, but this time, the two companies were able to afford a 50 × 40 foot booth, displaying different food presentations—

Mexican, Italian, a metropolitan café, Chinese. The booth was "knockout gorgeous," says Hallock.

And the traffic was heavy. "We were so busy," says Carlin Stamm, Vice President of Sales, "we had to get very efficient with our qualification strategy. We were looking for people who were involved in store development, or had plans for remodeling within a short time-frame. So as visitors approached, we'd query them about their titles, responsibilities, and the timing of any future projects. Based on these responses we made a quick judgment on their intentions before engaging in a real conversation."

Hubert generated $300,000 of sales directly from the trade show. Stamm points out the advantage of timing: "As with any show there were additional benefits more difficult to measure, as well. This was an era when retailers were investing heavily in capital used for building new stores, and improvements. I can't say we're able to repeat this strategy in a business downturn."

Another way Hubert partners with non-competitors is by taking advantage of its 2,000-square-foot facility in Harrison, known as the Center for Creative Merchandising. The space is like a show room, but more flexible, with lighting and a sound system that can be changed around for many uses. The room has thousands of products in it. The space is interactive, and the highlight of customer visits typically includes creating retail environments on the fly.

Hubert uses the Center to demonstrate its wares to customers, and for client conferences. But they also make it available to business partners for their own meetings. The International Dairy-Deli-Bakery Association uses the space to conduct user groups. Super-Valu, the largest U.S. food wholesaler, held a retailer conference at the Center. Sodexho, a global food service contractor, used the facility for a two-day marketing meeting. In exchange, Hubert gets some face time with their customers, and solidifies its relationships with its partners.

Hubert also manages a state-of-the-art photo studio for its own catalog shoots, and makes the facility available to customers for their use. For example, Westin Hotels brought in their own chefs and food stylists, and used the studio over three successive weekends to shoot their catering manual. Hubert products became an integral part of the displays shot, and their SKU numbers and prices were listed in the manual.

LAKE GROUP MEDIA: COMPETITIVE DIFFERENTIATION THROUGH BOOTH DESIGN

Summary: *In order to stand out in a crowded market, Lake Group Media developed a new booth environment every year for its major national trade event. The booth provided comfortable meeting space as well as a unique—but professional—design theme, setting the company apart from its many competitors who exhibit at the same show.*

Lake Group Media, a mailing list brokerage, list management, and interactive marketing firm in Rye, New York (*www.lakegroupmedia.com*), operates in a crowded marketplace. Most brokers have access to the same mailing lists, so list rental has become something of a commodity. In order to differentiate itself, Lake Group Media focuses on mirroring the business style and practices of its clients.

"Our business philosophy is that we consider ourselves to be an extension of our clients' staff," says Joyce P. Lake, Vice Chairman. "Thus, we need to reflect their standards and style in all aspects of our service to them." Lake's philosophy extends to her booth at marketing industry trade shows.

Lake Group Media's approach to booth design at its industry's largest show, the DMA Annual Convention every October, focused on creating an environment where their clients could feel completely comfortable doing business. Lake hired a professional designer, and instructed that the booth should provide two seating areas for a minimum of eight people, plus some flexibility to add extra seats if needed. The booth size was 10 × 30, wide and shallow, for maximum aisle exposure, with an entry area in the middle of the "block" and the seating areas at each end, fenced off by low walls. The booth was covered by an eight-foot open ceiling, which created an even more intimate feeling to the space.

Each year, Lake developed a new booth theme for their presence at The DMA, based on the "feeling" of the city where the show was located. For example:

- New Orleans. The booth resembled a balcony in the French Quarter, with wrought iron railings, wicker furniture, and plenty of hanging plants.
- Chicago. The theme was a classically appointed penthouse on Lake Shore Drive, with oriental rugs, table lamps, and book-lined walls that suggested a library. See Exhibit 12.4.
- San Francisco. A nautical look, with brick columns and back wall, wooden ship steering wheels and a model ship on display.

Exhibit 12.4

Source: Lake Group Media, Inc. Reproduced with the permission of Mary E. McFadden, Director of Corporate Communications, Lake Group Media.

The result was a richly appointed living-room feel, with two comfortable meeting spaces and a face on the trade show floor that was unusual and eye-catching. "Not only were our clients pleased with our ability to conduct business in such a setting," notes Lake, "But we were also able to convert much of the exhibit hall traffic into prospects, as they stopped by to comment on just how unique our booth was."

The meeting area is usually booked solid. "Prior to each show, our staff pre-schedules appointments with brokers, mailers, clients and prospects in the exhibit hall, thereby ensuring optimum use of our booth throughout the duration of the show." People in the industry began to talk about the Lake Group theme, and make a note to stop by the following year to see what ideas they had developed.

Thanks to an unusual design and a welcoming atmosphere, Lake Group Media was able to look different from all the other broker-manager companies on the trade show floor, and at the same time attract new prospects and conduct plenty of business on site. "It was hard work," observes Lake, "And we always went a bit over budget. But I always felt it was worth it."

MTS SYSTEMS: AN ANNUAL EVENT TO PROMOTE DISTRIBUTOR LOYALTY AND PRODUCTIVITY

Summary: *In order to motivate its key distribution channel, a sensor manufacturer runs an annual meeting, where distributors learn about new products, customer case studies and sales support programs. The corporate event also serves to deepen the relationship between the company and its distributors.*

Every year, the sensors division of MTS Systems Corporation (*www.mts.com*) runs a two-day meeting for its distributor network during the first quarter of the company's fiscal year. The primary objective of the Distributor Symposium is motivation: MTS competes with other distributed lines for distributor mindshare, so they do whatever they can to persuade the channel to spend more time selling MTS linear products. The strategy for the meeting is a combination of product information, applications (case studies), relationship building and delivering information about sales support programs.

Based in Cary, North Carolina, in the heart of Research Triangle Park, the sensors division of MTS Systems Corporation manufactures magnetostrictive position and level sensors that are sold to design and systems engineers in a wide range of industries, ranging from specialty machine manufacturers to process industries like pharmaceuticals and chemicals. The division sells through a field sales force that calls on key accounts, plus a network of independent distributors.

It is these distributors who are invited to the October corporate event. In alternative years, the Distributor Symposium is held in Cary, but every other year, they go to such destinations as Scottsdale and San Diego. In 2003, the corporate event took place in New Orleans.

The meeting schedule follows a well-tested formula each year. Attendees arrive on Thursday evening and check into the hotel. The meeting kicks off at 8:00 the next morning, with presentations from company officials as well as the distributors themselves, who share first hand experience of solving their customers' problems. All the material is intended to support the meeting objective of exciting and educating the distributors. The typical agenda includes product updates, case studies on successful customer product installations, reviews of forthcoming marketing communications plans, and reports on sales trends and plans for the new fiscal year.

MTS Sensors Division also operates a Distributors Council, a group of 12 key distributors and senior MTS management that meet quarterly, to develop the relationship between manufacturer and sales channel by sharing plans, product capabilities, future designs, and sales programs. The council's meeting will be scheduled for the previous Thursday at the business event site, and council representatives' report on their findings at the plenary event as well.

Friday night is the scene of the annual Awards Dinner, usually held at the hotel. Plaques and bonuses are handed out to both distributors and MTS sales people in such categories as highest growth year on year, and top sales record by region. Saturday brings another full day of presentations and discussion, ending with distribution of door prizes drawn from a pool of business cards collected from attendees who came on time to each session. (The more often distributors show up at sessions on time, the greater their chance of winning a door prize at the end of the corporate event. This has proven to be an effective method of ensuring that sessions start promptly.)

Dinner on Saturday night is a less formal, more relaxed occasion, such as a barbecue or boat ride, and usually includes some kind of entertainment such as a comedian or a magician. On Sunday, attendees head home, although some might stay on for sightseeing or golf on their own.

Janet Rapp, Senior Marketing Communications Specialist for the division, plans and executes the entire meeting. She notes that the meeting format is designed to suit the preferences of the audience. "Many of our distributors run their own small businesses, and are very time and cost conscious. So, we hold the event in a way that keeps their time away from the office to a minimum, and, with a Saturday overnight, their airfare is manageable. We have discovered that our audience, which is mostly men, prefers a hearty breakfast and substantial dinners. We keep the lunch light to overcome the low patch that often occurs in the early afternoon."

The attendees at the corporate event comprise a mixture of distributors and MTS executives. Although Tier One distributors are contractually obligated to attend, Rapp is heartened to note how many send more than one attendee. "The distributors recognize the value of the material communicated, the product training and hands-on interaction at the meetings," she observes. From MTS's side, the regional sales managers, customer service manager, sales director, marketing manager and marketing communications specialist attend every year. Then depending on the year and the need, other senior MTS officials, the CEO, or certain product managers, will attend.

For the New Orleans version of the Distributor Symposium, Rapp built on the city's colorful history by decorating the invitations and the dinner tables with masks, beads and other Mardi Gras images. The second night's dinner was held on a Mississippi riverboat, and included jazz music. Rapp's total budget was $85,000 for the New Orleans event, which attracted 145 attendees—50% more than the years when it is held in Cary.

Rapp evaluates the corporate event's success based on two sources of input. First, she considers the attendance levels. Although the distributors are obligated to attend, the number of people they send is an important variable. Second, she collects a detailed questionnaire from attendees, asking about their satisfaction with the hotel, the food, and the content of the program. A lesson about survey methodology: "I have learned over the years to limit the survey questions to areas I can actually control. For example, whether or not they liked the CEO's presentation is not going to mean that we'd ever eliminate it."

Rapp believes that the most important success factor for the meeting is quality. "It's not always necessary to provide the most expensive event," she says. "It's really about value, about high quality materials, and superb presentation content."

SAAB AIRCRAFT:
A FULLY LOADED CLIENT CONFERENCE

Summary: *Saab Aircraft's Operators Conference combines elements of education, entertainment, relationship building, and a trade-show-style exhibit hall, focusing on maintenance, repair and upgrades.*

Every two to three years, the U.S. division of Saab Aircraft (www.saabaircraft.com), based in Sterling Virginia, hosts a customer conference called the Saab Operators Conference, which is attended by operators of the Saab 340 turboprop aircraft and the vendor community that supports it. In the U.S. there are about 300 Saab 340 aircraft in operation, and there are another 150 throughout the rest of the world. Currently, the largest U.S. customer is Mesaba Airlines, which has over 60 of the planes. The bulk of the customer base, however, comprises smaller regional airlines and corporate owners. From Saab Aircraft's perspective, the marketing strategy is all about customer retention. So, at this conference there is less focus on leasing new aircraft and more on keeping them running smoothly.

The conference is organized by various members of the Saab management team, including Patrick McGuiness, Director of Spares (meaning spare parts). Their objective is to combine elements of an educational conference, an entertainment event, and a trade show to attract and serve 75 airline purchasing and maintenance personnel plus 100 to 125 vendor partners.

The conference format has evolved over the years, to kick off on a

Monday evening with cocktails, and the rest of the conference extending through Thursday lunch. On arrival, clients are greeted with a welcome kit—a backpack containing a promotional gift and a conference session guide. Tuesday morning brings a welcoming speech by the president of Saab Aircraft of America as well as comments from the president of the Sweden-based Saab operation. Tuesday afternoon and Wednesday morning consist of breakout sessions, where customers can learn about product improvements or specialized maintenance practices. During the frequent breaks, clients head for the ballroom, where vendor tabletop exhibits are on display. An entertainment or sports outing is scheduled for Wednesday afternoon, with teambuilding as its objective. A formal dinner takes place on Tuesday evening, and a more casual dinner is scheduled for Wednesday. Thursday lunch includes a wrap-up and farewell speech by a senior Saab executive.

The exhibit hall is populated by Saab business partners who also sell to the aircraft operators. These are suppliers of such categories as instrumentation, propellers, landing gear, and aircraft lavatories, galleys, and seats. For them, the operators represent a rich source of aftermarket sales opportunity, whether replacement parts, repairs, or modifications. Saab charges the vendors a fee to exhibit, and usually attracts, on average, 30 vendors to participate. Recently, McGuiness introduced a "passport" program to help the vendors get more value for their money. He had 30 stamps made up, one for each vendor, and created a booklet (passport) for each client walking the exhibit hall floor. When clients collected stamps on their passports at each booth, they became eligible for a variety of prizes. McGuiness has learned that interaction is key to exhibit hall success. "We always place refreshments and snacks in the exhibit hall to draw traffic throughout the day."

In 2001, when the event was held in Phoenix, McGuiness took advantage of the desert atmosphere to schedule several special events. The Tuesday evening formal dinner was set up atop of a mountain overlooking an air force base, and the party could watch the F-15s taking off and landing. After dinner, the guests enjoyed a Wild West show, which was particularly appreciated by the visitors from Europe and Asia. On Wednesday afternoon, clients had their choice of a desert tour in Humvees, a pool party, or a golf outing.

Would Saab run the event in Phoenix again? Probably not, since that venue was higher end than necessary, according to McGuiness. "We try to strike a balance between having a destination that attracts domestic and international operators of the Saab 340 aircraft, and at the same time focusing on the costs of the conference," he says. "We don't want the destination to be too appealing. Our targets for the event are the directors of maintenance and purchasing staff. If the venue is too attractive, our target audience has a harder time getting approval to attend. Instead, we end up with the senior managers, and they may not be as well versed in the day-to day-issues that we address at our conference. In 2004 we are heading to Clearwater."

Saab measures its Operator Conference success with a post-event questionnaire, where feedback is solicited. The survey also asks for suggestions for future events, session topics, and entertainment activities. "It's tough to get a lot of input after the fact," observes McGuiness. "A much better gauge of success or failure is feedback while the conference is in session, and we take this feedback very seriously. We can tell from their comments throughout the event whether or not it's working."

McGuiness figures the corporate event costs a total of $250,000, with his share coming to about $100,000. The customers pay their own travel and hotel room, and the vendor registration fees and exhibits fund a significant part of the rest of the budget.

WOOLPERT: INTEGRATED EVENT MARKETING

Summary: *An architectural and engineering firm extends its trade show presence by leveraging opportunities in special events and meeting, PR, promotions, and hospitality.*

Woolpert (www.woolpert.com) is a 650-person architectural and engineering firm that targets government buyers at all levels—city, state, and federal. Trade shows and corporate events make up a large part of Woolpert's marketing strategy, but the company has evolved a highly integrated approach to business event marketing that takes advantage of the wide variety of sales, marketing, and PR levers available.

Typically, the Woolpert business event calendar combines exhibits, speaking engagements, client appreciation events, prospecting events, and sales appointments. Marci R. Snyder, Marketing Facilitator for three Woolpert service groups, pays special attention to the publicity angles available in business event marketing. She helps Woolpert architects and engineers secure speaking engagements at a wide range of state and national conferences, whether Woolpert is exhibiting there or not. The engagements run the gamut from giving a scholarly paper to presenting a case study with a client. After the business event, Snyder works to arrange for the paper or session content to be published in industry journals.

When Woolpert does exhibit, it is business developers and technical staff who are the likely choices for booth duty. The business developers also do their best to take advantage of the client and prospect contact opportunity by arranging a series of breakfasts, lunches, and dinners. A mixture of current clients and prospects will be invited. "What better way to sell than to have an existing client give an unrehearsed testimonial to a prospective client," says Snyder.

In recent years, Woolpert marketers have added special events to their conference calendar. ESRI, the giant geographic information systems (GIS) research and development firm, runs their International User Conference in San Diego every summer that attracts 17,000 attendees. Woolpert began organizing a golf outing the day before the conference, and inviting its clients and prospects. "Invitations to our golf event have become highly prized, a source of prestige, in the GIS industry," notes Snyder.

The ESRI conference showcases Woolpert's integrated event marketing program, including such tactics as:

- Exhibiting with a 10 × 20 booth in the ESRI exhibit hall.
- 15 presentations by Woolpert experts and clients on the conference program.
- Proprietary invitation-only golf outing the day before the conference.

- Pre-show promotions to client and prospect lists about the golf outing.
- Hospitality suite.
- Full schedule of client and prospect breakfasts, lunches, and dinners.
- Booth-based signage promoting the speaking engagements.
- Running demos on the latest GIS technology.
- Exclusive client and prospective client invitation-only dinner.

How did Woolpert decide on its entertainment strategy? By asking their clients. According to Kathryn Munn, Director of Marketing Communications, Woolpert regularly conducts focus groups among clients to elicit their preferences. "When we asked a client panel about how they like to interact with us, they told us very clearly that they find it difficult during the regular course of business to go out for semi-social dinners and other entertainment-type events. At home, they need to focus on office and family. They much prefer to schedule the dinners and lunches during conferences, when they are out of town and completely available. So this is why we pack so many meal events into our conference plans."

Munn also points out that Woolpert has changed its trade show premium strategy over time. "Used to be, we would always have a giveaway of a small item, and we'd give it to everyone. But recently, we have migrated to a more targeted approach. We will have a valuable giveaway, like a Palm Pilot or a GPS system, and we'll conduct a drawing for it instead," she says. "People want something they can really use, and the $200 or $250 item is more appealing."

Woolpert also adjusts its promotional strategy to the quality of the attendee level. For a national show like The National League of Cities, which attracts city council members and city managers from all over the country, Munn estimates that perhaps 50% of the attendee population is a target for Woolpert. The rest are from states where Woolpert is not interested in pursuing, or representing business that is too small to serve. So with such a show, Woolpert will conduct more targeted promotions, such as mailing to its customer file and perhaps holding an invitation-only hospitality suite or dinner.

For a more targeted trade show, like the North Carolina Recreation and Park Society, where as much as 75% of the attendees are likely to be prospects, Munn will develop a broader promotional plan, such as mailing out a key to a treasure chest to the entire pre-show attendee mailing list from the show organizer.

As for measuring the success of its business event strategy, it's all about relationship building and sales. Notes Snyder, "Our business developers know what opportunities to pursue, based on their relationships in the industry. Not every project out there is going to get funded. So, they work the conference leads with care. Our sales cycle can be as much as several months to four years long. We need to be in there, consulting with the prospects, helping them develop the RFPs, building support for the projects, and positioning ourselves to get the projects when they are funded."

XMPIE: EAT YOUR OWN COOKING

Summary: *By partnering with a large manufacturer, a start-up software company was able to make a big splash with a small budget. Using their own software, XMPie drove traffic to the booth with an integrated direct marketing campaign that clearly demonstrated their product's capabilities to the audience of marketing professionals.*

XMPie (*www.xmpie.com*) is a U.S. technology company with its R&D based in Israel. XMPie's PersonalEffect™ software makes data-driven customized messaging easy to produce in multiple media formats, like email, digital variable color printing, or websites. In 2002, XMPie entered into a marketing agreement with Xerox, a leading manufacturer of variable printing solutions. Xerox was planning to exhibit at the newly launched Digital Printing Pavilion at the Direct Marketing Association's annual convention in San Francisco in October 2002, and invited XMPie to join them.

This presented an enormous opportunity to XMPie, who was not only new to the market, but also had limited budget to invest in marketing and sales promotion. So Phil Asche, Executive Vice President at XMPie, decided to take full advantage. His objective for the show was three-fold: 1) exposure (awareness), 2) credibility, and 3) qualified sales leads.

Having come to XMPie after a 27-year career in advertising and integrated communications at Young and Rubicam, Asche was aware of the importance of planning. "You have to have a business plan, and a business strategy," he notes. "Everything else will follow from that. For example, if my plan is clear, it will also be relatively easy to evaluate the merits of various event and promotion ideas."

So Asche's first step was to write a corporate event plan that contained XMPie's objectives for the show, specific demographics, psychographics, and insights about the audience, including their needs and what they should get out of the XMPie show experience, the key messages, and the tone and manner of the exhibit communications (see Exhibit 12.5).

Asche's plan at the trade show involved a hands-on demo of the XMPie solution, enveloped in an automotive theme. Visitors could take a "test drive" of the XMPie system, entering information about themselves and their preferences, and receiving a four-color custom print-out from the Xerox DocuColor printer, minutes later. The printed flyer showed the type of car selected by the visitor, and the background photo was customized to the visitor's geographic region. When the visitor went home, he could stop by a unique URL on the Internet and see the same custom images online. XMPie also sent out a customized follow-up email to everyone who participated in the test drive.

To promote the demonstration at the booth, Asche conducted a pre-show postcard mailing to all conference pre-registered attendees, which was a list of about 2,000 (see Exhibit 12.6). The postcard was digitally printed, using a design that highlighted the customized elements. "We wanted everything in the pre-show campaign to replicate the direct marketing campaign experience," says Asche. "Our strategy was to eat our own cooking. As a business, XMPie's issue is how to make our solution an everyday part of our customers' marketing activity, and not a special event. So we needed a straightforward campaign format and message—no die cuts, nothing wacky. We wanted an example of an integrated campaign that would make sense for the audience."

Exhibit 12.5: Promotion Brief

2002 DMA CONFERENCE
PROMOTION CAMPAIGN CREATIVE STRATEGY

Key Fact

Xerox is exhibiting at the DMA Conference for the first time and has asked XMPie to join with them to demonstrate the direct marketing potential of VI color printing. National Car Rental is giving away long weekend rentals to Conference attendees who take a test drive of the XMPie Xerox 1 to 1 solution.

Target Audience

DMA attendees are a mixture of enterprise marketing clients, DM agency personnel and DM production/fulfillment suppliers. They are mostly senior and middle managers who are influential in decisions to develop and recommend DM programs as well as workflow and production system decisions.

Customer Problem Our Exhibit & Communications Should Solve

Most attendees have limited first hand knowledge and experience of true 1 to 1 marketing, VI digital color applications and workflow. They probably have somewhat negative legacy perceptions of the applicability of color VI printing to most DM print campaigns.

Communications Objective

To encourage Conference attendees to visit the Xerox exhibit and experience how the XMPie-Xerox solution makes 1:1 marketing a tool you can now use everyday – for print, Web, e-mail and wireless – using a single and unique software solution.

Customer Benefits

Visit the Xerox booth and experience first hand how XMPie PersonalEffect™ software effortlessly blends creative concepts with database information to produce powerful 1 to 1 campaigns. And you can win a free weekend National® car rental of your choice.

Reasons Why

You'll see powerful, personalized, full color print produced with a Xerox DocuColor Digital Color Press. You also see how XMPie enables you to easily extend campaigns to e-mail, wireless and Web with enhanced brand consistency across media channels.

PersonalEffect™ is unique in combining Ease of use yet highly Professional; Distributed workflow with modular and specialized desktop tools for each professional (Fosters teamwork); Industrial Strength with Powerful Data and Media capabilities; Cross Media Solution; PC & Mac plus Multi-lingual.

Every hour of the Conference there will be an on-site random drawing of a free weekend car rental for those attendees taking a test drive of the XMPie-Xerox solution.

Tone & Manner

Look and feel of a "real" DM campaign with quality auto assets
Industrial strength, but approachable and easy to use

Source: XMPie. Reproduced with permission.

Exhibit 12.6: Pre-Conference Mailer

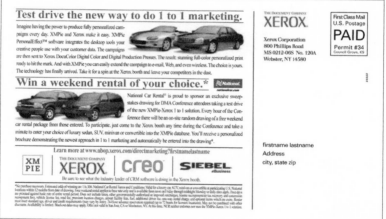

Source: XMPie. Reproduced with permission.

Asche recruited National Car Rental to provide free long-weekend rentals as an incentive at the booth, with a drawing every hour among visitors who took the test drive of the XMPie-Xerox solution.

XMPie was very happy with the results. Of total booth attendance, 600 participated in the "test-drive" demo and provided XMPie with their business segment and contact information. These contacts resulted in 70 qualified leads, and the sales team began following up on them immediately after the show.

APPENDIX

1. TRADE AND PROFESSIONAL ASSOCIATIONS FOR BUSINESS EVENT MARKETERS

Association	Website
The Computer Event Marketing Community (CEMA)	cemaonline.com
Center for Exhibition Industry Research (CEIR)	ceir.org
Convention Industry Council	conventionindustry.org
Exhibit Designers & Producers Association	edpa.com
Exhibition Services & Contractors Association	esca.org
Healthcare Convention & Exhibitors Association	hcea.org
International Association for Exhibition Management (IAEM)	iaem.org
Meeting Professionals International (MPI)	mpiweb.org
Professional Convention Management Association	pcma.org
Promotion Marketing Association (PMA)	pmalink.org
Society of Independent Show Organizers (SISO)	siso.org
Trade Show Exhibitors Association (TSEA)	tsea.org

2. INDUSTRY PUBLICATIONS

Publication	Website
Corporate Meetings & Incentive	meetingsnet.com
Event Marketer	eventmarketermag.com
Event Solutions	event-solutions.com
Exhibit Builder magazine	exhibitbuilder.net
Exhibit City News	exhibitcitynews.com
Exhibitor magazine	exhibitornet.com
EXPO magazine, for show organizers	expoweb.com
Meeting News	meetingnews.com
Meetings & Conventions	meetings-conventions.com
Successful Meetings	successmtgs.com
Technology Meetings Magazine	technology meetings.com
Tradeshow & Exhibit Manager	tradeshowpub.com
Tradeshow Blues newsletter	attendsource.com/tsb
Tradeshow Week	tradeshowweek.com

3. WEB-BASED RESOURCES

Website	Comments
event-planner.com	Resources for event planners
exhibitauction.com	Buy and sell used exhibits and materials
expoworld.net	Search among 11,000 trade shows worldwide
mim.com	Discussion board for meeting professionals
mpoint.com	Site selection and other tools for meeting planners
TSNN.com	Search for venues, events, suppliers, travel deals and more

4. PROFESSIONAL CERTIFICATION PROGRAMS FOR EXHIBITORS

Certification	Description	Sponsor	Website
CTSM	Certified Trade Show Manager	Exhibitor Group	exhbitornet.com/ctsm
CME	Certified Manager of Exhibits	TSEA	tsea.org
CEM	Certified in Exhibition Management	IAEM	iaem.org
CMP	Certified Meeting Professional	Convention Industry Council	conventionindustry.org/cmp
CMM	Global Certification in Meeting Management	Meeting Professionals International	mpiweb.org/education/cmm

INDEX

About TEXERE

TEXERE, a progressive and authoritative voice in business publishing, brings to the global business community the expertise and insights of leading thinkers. Our books educate, enlighten, and entertain, and provide an intersection where our authors and our readers share cutting edge ideas, practices, and innovative solutions. Texere seeks to cultivate, enhance, and disseminate information that illuminates the global business landscape. This book was set in Minion, 10.5/14.

www.thomson.com/learning/texere

1/10 added
back.
2010